Contents

General Editors' Preface

The outlines of contemporary critical theory are now often taught as a standard feature of a degree in literary studies. The development of particular theories has seen a thorough transformation of literary criticism. For example, Marxist and Foucauldian theories have revolutionized Shakespeare studies, and 'deconstruction' has led to a complete reassessment of Romantic poetry. Feminist criticism has left scarcely any period of literature unaffected by its searching critiques. Teachers of literary studies can no longer fall back on a standardized, received, methodology.

Lecturers and teachers are now urgently looking for guidance in a rapidly changing critical environment. They need help in understanding the latest revisions in literary theory, and especially in grasping the practical effects of the new theories in the form of theoretically sensitized new readings. A number of volumes in the series anthologize important essays on particular theories. However, in order to grasp the full implications and possible uses of particular theories it is essential to see them put to work. This series provides substantial volumes of new readings, presented in an accessible form and with a significant amount of editorial guidance.

Each volume includes a substantial introduction which explores the theoretical issues and conflicts embodied in the essays selected and locates areas of disagreement between positions. The pluralism of theories has to be put on the agenda of literary studies. We can no longer pretend that we all tacitly accept the same practices in literary studies. Neither is a *laissez-faire* attitude any longer tenable. Literature departments need to go beyond the mere toleration of theoretical differences: it is not enough merely to agree to differ; they need actually to 'stage' the differences openly. The volumes in this series all attempt to dramatize the differences, not necessarily with a view to resolving them but in order to foreground the choices presented by different theories or to argue for a particular route through the impasses the differences present.

The theory 'revolution' has had real effects. It has loosened the grip of traditional empiricist and romantic assumptions about language and literature. It is not always clear what is being proposed as the new agenda for literary studies, and indeed the very notion of 'literature' is questioned by the post-structuralist strain in theory. However, the uncertainties and obscurities of contemporary theories appear much less worrying when we see what the best critics have been able to do with them in practice. This series aims to disseminate the best of recent criticism, and to show that it is possible to re-read the canonical texts of literature in new and challenging ways.

RAMAN SELDEN AND STAN SMITH

Acknowledgements

I should like to acknowledge the helpfulness of my publishers, Longman, and of Stan Smith and Ray Selden, the General Editors for the Longman Critical Readers Series. I am grateful to Bruni de la Motte and Judy Giles for careful and perceptive readings of the Introduction. The Library staff at the College of Ripon and York St John, particularly Sandra Huxley and Tony Chalcraft, have given ample proof of their efficiency and professionalism. My major debt, as ever, is to David Pierce for daily encouragement, advice and humour.

We are grateful to the following for permission to reproduce copyright material:

Marion Boyars Publishers Ltd for extracts from *About Chinese Women* by Julia Kristeva (Marion Boyars, London, New York, 1977); The Johns Hopkins University Press for the article 'Is There a Woman in This Text?' by Mary Jacobus from *New Literary History*, Autumn 1982, Vol 14 (1), & the articles 'Replacing Feminist Criticism' by Peggy Kamuf & 'The Text's Heroine: A Feminist Critic & Her Fictions' by Nancy K Miller from *Diacritics*, Vol 12, 1982; Methuen & Co, a division of Routledge, Chapman & Hall Ltd, for an extract from *Sexual/Textual Politics* by Toril Moi (Methuen, 1985); the author's agent for an extract from *Sexual Politics* by Kate Millett, copyright © 1969, 1970 by Kate Millett; Princeton University Press for extracts from *A Literature of Their Own* by Elaine Showalter, copyright © 1977 by Princeton University Press; Routledge, Chapman & Hall, Inc for the essay 'Male Feminism' by Stephen Heath & the article 'French Feminism in an International Frame' by Gayatri Chakravorty Spivak from *In Other Worlds* (1987); University of Minnesota Press for extracts from *The Newly Born Woman* by Hélène Cixous & Catherine Clément, English translation & Introduction copyright © 1986 by the University of Minnesota; Verso Ltd for an extract from *Sea Changes* by Cora Kaplan (1986).

Note, a Glossary has been provided to explain any specialist terms.

Introduction

This selection of essays on feminist literary theory begins with a consideration of Virginia Woolf, the founding mother of the contemporary debate. In a second-hand bookshop I once saw a notice which stated that all fiction was shelved alphabetically with the sole exception of Woolf who was to be found under 'Women's Studies'; though the arrangement was unorthodox, the bookshop owner had evidently recognized Woolf's significance for feminists. In some ways it is difficult for feminist criticism to get beyond Woolf. So acutely did she foreshadow future developments that feminists from a variety of critical positions – Marxist, psychoanalytical, post-structuralist – turn to her as their starting-point. In this volume Elaine Showalter develops Woolf's interest in a tradition of women authors and explores Woolf's own status within that tradition, while Toril Moi relates Woolf's avant-garde textual practice to recent French critical theory. From the writing of literary history to a more abstract theoretical debate, Woolf's work has relevance for feminists.

Kate Millett proves to be a less dutiful daughter. Her passing and dismissive reference to Woolf in *Sexual Politics* (1970) reads: 'Virginia Woolf glorified two housewives, Mrs Dalloway and Mrs Ramsay, recorded the suicidal misery of Rhoda in *The Waves* without ever explaining its causes, and was argumentative yet somehow unsuccessful, perhaps because unconvinced, in conveying the frustrations of the woman artist in Lily Briscoe. Only in *A Room of One's Own*, essay rather than fiction, could she describe what she knew'.[1] I suppose we have to be grateful for the final sentence. Yet in its own way Millett's book is as historically important to feminism as Woolf's *oeuvre* and these two critics – Woolf and Millett – are determining voices in the development of feminist literary studies. Published seven years after Betty Friedan's *The Feminine Mystique* (1963), five years after Tillie Olsen's essay 'Silences' first appeared in *Harper's Magazine* (1965), two years after Mary Ellmann's *Thinking About Women* (1968), and concurrent with Eva Figes's *Patriarchal Attitudes* (1970) and Germaine Greer's *The Female Eunuch* (1970), *Sexual Politics* marks, with these other texts, that moment when the present women's

…nent established itself as a widespread, self-aware, activist …ization. The audacity and élan of Millett's writing testifies to the excitement of that juncture, and in somewhat greyer, less militant times we could all feed from her energy and sense of urgency. The measure of her achievement is indicated in the very term 'sexual politics' – a concept strange and contentious twenty years ago but one which we now find both self-evident and indispensable to critical analysis.

Two facets of *Sexual Politics* remain characteristic of feminist thinking: firstly, its comprehensiveness. Though her Introduction admits to some hesitancy about the task in hand, once into her thesis Millett moves with confidence – later critics have suggested, a rather too easy confidence – across literature, history, sociology, psychoanalysis and several other disciplines. She exemplifies a revolutionary scope intrinsic to feminism: the whole world needs changing and all established canons must be challenged. Secondly, within this comprehensive critique, *Sexual Politics* evinces a particular attention to cultural matters, an aspect about which Cora Kaplan asks searching questions in her comments on Millett. The frequency with which books and courses in the early 1970s took as their subject 'images of women' indicates how crucial for feminism have been debates on visual and verbal representation. In many feminist circles protests against pornography or the imaginative feminist graffiti on advertising hoardings have been given the same priority as campaigns for reproductive rights or equal pay. From the start feminists felt that writing, literature, criticism were places for them to be. Now, twenty years after Millett, we can see how the proliferation of writing by and about women has had a decisive effect on the publishing industry, academic institutions, the nature of critical theory, the practices of teaching and literary criticism. Of course this is not necessarily a sign of the end of patriarchy. It may instead be a sign of the ability of publishers to recognise the marketable, or criticism's capacity for absorbing the radical. Yet it is, equally, an indication of feminism's pervasive and – to date – sustained impact.

This book is designed to capture something of the variety of critical positions that have developed since 1970. Feminist theory is a broad church with a number of co-operating and competing approaches; it is probably more appropriate to talk of feminist theories rather than feminist theory. For those who are looking for a consolidated political position, or a uniform feminist practice, or even simply for clarity, such diversity is distressing. For others, pluralism is an indication of feminism's creativity and flexibility. Annette Kolodny's influential essay, 'Dancing Through the Minefield: Some Observations on the Theory, Practice, and Politics of a Feminist Literary Criticism' (1980), poses the dilemma. Does diversity render feminist literary criticism 'woefully deficient in system, and painfully lacking in program', or does it lead us to our true political and literary home, 'camped out on the far side of the minefield, with the other pluralists and pluralisms'?[2] Alternatively, Jane Marcus sees in Kolodny's pluralism a 'liberal relaxation of the tensions among us and the tensions between feminists and the academy'. In her opinion the necessary activity for feminists is not 'dancing through the minefield' but 'storming the toolshed' so as to wrest from male hands the implements of literary criticism.[3] Similarly, Gayatri Chakravorty Spivak is less concerned with the unsystematic aspect of pluralism than with its tendency 'to espouse the politics of the masculinist establishment': 'Pluralism is the method employed by the *central* authorities to neutralize opposition by seeming to accept it. The gesture of pluralism on the part of the *marginal* can only mean capitulation to the center.'[4]

The variety within feminist literary studies can be accounted for, partly, by the facility with which feminism has interacted with other critical discourses, both influencing and being influenced by them. This collection illustrates the effect of Marx on Cora Kaplan, of Michel Foucault on Peggy Kamuf, of Julia Kristeva on Moi, of Jacques Derrida on Spivak, of Freud on seemingly everybody – Millett, Kaplan, Mary Jacobus, the French feminists. What I think distinguishes many of the feminists listed above is their openness and suppleness of thinking. They exhibit a capacity to synthesize and move between different critical viewpoints without evading any of the problems or, as Marcus and Spivak warn, sinking into a pluralism that has no political stringency. The diversity indicates the ongoing nature of the debate: we are still in the throes of it. Inevitably, it also fuels a demand for retrospective surveys and collections of essays to organize the material.

The shape I have imposed on this collection is that of the dialogue. I hope that such a structure captures a sense of the vigour of feminist debate, of momentum and interchange. Some of the essays are divided by a clear historical and ideological space. Eight years, 1977–85, separate Showalter's and Moi's essays, during which period the writings of Derrida and Kristeva made their entry into the English and American academies. In a similar way, Kaplan's response to Millett is marked by a feminist rethinking on Freud in the years between 1970 and 1979. The tendency has been to read these pairings in a hierarchical manner – Moi as the theoretical superior to Showalter, or Kaplan as the definitive refutation of Millett. Though I have little control over how others approach the material, such prioritizing is not one of my interests; I am concerned rather with understanding the historical and theoretical contexts which produce these varied critiques and with the interplay between them. In other pairings the clash of contrary opinion is more muted. Nancy Miller, for instance, finds herself in 'a discursively polemical (but personally irenic) relation to Peggy Kamuf's questions'. Between these two essays there is no historical gap; both authors are equally aware of the spectrum of critical discourses within which their discussion is set, and yet Miller and Kamuf come to significantly different conclusions about the practice of feminist criticism. Repeatedly, I find, the juxtaposition of essays or, as in the case of Hélène Cixous and Catherine Clément, two viewpoints within a single essay can clarify both the convergence and divergence of feminist literary theories: each essay encourages the reader to question more sharply the thesis of its companion.

In this Introduction I should like to proceed on two fronts, noticing the distinctiveness of the separate dialogues *and* the value of ranging across the essays to uncover changing responses to key issues. I begin by considering the relationship of feminist literary studies to critical theory in general and, then, through a comparison of Showalter's and Moi's views on Woolf, move to the complex debate of recent years between Anglo-American and French feminisms. Many of the essays in this selection consciously speak within the context of this debate and some of the most illuminating voices for me are those which are subtly alive to the problems and possibilities of both positions. For example, Stephen Heath's range of secondary material seems commendably catholic and Jacobus's summary of the two critical approaches at the end of her essay is astute and succinct. The nomenclature, 'Anglo-American' and 'French', is problematic. Not all Anglo-American writers expound Anglo-American criticism, nor all French feminists French criticism; the generalized terms disguise the multiplicity of critical practices coexisting within each tradition; Black critics have rightly pointed out how establishing the debate in this way presumes that, theoretically at least, most of the world has nothing to offer; finally, the binary terminology perpetuates an oppositional logic which many commentators would want to challenge. Moi, however, outlines what has become a working definition in this] area: 'the terms "Anglo-American" and "French" must not be taken to represent purely national demarcations: they do not signal the critics' birthplace but the intellectual tradition within which they work. Thus I do not consider the many British and American women deeply influenced by French thought to be "Anglo-American" critics.'[5]

Miller and Kamuf take further those questions of identity and subjectivity that are inherent in the disagreement between Showalter and Moi and they remind us forcefully of the political meaning of feminism: if feminist literary studies fail to promote wide political change, then what is the point of them? I see the problems of identity as particularly relevant to Black feminists, and I view the writing of Spivak – an Indian working in the American university system, and the translator of the French philosopher, Derrida – as uniquely placed to comment on both Anglo-American and French perceptions of Black people. Spivak is equally alert to the incipient imperialism of some

Anglo-American critics and to the anti-materialism of some French commentators. In an attempt to bridge that cultural chasm signified in the essays of Showalter and Moi, the four voices of Spivak, Kristeva, Cixous and Clément interact in complex ways. The Introduction ends with a résumé of one of the most pressing and querulous feminist issues of the late 1980s, the relationship of men to feminism. From Millett's trenchant critique of male influence in her rejection of Freud, through the French preoccupation with 'l'écriture féminine' written by male authors, to current debates on the legitimacy of Gender Studies as opposed to Women's Studies and the part that men may play in those studies, the 'problem' of men has rumbled through feminism.

Feminism and critical theory

Why theorize? How to theorize? A suspicion of theory is widespread throughout feminism. Faced as we are with a long history of patriarchal theory which claims to have proved decisively the inferiority of women, this caution is hardly surprising. Many feminists see theory as, if not innately male – women are capable of doing it – then certainly male-dominated in its practice and masculinist in its methods. In the same year, 1973, from either side of the Atlantic, Mary Daly and Marguerite Duras expressed the view that theorizing was oppressive to women and sought chiefly to consolidate male power:

> It should be noted that the god Method is in fact a subordinate deity, serving Higher Powers. These are social and cultural institutions whose survival depends upon the classification of disruptive and disturbing information as nondata. Under patriarchy, Method has wiped out women's questions so totally that even women have not been able to hear and formulate our own questions to meet our own experiences. Women have been unable even to experience our own experience.[6]

> Men must learn to be silent. This is probably very painful for them. To quell their theoretical voice, the exercise of theoretical interpretation. They must watch themselves carefully. One has scarcely the time to experience an event as important as May '68 before men begin to speak out, to formulate theoretical epilogues, and to break the silence. Yes, these prating men were up to their old tricks during May '68 . They are the ones who started to speak, to speak alone and for everyone else, on

behalf of everyone else, as they put it. They immediately forced women and extremists to keep silent. They activated the old language, enlisted the aid of the old way of theorizing, in order to relate, to recount, to explain this new situation: May '68.[7]

Feminism would argue that the impersonality and disinterestedness of theory is fallacious, masking the needs and partiality of the theoretician and that it partakes in the kind of hierarchical binary opposition to which Cixous refers in her essay 'Sorties: Out and Out: Attacks/Ways Out/ Forays' (1986): theory is impersonal, public, objective, male; experience is personal, private, subjective, female.[8] The anti-theorists undermine the primacy of theory by valorizing the subordinated term, variously styled as the experiential, the body, *jouissance*, the Mother.

The aggressive competitiveness of much male theoretical writing enacts an Oedipal struggle as each practitioner strives to supplant his master/father. Whereas feminism's aspirations are towards the collective and supportive, Jacobus detects in male theory an 'adversarial relation between rival theorists'. However judicious feminism may try to be in its use of theory there remains a certain disquiet about the effect of 'a long apprenticeship to the male theoretician' and a conviction that 'the master's tools will never dismantle the master's house'.[9] Theory holds a privileged location within an élitist institution, the academy; its female practitioners share in that status. How, then, certain feminists ask, can it ever give expression to the mass of women or facilitate a change in their circumstances? As Lillian Robinson laconically remarks: 'The revolution is simply not going to be made by literary journals.'[10]

On the other hand, feminists who are engaged in debates with other critical theories, particularly Marxism, post-structuralism, and psycho-analytical theory, believe they have no alternative. How can one be 'outside' theory? To look for some pure, experiential, non-theoretical space is utopian. Though the personal is political, the political isn't only the personal; an untheorized politics of personal experience may never get beyond subjectivism. What disturbs the pro-theorists is the refusal of the anti-theorists to analyse their own theoretical positions: witness Moi's complaint that 'Showalter's theoretical framework is never made explicit'. This lack of awareness, this belief in a straightforward authenticity of statement can encourage feminism into complicity with a reactionary politics. 'Unless one is aware that one cannot avoid taking a stand, unwitting stands get taken' (Spivak). From this perspective to value the experiential over the theoretical is not fundamentally to challenge the binary opposition, merely to reverse it. The oppositional structures of patriarchal thinking remain firmly in place and hierarchical modes of categorization are sustained.

Woolf/Showalter/Moi

The debate between pro- and anti-theorists provides an entrée into understanding the strikingly different assessments of Woolf by Showalter and Moi. Though Showalter has always been notably cautious about theorizing, it would be an injustice to dismiss her as a mere anti-theorist. Indeed, in recent years, she has moved towards a fuller engagement with theory. Her latest collections, *The New Feminist Criticism* (1986) and *Speaking of Gender* (1989), though still largely American both in terms of contributors and critical approach, have nevertheless included essays from several critical positions, and Showalter in her introductory assessments has clearly tried to be even-handed. But it does seem that whenever Showalter turns to a consideration of Anglo-American versus French perspectives a curiously uncertain tone enters her writing. For instance in 'Women's Time, Women's Space: Writing the History of Feminist Criticism' (1985) she mentions two groups of 'pioneering practitioners' of feminism – firstly, those who 'have been driven to ask theoretical questions and to accept the modern idea that there can be no practice without theory', and secondly, those who raise the spectre of the post-structuralist feminist as 'a rhetorical double agent, a little drummer girl who plays go-between in male critical quarrels'. In which group does Showalter, undoubtedly a 'pioneering practitioner', place herself? Ostensibly, in this essay, as in the recent collections, she sees herself not as a group member but as a mediator, opposing 'such a hostile polarization of French and American feminist discourse, arid theory and crude empiricism, obscurantism or essentialism'. Yet at times her appeal for work to proceed 'on both fronts... enriched by dialectical possibilities' sounds laudable but strained, as if neither her head nor her heart is quite convinced of the possibility of dialogue.[11]

Moi believes that a theoretical incompatibility is at the root of Showalter's problem with Woolf, but in many ways Woolf and Showalter are united in common pursuits. Showalter's volume, *A Literature of Their Own* (1977), not only acknowledges its lineage by playing on the title of Woolf's *A Room of One's Own* (1929) but also explores similar interests. Both critics are discerning in their analyses of that configuration of material, ideological and psychological factors that situate the woman writer. What defeats Woolf's Judith Shakespeare is not lack of effort or ability but the absence of material support – no education, no money; an ideological antipathy – women are unoriginal, private and domestic, creative only in their biology; and the psychological consequences of this situation – the self-doubt, the remorse, the fear. In her turn Showalter traces the effect of male criticism on nineteenth-century women novelists. Again, the problem is not the women's inadequacy but a criticism which is patronizing, scathing, or anxiously self-protective. A passion for women's writing and feminist research also links both critics. Aware of the invisibility of women's lives, they are active in the essential work of retrieval, trying to find the forgotten precursors. In her 1979 essay 'Toward a Feminist Poetics', Showalter recommends that literary feminists should follow the example of their sisters in other disciplines and begin to study female literary sub-cultures.[12] In a sense Showalter simply reiterates what Woolf had herself proposed half a century earlier. Constantly stymied by the absence of facts about women's lives, Woolf's narrator in *A Room of One's Own* proposes for the women of Newnham and Girton a series of useful research projects. What is needed, she believes, is: 'a mass of information; at what age did she marry; how many children had she as a rule; what was her house like'[13] or some study of the psychological effect that the absence of a tradition may have on women writers. With their empirical method, their concern with literary and social history, their woman-centred focus, these projects concur closely with Showalter's research aims.

Yet, despite so much agreement, Woolf, in Showalter's eyes, falls short. Her tetchiness is roused by what she observes as an evasiveness in Woolf. For example, Woolf's interest in androgyny is a failure to confront 'her own painful femaleness', a desire 'to choke and repress her anger and ambition'; it is 'a strategic defeat' and 'a denial of feeling'. Woolf's use of multiple personae in *A Room of One's Own* is repudiated as 'impersonal and defensive'. Her style is similarly 'teasing, sly and elusive' and full of 'gamesmanship'. In Showalter's opinion Woolf needlessly dissipates, amidst a range of literary strategies, her just feminist anger, her sense of herself as an oppressed women. Showalter finds Woolf not only shifting but shifty, almost too clever by half. Moi invites a different perspective. Where Showalter detects flaws, Moi discovers qualities; what Showalter sees as an avoidance of a declared and explicit political commitment, Moi views as the potential for a revolutionary practice; while Showalter believes Woolf's use of multiple personae represents a refusal to stand up and be counted, Moi welcomes Woolf's willingness to 'radically undermine the notion of a unitary self, the central concept of Western male humanism'.

Anglo-American feminism/French feminism

How two equally perceptive feminist critics can come to such contrary conclusions about the significance of Woolf's work needs explanation. Moi's suggestion is that Anglo-American feminism does not possess the necessary theoretical apparatus to respond adequately to Woolf. Since the mid-1970s the dominant mode in Anglo-American criticism has been concerned with the specificity of women's writing, a tradition of women authors and an exploration of women's culture. Showalter, who is among the most consistently illuminating exponents of this approach, has coined for it the term 'gynocriticism'.[14] The gynocritic dedicates herself to the female author and character and develops theories and methodologies based on female experience, the touchstone of authenticity. The gynocritic discovers in her authors and characters an understanding of female identity – not that she expects her authors and heroines to be superwomen, but the essential struggle will be towards a coherent identity, a realization of selfhood and autonomy. The most popular sequence in a gynocritical reading is from reality, to author, to reader, to reality: there is an objective reality which the author apprehends and describes truthfully in her text; the reader appreciates the validity of the text and relates it to her understanding of her own life. In this paradigm author, character and reader can unite in an exploration of what it means to be female – they can even assert a collective identity as 'we women' – and the reader is gratified by having her anger, experience, or hopes confirmed by the author and narrative. If this description approximates Showalter's expectations as a reader, one can understand why she found reading Woolf so unsatisfactory.

Moi's resurrection of Woolf is based on French theory; it is Derrida and Kristeva, she tells us, who can rescue Woolf for feminism. Interestingly – and for some alarmingly – French theory disputes almost every point in the Anglo-American thesis. It has also found its own neologism. Alice Jardine has set alongside gynocriticism, 'gynesis':

...a reincorporation and reconceptualization of that which has been the master narratives' own 'nonknowledge', what has eluded them, what has engulfed them. This other-than-themselves is almost always a 'space' of some kind (over which the narrative has lost control), and this space has been coded as *feminine*, as *woman*...

...gynesis – the putting into discourse of 'woman' as that *process* diagnosed in France as intrinsic to the condition of modernity; indeed, the valorization of the feminine, woman, and her obligatory, that is historical connotations, as somehow intrinsic to new and necessary modes of thinking, writing, speaking.[15]

The different meanings that Anglo-American and French feminisms give to the terms 'women', 'woman' and 'feminine' are crucial to understanding this interchange. Anglo-American feminism centres on 'women' – real, biological entities who, at this moment in history, are

forging a politics based on shared experience and needs. French interest
converges not on women but on 'woman' who, as Jardine points out, is
not a person but a 'writing-effect'. Jacobus in her essay makes the same
distinction: 'the French insistence on *écriture féminine* – on woman as a
writing-effect instead of an origin – asserts not the sexuality of the text but
the textuality of sex. Gender difference, produced, not innate, becomes a
matter of the structuring of a genderless libido in and through patriarchal
discourse. 'When the French talk of 'l'écriture féminine' they do not mean
the tradition of women's writing that Woolf and Showalter have laboured
to uncover, but a certain mode of writing which unsettles fixed meanings.
On the other hand, when Anglo-Americans use the term 'feminine' they
are usually referring to that cultural stereotype which patriarchy tells us is
the appropriate, even 'natural' form of behaviour for women.

Though both gynesis and gynocriticism would agree that the master
narratives are bankrupt, gynesis does not want to substitute mistress
narratives. That strategy, gynesis would argue, is ostensibly attractive but,
at the level of structure, changes nothing; it is simply to replace man at the
centre of the humanist endeavour with woman. Therefore gynesis gives
no special emphasis to female authors and characters; most of the
examples of 'feminine writing' it considers are by men. It is not necessarily
preoccupied with women's achievements in history or with women's
groups; on the contrary, Jardine stresses, the location that concerns gynesis
is a space, an absence. Gynocriticism's belief in the control of the author,
finding her unique voice, is refuted by gynesis. The author is dead: long
live the text – and the reader. Under the influence of Roland Barthes and
Derrida, gynesis points to a textual free play of meaning which cannot be
bound by authorial intention or critical analysis. Thus, what Moi likes
about Woolf is that her writing 'continually escapes the critic's
perspective, always refusing to be pinned down to one unifying angle of
vision'. Where Showalter sees a troubling hesitancy, Moi finds a welcome
deconstruction. To gynesis, gynocriticism's emphasis on the sisterhood of
author and reader ignores the complexity and duplicity of textuality.
Hence Moi's belief that 'Showalter's recommendation to remain detached
from the narrative strategies of the text is equivalent to not reading it at
all.'

Gynesis is not looking for an account of female experience – that is
dangerously close to biologism. Shoshana Felman asks what it means to be
'speaking as a woman': 'Is it enough to *be* a woman in order to speak as a
woman? Is 'speaking as a woman' a fact determined by some biological
condition or by a strategic, theoretical *position*, by anatomy or by culture?
What if 'speaking as a woman' were not a simple, 'natural' fact, could not
be taken for granted?'[16] In gynesis belief in the individual as a fully-

conscious, rational, secure identity gives way to a 'subject' which is unstable and constantly reformed. Kristeva uses the phrase 'subject in process' to convey how 'our identities in life are constantly called into question, brought to trial, over-ruled'.[17] Following this interpretation, Moi considers Woolf's exploration of multiple selves not as a loss of integrity, but as an interrogation of humanism's obsession with the individual, and an opening up of subjectivity to change. For gynocritism, liberation is to find one's true self; for gynesis, liberation is to abandon one('s) true self.

The French would deny that they are ignoring the historical predicament of women: to attack such notions as 'the natural', 'the real', 'the human' is in the interests of feminism, for it destabilizes the very order which keeps women oppressed. Furthermore, their emphasis on female desire can be judged as both woman-centred and potentially deconstructive. The Anglo-Americans also would deny that they are so fixed in the existing order that they are incapable of doubting its concepts and terminology. Few feminists of any persuasion would be convinced by statements such as: 'It's natural for women to be mothers', or 'Real women aren't ambitious', but beyond this baseline opinions differ considerably. Some radical feminists *would* subscribe to a belief in the 'natural' pacifism of women and the 'natural' aggression of men. Though doubts about the meaning of 'real' women are widespread, French feminism's questioning of realism as a literary form (the disagreement between Showalter and Moi could be seen as a debate between realism and modernism) and its insistence on reality as a 'construct' would not be supported in the Anglo-American concern for 'truth to life' and 'realistic' portrayals of female characters. While feminists generally will dispute a phrase such as 'the human condition', indicating how frequently women are lost within this seemingly all-embracing term, they will not all go along with the fundamental attack on humanism offered by gynesis.

Instead of speaking to each other, the Anglo-Americans and French seem frequently to be speaking past each other. For gynocritics or, more widely, for many who hold the political programme of feminism as central, gynesis contains a troubling potential for anti-feminism. Just at the moment when women are discovering a sense of identity, history and the credibility of their experience, gynesis tells them that it is illusory, and that their extensive work on the woman author, the female tradition, images of women is at best an interesting cul-de-sac. For the feminists at the chalk face of Women's Studies, those who are planning courses, and hoping for tenure, the distinction between the anti-feminists, who never thought feminism was academically respectable anyway, and the post-structuralists, who see the project as misconceived, may appear minimal.

The personal and the political

The dialogue between Kamuf and Miller is located firmly within the debate outlined above and the quality of the discussion lies partly in their close understanding of each other's point of view. As with the dialogue between Cixous and Clément, these essays represent not voices shouting to each other across the ocean, but colleagues jointly exploring common problems – most notably the significance of a text's signature and the institutional place of feminism within the university. Again, these are issues that occur in other essays in the collection. On the female signature, one could compare Showalter's understanding of the female tradition (definitely written by women) with Cixous' understanding of feminine discourse (possibly written by women), or follow Kamuf and Miller's comments on the university with Spivak's observations on academic feminism and Cixous' and Clément's discussion of the use, for pedagogic purposes, of the discourses of mastery. This in turn could lead to a consideration of the place of men in feminism; if men in feminism usually means men in feminism in the university, what are the consequences of this for women and feminism?

Kamuf's article opens with the requisite question: 'What is the place of feminist critical practice in the institution, in particular, the university?' Among Anglo-American critics the most frequent replies have been either to agitate for women's inclusion within the existing academy – essentially a liberal, reformist stance – or, more radically, to demand the transformation of the institution along woman-centred lines; the relevant essays of Adrienne Rich would be a good example of the latter response.[18] To Kamuf both strategies 'rest on the same analysis of phallocentrism's most readily evident feature – the order of women's exclusion – and proceed in practice to attempt to correct or reverse that feature at the same level at which it appears'. The predicament recalls our earlier discussion on the respective merits of theory versus experience: what appears to be a clearly oppositional move – to value women's experience over abstract masculinist theory, or to campaign for the full participation of women in the university – may in practice be open to fairly ready recuperation. In the extended metaphor of Kamuf's final two paragraphs, feminist practice is placed neither centrally within the institution, nor in some separatist enclave outside, but on the margins, delighting in 'its own inevitable inaccuracy and lack of finality', constantly pushing against what is fixed and circumscribed.

Miller locates herself differently. She aligns herself with those who wish to 'rectify or reverse women's exclusion'; speaks in the collective term Kamuf queried – 'we women'; and, using the same text that Kamuf once used, the anonymous *The Portuguese Letters*, comes to the opposing conclusion, namely that the sex of the author matters.[19] Yet she is well aware of the dangers in some branches of Anglo-American feminism: she rebukes any form of prescriptive feminism or any belief in the ethical superiority of reading works by women, and she is attentive to the arguments of gynesis. It is basically the pressure of politics that urges Miller to two conclusions. Firstly, the involvement with the woman author 'may betray a naïve faith in origins, humanism, and centrality', but it also makes visible 'the marginality, eccentricity and vulnerablity of women' and challenges 'the confidence of humanistic discourse as universality'. One could note here the different uses made by Kamuf and Miller of the concept of 'margins'. For Kamuf it is a position where the feminine can discover its most disturbing potential; for Miller it is a place where women have been restricted and confined. Secondly, Miller considers how, for people without power, questions about who is speaking, about authorship and authority are of daily relevance. The deconstruction of identity is only possible for those with a firm psychological and political hold on who they are and the status they have attained. To choose the marginal as a subject-position is a markedly different proposition from being discarded at the margins of society. Kamuf makes a brief (perhaps too brief?) reference to this materiality and the need to engage with the 'political – social distribution of effects that shapes our institutions', but she places her emphasis elsewhere, believing that any liaison with 'patriarchal meaning structures' must always 'keep in view its own contradictory disengagement of that meaning'.

The essays of Jacobus and Heath reproduce certain aspects of Kamuf and Miller's argument. Jacobus's conclusion, like Kamuf's, favours textuality over sexuality. To rely on signature is to risk biologism. Heath is well versed in the theories which warn us 'not to confuse the sex of the author with the sexuality and sexual positioning inscribed in the text'. Yet he is wary about idealizing textuality. His responsibilities, his connivance even, as a man in a phallocentric society cannot be jettisoned in favour of a world of playful deconstruction; the danger that his writing continues 'reinscribing, confirming, prolonging' his male authority is still to be reckoned with. Heath reminds us that, amidst the talk about reading 'as a woman' or writing 'as a woman', we must not forget to consider the meanings of 'being a woman'. Like Kamuf and Miller, Heath too finds fruitful a consideration of marginality. Is the marginal a positive position for men to take in relation to feminism? Heath offers this option, not in the old, unreconstructed sense where men's marginal relation to feminism indicated simply their negligible interest in it, but as a recognition that 'feminism has decentered men'; feminism is the one discourse where men cannot play the star part.

Black feminists have been deeply engaged in debates on the nature and significance of identity. Many would agree with Miller that a sense of identity and a valuing of personal experience can be life-lines for the invisible woman. Thus Nancy Hoffman, an Afro-American critic, writes: 'How do I invent an identity for myself in a society which prefers to behave as though I do not exist?'[20] and Alice Walker believes: 'that naming our own experience after our own fashion (as well as rejecting whatever does not seem to suit) is the least we can do – and in this society may well be our only tangible sign of personal freedom.'[21] Spivak, though, is concerned not only with how the Black woman names herself, but also with how her identity is constituted by the white woman, in particular First World feminists. She has been acerbic in her criticism of Anglo-American feminism and its reproduction of 'the axioms of imperialism': 'A basically isolationist admiration for the literature of the female subject in Europe and Anglo-America establishes the high feminist norm. It is supported and operated by an information-retrieval approach to "Third World" literature which often employs a deliberately "non-theoretical" methodology with self-conscious rectitude.'[22] But, as her comments on Kristeva indicate, she is equally critical of approaches within French feminism.

Politics and the poetic

One cannot accuse Kristeva, as one could some Anglo-American critics, of being blandly unaware of the need to interrogate one's own position. However, one can accuse her, Spivak believes, of neglecting the necessary dialectic between herself and Chinese women – 'not merely who am I? but who is the other woman? How am I naming her? How does she name me?' – in favour of a questioning which is 'obsessively self-centered'. Jane Gallop's conclusion is that Kristeva so positions herself within the text that 'she alone might be able to bridge the abyss of otherness, to contact and report the heterogeneous', and this in a book 'precisely about the dangers of using oneself as a measure for the other'.[23] Spivak's contention is that Kristeva not only privileges herself but elides others; in setting the 'Indo-European' world against China, Kristeva writes out the specificity of Indian history and culture, the very place to which Spivak, in her memories of childhood, needs to return.

There are similarities between Spivak's critique of Kristeva and Clément's responses to Cixous. Clément wants to bring together psychoanalysis, Marxism and feminism; Spivak is not greatly captivated by psychoanalysis but would like to conjoin Marxism, feminism and deconstruction. Spivak introduces Clément into her essay to voice one of her own objections about French feminism, its tendency to disengage from the particularities of the historical and political world. Thus, Spivak's complaints about Kristeva's generalized view of history – passing references to whole millenia – and her unsophisticated literary analysis of certain Chinese texts register not simply the objection of a 'Western-trained Third World feminist' to sloppy scholarship, but her desire to keep a firm materialist grasp on any analysis. Clément seems to function in a similar way in her dialogue with Cixous. It is Clément who is historically more precise, pointing to shifts in history when 'women had mastery'; she has a less monolithic view of ideology – for Cixous, ideology is a 'vast membrane enveloping everything' whereas for Clément there is always 'the power to change – or to inhibit'; it is she who makes the connection between the oppression of women and the development of capitalism, and she who repeatedly introduces into the debate the relevance of the class struggle. This final point returns us to Spivak's opposition to a 'principled "anti-feminism"', which puts its trust in the individualistic critical avant-garde rather than anything that might call itself a revolutionary collectivity'.

In Lacanian theory the moment of the Oedipal crisis and the repression of desire for the mother is also the moment of the acquisition of language and the entry into the symbolic order. 'To speak as a subject is therefore the same as to represent the existence of repressed desire.'[24] In her study of the Chinese language, Kristeva detects a 'pre-Oedipal, pre-syntactic, pre-symbolic register'. In her analysis of the manuals of the 'Art of the Bedchamber' she finds traces of an earlier matriarchal society where female pleasure, the woman's 'right to *jouissance* is incontestable'. Kristeva discovers here what she terms the 'semiotic', a process close to the maternal body, though not a female essence, and able to disrupt the symbolic order. As Kristeva suggests later in *About Chinese Women* (1977), patriarchal society 'protects itself from the *jouissance* that can drive it to madness or revolution: it keeps itself stable, permanent, eternal'.[25] Cixous and Clément are also interested in these potentially unsettling forces, though their example of repressed desire is the body of the hysteric. For Cixous, Freud's patient, Dora, is both 'the typical woman' and 'a force capable of demolishing those structures'. For Clément, Dora offers 'challenging positions', 'challenging functions', but she 'doesn't change the structures'; on the contrary, the family regroups around the hysteric, containing her. Using Flaubert as her example, Clément maintains that the progressive and necessary move is to enter 'symbolic inscription'. One can't make revolution at the level of language and desire, says Clément; one can't make revolution without a consideration of language and desire, replies Cixous.

This difference of approach can be interpreted not as a radical impasse but as a creative ambiguity. Clément herself defines her task as looking for the 'missing links' that relate politics to the poetic, the social and collective to the personal and familial, the class struggle to the language of desire.

However paradoxical it might seem, feminists must walk in two directions at once. The history of women and their political needs in the present are too important to be ignored. Nevertheless, our understanding of masculinity and femininity must be profoundly deconstructed; what we now understand as 'we women' will not survive patriarchy. As Mary Poovey has remarked so appositely, feminism needs to 'work out some way to think both women and "woman"'.[26] It is in this context that we can understand Moi's careful explanation of Kristeva's three-stage description of feminism: the second stage where feminists 'defend women *as* women' must work alongside a deconstruction of 'the metaphysical nature of gender identities'. Miller undertakes a similar balancing of priorities. For her the pursuit of a post-humanist theory is to be coupled with a sharp awareness of the political position of women within the institution; she calls for 'a decentered vision (*theoria*) but a centered action'. To put it crudely, there is no great advance in having numerous courses in feminism and deconstruction if only the men get promoted.

Predictably this twin perspective expresses itself in an imagery of margins, as we have already seen in Miller and Kamuf, and of borders, bridging and dialectical movement. Despite all her keen objections to elements within French feminism, Spivak recognizes the shrewdness of the French double agenda, both against sexism and for feminism. She sees in it the potential to 'straddle' a whole series of sexual, racial and cultural oppositions. In an earlier section of *About Chinese Women*, Kristeva offers women 'an impossible dialectic: a permanent alternation' as a strategy for attaining a public voice while still remaining critical and heedful of the repressed and unspoken.[27] It is precisely this passage which Spivak attacks for speaking only to 'class- and race-privileged literary women', for ignoring 'the micrology of political economy', and for being 'individualistic'. A shared imagery is evidently not the same as a shared politics.

Men in feminism

In several of the discussions so far questions of positionality have been crucial. How does an Indian woman living in America comment on a Bulgarian women living in France who is, in turn, commenting on Chinese women (Spivak and Kristeva)? What happens to femininity when women find themselves in 'the position of mastery' (Cixous and Clément)? And now, with the essays of Jacobus and Heath, we face another conundrum: how might the sex of the author affect his/her relationship with theory in general and feminism in particular? A rough schema of feminism's relationship with male writers since 1970 would oscillate between involvement, separatism and a return to a rather different kind of involvement. Men's relationship to feminism, on the other hand, has until recently been characterized by a lack of interest; currently feminism is experiencing a flurry of male attention. Millett's *Sexual Politics* belongs to that early phase of feminism's close association with the male author; D.H. Lawrence, Henry Miller, Norman Mailer, Jean Genet and Freud are the protagonists of *Sexual Politics*. Millett's Acknowledgements of authors quoted at length contain no women at all, and the reader is over a third of the way through the book before encountering any consideration of what female authors may have felt about changes in sexual relations: 'So far we have observed the sexual revolution as it was reflected in the mind of male writers responding to it with gallant enthusiasm or dubious ambiguity. But the period did provide something more informative than this: it permitted the first expression of a feminine point of view.'[28] Even then, in less than ten pages, it is back to the men and a critique of male Victorian poets. Millett maps out her terrain in the Preface. Her proposition is that 'sex has a frequently neglected political aspect' and that literature can effectively 'illustrate' this assertion. Lawrence, Miller and Mailer are chosen as 'representative' of a reactionary impulse that has attempted to stifle progressive moves in sexual politics; Genet is included as 'a contrast'. From the start Millett makes clear that she intends to set herself into ideological combat with her adversaries; she will take 'an author's ideas seriously', she tells us, and where she has 'substantive quarrels with some of these ideas' she will 'argue on those very grounds'. By the end of the Preface the indication is strong that Lawrence, for one, will be found 'inadequate, or biased, or his influence pernicious'. [29]

Kaplan is provoked into asking a series of questions about Millett's work: why the emphasis on literature – indeed, why in general do so many feminists look to literature as 'the particular object of their analysis of female subordination'; why the focus on male writers; and why the selection of these particular male writers? Kaplan suggests that socialist feminism, as opposed to Millett's radical feminism, would place less stress on high culture, but she also implies that an analysis of the class/educational background of academic feminists is not in itself sufficient to explain the precedence given to literature. Kaplan deduces that it is especially Millett's belief in the homologous nature of patriarchal institutions that encourages her emphasis on literature; for Millett, what is happening in literature parallels what is happening in other areas of society. Thus, so the argument goes, if one finds examples of sexism in literature, then these are a good indication of a wider malaise.

Kaplan's more subtle understanding of social structures warns her against any easy equation between one social institution and another. Her careful literary analysis also points out an inconsistency in Millett's thinking. Millett subscribes to a reflectionist theory of literature: she claims that literature has a mimetic function and that certain authors are 'representative'. Consequently, literature can provide the reader with a 'true' indication of the misogyny both of certain individual writers and of our culture generally. At the same time, however, Millett discovers that the authors under observation fail in their mimetic task and give a 'false' image of the nature and potential of women. As Kaplan concludes 'the author can be represented as telling the truth about his desires and gross falsehoods about cultural reality': literature can be at once mimetic and manipulative. At the heart of Kaplan's dispute with Millett is a debate about ideology. Millett is quite right to express her disgust at brutal and exploitative portrayals of female characters, but where she is in error , Kaplan argues, is in her 'unproblematic identification of author, protagonist and point of view, and the unspoken assumption that literature is always a conscious rendering of an authorial ideology'. Does Millett therefore set up straw men only so that she can knock them down? Would the selection of a different group of men as 'representative', or an exploration of the contradictory elements within her chosen group have made men a less easy target? Would a critique of the ambiguous ideological positions of a group of female authors render women less heroic, less victimized?

Millett perceives that there exists in the male word a source of power to be assailed. One of the most enduring qualities of *Sexual Politics* is the wit and anger with which Millett takes on the male intellectual establishment. Reverential readings, deference to canonical status or critical acclaim are all swiftly debunked. But by the mid-1970s even this combative approach had become unacceptable, and quarrying male works for examples of sexism deferred to studies of the variety and uniqueness of women's writing. Showalter's creation of gynocriticism provided a theory for this swing of interest and signalled a rejection of what she called the 'feminist critique', 'this angry or loving fixation on male literature'.[30] Whereas in Millett there seemed no way for women to read many male authors except to condemn them, in Showalter's theory there seemed to be no way for women to read men at all. In certain circles it was more than bad form – collusion with the enemy in fact – to study male authors. Such study manifested a lack of commitment to women and an unreconstructed psychological dependence on men. Any pleasure the woman reader gained from the male text was ascribed to false consciousness, masochism, or an infantile desire to continue pleasing daddy. Reading became a separatist activity; heterosexuality in bed or books was frowned on.

For most of the 1970s the response to feminist criticism by male readers and critics veered from the vitriolic, to lack of interest or mild tolerance. In academic circles, once the first wave of vituperation had died down, two reactions became customary: the first, a conservative position which ignored feminism in the hope that one day it would go away; the second, a progressive posture which agreed with female demands for a space, both physical and ideological. The irony of the second stance, although superficially liberal, is that it compounded male reluctance to participate in debates about gender or feminism. Gender became a woman's issue, indeed deeply problematic for women; men, it appeared, continued to enter the world whole, complete, fully gendered and not needing to discuss the matter. As Heath indicates, in Freud's writing on sexuality it is *female* sexuality that is deviant and controversial; male sexuality is 'the norm, the point of departure'.

The alacrity with which male theorists responded to other new theoretical developments can be contrasted with the notable lack of urgency about participating in feminism. If masculinity was unquestionable and femininity and feminism were for women only, then there was really nothing to say. This situation led to a series of untenable conclusions: as we have seen, that women couldn't read men's texts without collusion; in addition that men couldn't read women's texts without expropriation; and that women's texts spoke directly to women and men's directly to men. One of the deleterious consequences of gynocriticism was that the male text remained inviolable; the more we refused to query it, the larger its power loomed. But from the early 1980s a new state of wary negotiation permitted the woman critic to return to the male text, not enthralled with it, as Showalter feared, but often taking Nina Auerbach's advice about 'demystifying, diminishing and finally engorging that power'.[31] For their part, men began to come to the tardy apprehension that in feminist criticism was a body of work that could no longer be ignored. Both groups started focusing on some pivotal questions. What does it mean to talk of a 'male' text or a 'female' text? How does a 'female' text differ from a 'feminist' text, or from 'feminine' writing? Can a man read 'as a woman', Jonathan Culler asked? In patriarchal society are women coerced into reading 'as a man'?[32]

The arrival of men on the feminist scene has not been without problems. *Pace* Freud, the questions now are 'What does man want?' and 'Are we (female feminists) prepared to give it to him?' Heath identifies the relationship between men and feminism as 'an impossible one'; no matter how sympathetic or, indeed, knowledgeable about feminism the male critic may be, he always brings to his criticism 'all the implications of domination and appropriation'; however sincerely he tries to find the answer, he still remains part of the problem. Heath wisely realizes that this very 'impossibility' can be transformed into an advantage for men. Men must resist seeing themselves as part of an 'existential tragedy', writing men's relation to feminism as an heroic struggle against the odds, and face the historical and political moment. Heath's willingness to question scrupulously, to encourage male self-effacement, to read closely and with enjoyment women writers and critics justifiably wins him approbation from many female feminists. Yet there are dangers – and Heath would the first to appreciate these – in allowing oneself to become the favoured son. The engaging feminine qualities in Heath's work – its reluctance to assert, its receptivity – could play their own oppressive part: Heath as more feminist than the feminists, the new literary ladies' man. Although men's relation to feminism is 'impossible', there are occasions when men gain credit from feminism in a way that women do not. For example, in radical circles, men can achieve status by declaring their feminism; in the academy, the arrival of men into feminism is sometimes viewed as feminism's coming-of-age; female protestations have had to wait for the male imprimatur. To some extent, for Heath to say that the relation between men and feminism is 'impossible' carries more weight than an identical comment from a woman. Is this because his experience as a man validates his remarks on this particular relationship, or is it because, even now, male interpretations of feminism are perceived as more reliable than female interpretations?

Feminists fear that the involvement of men in feminism will lead to yet one more displacement of women, possibly supplanting women as the critics, teachers and practitioners of feminism, and eroding its political agenda. Ken Ruthven's volume, *Feminist Literary Studies* (1984), would give credence to both fears. Billed by its publishers as 'the first broad survey' of its kind, it informs its audience that feminism 'by the time it enters literary studies as critical discourse is just one more way of talking about books'.[33] So much for any hopes about changing the world! Jacobus continues to search for the woman. Her opening anecdote illustrates how the female is erased, becoming the 'mute sacrifice on which theory itself may be founded'. The important relationship is the male bonding between theorist and theorist or, as in *Frankenstein* (1818), between the scientist and his creation. The woman is disposable, silenced, a reference point, an object of exchange between men. Heath too is alert to instances of male bonding. Is there in male feminism, he wonders, 'always potentially a pornographic effect' in 'the rebonding of men round "the feminine" '? The regrouping is also a reclamation taking many forms, from the 'textual harassment' Jacobus isolates, to the 'sympathy-reconfirmation' of the right-on man. In the latter case, by identifying with female oppression, men can again become benign fathers to whom women are grateful.

Heath's essay is included in a volume entitled *Men in Feminism* (1987). The editors, Alice Jardine and Paul Smith, propose in their Introduction that the most difficult word in that title is 'in'. To some extent the whole problem of men's relation to feminism can be interpreted as a problem of prepositions and conjunctions.[34] For me 'in' suggests a series of invasive and penetrative connotations; for Richard Ohmann it implies an unpleasant exclusion: ' To speak of men (or women) as in feminism surely does not (yet?) imply the sort of academic reduction of the person to a specialism, but it does smack of guild credentials – of an intellectual membership earned through writing centripetally toward an established group that has the authority to admit or exclude.'[35] Is the contrast in our responses a sign of the different positions of men and women in coming to feminism? Men 'on' feminism intimates to me both an oppressive weight and a superior mode of disputation. For instance, Denis Donoghue's summary of feminist criticism in the Jardine and Smith volume is notable for its tone of airy disdain, of speaking *de haut en bas*. His frequent laments that he does not understand the material he is reviewing – 'I allude to this agenda so far as I can understand it... I give the passage in English, but the French to me is just as opaque... I'm not sure what she means... I have no answer...' – are either disingenuous or an indication that he should put greater effort into his research. [36] Men 'and' feminism hides more than in reveals, suggesting an equilibrium which hardly does justice to the fraught relationship of the moment. Men 'with' feminism sounds supportive and egalitarian, but could also imply fellow-travelling. The problem is at once semantic and political. Is there no preposition that could hint at a more productive future relationship? Perhaps men 'for' feminism?

Notes and references

1. KATE MILLETT, *Sexual Politics* (London: Virago Press, 1977), pp. 139-40.

2. ANNETTE KOLODNY, 'Dancing Through the Minefield: Some Observations on the Theory, Practice, and Politics of Feminist Literary Criticism', in *The New Feminist Criticism: Essays on Women, Literature and Theory*, ed. Elaine Showalter (London: Virago Press, 1986), p. 159.

3. JANE MARCUS, 'Storming the Toolshed', in *Feminist Theory; A Critique of Ideology*, ed. Nannerl O. Keohane, Michelle Z. Rosaldo, Barbara C. Gelpi (Chicago: University of Chicago Press, 1982), p. 218.

4. GAYATRI CHAKRAVORTY SPIVAK, 'A Response to Annette Kolodny' (unpublished essay). Quoted in Jane Marcus, op. cit., p. 218 note.

5. TORIL MOI, *Sexual/Textual Politics: Feminist Literary Theory* (London: Methuen, 1985), p. xiv.

6. MARY DALY, *Beyond God the Father: Toward a Philosophy of Women's Liberation* (Boston, Mass: Beacon Press, 1973), pp. 11-12.

7. MARGUERITE DURAS, 'An Interview', in *New French Feminisms: An Anthology*, ed. Elaine Marks and Isabelle de Courtivron (Brighton: Harvester Press, 1981), p. 111.

8. HÉLÈNE CIXOUS, 'Sorties: Out and Out: Attacks/Ways Out/Forays', in *The Newly Born Woman*, Hélène Cixious and Catherine Clément (Manchester: University of Manchester Press, 1986).

9. ELAINE SHOWALTER, 'Toward a Feminist Poetics', in *The New Feminist Criticism*,

op. cit., p. 130. 'The Master's Tools will Never Dismantle the Master's House' is an essay title from Audre Lorde, *Sister Outsider: Essays and Speeches* (New York: Crossing Press, 1984).

10. LILLIAN ROBINSON, *Sex, Class, and Culture* (London: Methuen, 1986), p. 52.

11. ELAINE SHOWALTER, 'Women's Time, Women's Space: Writing the History of Feminist Criticism', in *Feminist Issues in Literary Scholarship*, ed. Shari Benstock (Bloomington and Indianapolis: Indiana University Press, 1987), pp. 36 – 7.

12. ELAINE SHOWALTER, 'Toward a Feminist Poetics', in *The New Feminist Criticism*, op. cit., p. 131.

13. VIRGINIA WOOLF, *A Room of One's Own* (London: Grafton Books, 1987), p. 44.

14. ELAINE SHOWALTER, 'Toward a Feminist Poetics', in *The New Feminist Criticism*, op. cit., p. 128.

15. ALICE A. JARDINE, *Gynesis: Configurations of Woman and Modernity* (Ithaca and London: Cornell University Press, 1985), p. 15.

16. SHOSHANA FELMAN, 'Women and Madness: The Critical Phallacy', *Diacritics*, 5, no. 4 (Winter, 1975), p. 3.

17. JULIA KRISTEVA, 'A Question of Subjectivity', *Women's Review*, 12 (Oct. 1986), p. 19.

18. See RICH's essays on women's education in *On Lies, Secrets, and Silence: Selected Prose 1966 – 1978* (London: Virago, 1980), and *Blood, Bread and Poetry: Selected Prose 1979 – 1985* (London: Virago 1987).

19. Miller's analysis of *The Portuguese Letters* is a reply to Kamuf's exposition in 'Writing Like a Woman', in *Women and Language in Literature and Society*, ed. Sally McConnell-Ginet, Ruth Borker, Nelly Furman (New York: Praeger Publishers, 1980).

20. NANCY HOFFMAN, 'White Woman, Black Woman: Inventing an Adequate Pedagogy', *Women's Studies Newsletter*, 5, nos 1,2 (Winter/Spring, 1977), p. 21.

21. ALICE WALKER, *In Search of Our Mothers' Gardens: Womanist Prose* (London: Women's Press Ltd, 1984), p. 82.

22. GAYATRI CHAKRAVORTY SPIVAK, 'Three Women's Texts and and a Critique of Imperialism', in *The Feminist Reader: Essays in Gender and the Politics of Literary Criticism*, ed. Catherine Belsey and Jane Moore (Basingstoke and London: Macmillan, 1989), pp. 175 – 6.

23. JANE GALLOP, *Feminism and Psychoanalysis: The Daughter's Seduction* (London: Macmillan, 1982), p. 119.

24. TORIL MOI, *Sexual/Textual Politics*, op. cit., pp.99 – 100.

25. JULIA KRISTEVA, *About Chinese Women* (London: Marion Boyars, 1977), p. 76.

26. MARY POOVEY, 'Feminism and Deconstruction', *Feminist Studies*, 14, no. 1 (Spring, 1988), p. 53.

27. JULIA KRISTEVA, *About Chinese Women*, op. cit., p. 38.

28. KATE MILLETT, *Sexual Politics*, op. cit., p.38.

29. KATE MILLETT, Ibid., pp. xi -xii.

30. ELAINE SHOWALTER, 'Toward a Feminist Poetics', *The New Feminist Criticism*, op. cit., p. 131.

31. NINA AUERBACH, 'Why Communities of Women Aren't Enough', *Tulsa Studies in Women's Literature*, 3 nos 1,2 (Spring/Fall, 1984), p. 156.

32. JONATHAN CULLER, *On Deconstruction: Theory and Criticism after Structuralism* (London: Routledge & Kegan Paul, 1983).

33. K. K. RUTHVEN, *Feminist Literary Studies: An Introduction* (Cambridge: Cambridge University Press, 1984), p. 8.

34. Note how Toril Moi deftly side-steps the problem of men's relation to feminism by redefining the issue as men's relation to patriarchy. See 'Men Against Patriarchy', in *Gender and Theory: Dialogues on Feminist Criticism*, ed. Linda Kauffman (Oxford: Basil Blackwell, 1989).

35. RICHARD OHMANN, 'In, With', in *Men in Feminism*, ed. Alice Jardine and Paul Smith (New York and London: Methuen, 1987), pp. 182 – 3.

36. DENIS DONOGHUE, 'A Criticism of One's Own', in *Men in Feminism*, op. cit., pp. 147 – 9.

1 Elaine Showalter and Toril Moi

ELAINE SHOWALTER *A Literature of Their Own**

Elaine Showalter's *A Literature of Their Own: British Women Novelists from Brontë to Lessing* (1977) traces a history of women's writing through three phases – the 'feminine' from 1840–80, the 'feminist' from 1880–1920 and the 'female' from 1920 onwards. The two extracts included here are from the female phase, from Showalter's chapter on Woolf, entitled 'Woolf and the Flight into Androgyny'. The chapter title is suggestive. Showalter finds Woolf's concern with an androgynous ideal escapist, a way of avoiding confrontation with her family, her critics and readers, her social class. Similarly, Woolf's 'room of one's own' has certain creative and protective possibilities, but is more often viewed by Showalter as a sign of Woolf's retreat from a necessary interaction with the material world and with her own psychosexual dilemmas. The section of the chapter excluded focuses on Woolf's sexual and psychiatric history, relating her mental crises to biological factors – the onset of menstruation, her childlessness, the menopause – and to her relationship with her husband, Leonard. The link is not one of crude biologism – women because of their biological make-up are periodically unstable and hysterical – but one that points to the excessive and irreconcilable pressures that Woolf felt at such moments of crisis. Fuelled by a feminism that believes in a forthright declaration of one's needs as a woman, Showalter contends that androgyny, private space, aestheticism are inadequate answers to the problems of sexual politics. (See Introduction, pp. 7–11).

---

* Reprinted from Elaine Showalter, *A Literature of Their Own: British Women Novelists from Brontë to Lessing* (London: Virago, 1978), pp. 263–5, 282–97.

It needs little skill in psychology to be sure that a highly gifted girl
who had tried to use her gift for poetry would have been so
thwarted and hindered by other people, so tortured and pulled apart
by her own contrary instincts, that she must have lost her own health
and sanity to a certainty.

A ROOM OF ONE'S OWN

If I were a woman I'd blow someone's brains out.

THE VOYAGE OUT

In recent years it has become important to feminist critics to emphasize
Virginia Woolf's strength and gaiety and to see her as the apotheosis of a
new literary sensibility – not feminine, but androgynous. Caroline Heilbrun
has described the members of the Bloomsbury Group as the first examples
of the androgynous way of life; she demands that we recognize: that they
were all marvelously capable of love, that lust in their world was a joyful
emotion, that jealousy and domination were remarkably sparse in their
lives.[1] Within this milieu, we are to understand, Virginia Woolf was free to
develop both sides of her nature, both male and female, and to create the
appropriate kind of novel for the expression of her androgynous vision.

The concept of true androgyny – full balance and command of an emotional range that includes male and female elements – is attractive, although
I suspect that like all utopian ideals androgyny lacks zest and energy. But
whatever the abstract merits of androgyny, the world that Virginia Woolf
inhabited was the last place in which a woman could fully express both
femaleness and maleness, nurturance and aggression. For all her immense
gift, Virginia Woolf was as thwarted and pulled asunder as the women she
describes in *A Room of One's Own*. Androgyny was the myth that helped her
evade confrontation with her own painful femaleness and enabled her to
choke and repress her anger and ambition. Woolf inherited a female tradition
a century old; no woman writer has ever been more in touch with – even
obsessed by – this tradition that she; yet by the end of her life she had gone
back full circle, back to the melancholy, guilt-ridden, suicidal women –
Lady Winchelsea and the Duchess of Newcastle – whom she had studied
and pitied. And beyond the tragedy of her personal life is the betrayal of
her literary genius, her adoption of a female aesthetic that ultimately proved
inadequate to her purposes and stifling to her development.

In Virginia Woolf's version of female aestheticism and androgyny, sexual
identity is polarized and all the disturbing, dark, and powerful aspects of
femaleness are projected onto maleness. Woolf deals with her most intimate
experience through biographical essays on other women writers, including

25

Jane Carlyle, Geraldine Jewsbury, Charlotte Brontë, and George Eliot. In her fiction, but supremely in *A Room of One's Own*, Woolf is the architect of female space, a space that is both sanctuary and prison. Through their windows, her women observe a more violent masculine world in which their own anger, rebellion, and sexuality can be articulated at a safe remove. Yet these narrative strategies, as in the novels of her predecessors Schreiner and Richardson, are ultimately unsuccessful. It is a man, of course, who speaks the line from *The Voyage Out* quoted above. The ambiguity of violence in Woolf's fiction is instructive; the vague target, the someone whom the sensitive woman is likely to destroy, is inevitably the woman herself. When we think about the joy, the generosity, and the absence of jealousy and domination attributed to Bloomsbury, we should also remember the victims of this emotional utopia: Mark Gertler, Dora Carrington, Virginia Woolf. They are the failures of androgyny, their suicides are one of Bloomsbury's representative art forms.

For the past fifty years, Virginia Woolf has dominated the imaginative territory of the English woman novelist, just as George Eliot dominated it the century before. The woman writer is urged to be as 'Woolfian' as possible, according to Joyce Carol Oates[2] – that is, to be subjective, and yet to transcend her femaleness, to write exquisitely about inner space and leave the big messy brawling novels to men. A similar idealization and mystification of Woolf's life style is extending her sphere of historical influence to personal relationships. I think it is important to demystify the legend of Virginia Woolf. To borrow her own murderous imagery, a woman writer must kill the Angel in the House, that phantom of female perfection who stands in the way of freedom. For Charlotte Brontë and George Eliot, the Angel was Jane Austen. For the feminist novelists, it was George Eliot. For the mid-twentieth-century novelists, the Angel is Woolf herself.

The most famous of Woolf's statements about androgyny is *A Room of One's Own*. A. J. Moody is in the minority when he objects that 'the title has enjoyed a fame rather beyond the intrinsic merits of the work' (Woolf's most conspicuous antagonists, the Leavises, found *Room* too flimsy to warrant their close attention).[3] What is most striking about the book texturally and structurally is its strenuous charm, its playfulness, its conversational surface. There is nothing here to suggest the humorless polemics of *Votes for Women* or *The Egoist*. The techniques of *Room* are like those of Woolf's fiction, particularly *Orlando*, which she was writing at the same time: repetition, exaggeration, parody, whimsy, and multiple viewpoint. On the other hand, despite its illusions of spontaneity and intimacy, *A Room of One's Own* is an extremely impersonal and defensive book.

Impersonality may seem like the wrong word for a book in which a narrative 'I' appears in every third sentence. But a closer look reveals that the 'I' is a persona, whom the author calls 'Mary Beton' and that her views are carefully distanced and depersonalized, just as the pronoun 'one' in the title depersonalizes, and even de-sexes the subject. The whole book is cast in arch allegorical terms from the start: 'I need not say that what I am about to describe, Oxbridge, is an invention; so is Fernham; 'I' is only a convenient term for somebody who has no real being.' In fact the characters and places are all disguised or delicately parodied versions of Woolf's own experience. 'Fernham' is Newnham College, Cambridge, where she had given the lectures that were the genesis of the book. Woolf's cousin Katherine Stephen was Vice-Principal of Newnham; she is the 'Mary Seton' who explains to Mary Beton why the women's colleges are so poor. Her mother, 'Mrs Seton', has had thirteen children (actually Mrs Stephen had seven). The narrator, Mary Beton, lives in a London house by the river. Before 1918 she made her living in the jobs open to untrained middle-class women: amateur society journalism, clerical work, and teaching. Then she inherited 500 pounds a year from an aunt, also named Mary Beton, who had fallen off a horse in Bombay. Woolf had inherited 2,500 pounds from her aunt Caroline Emelia Stephen, whose life was much less romantic.[4] The last Mary, Mary Carmichael, author of *Life's Adventure*, is probably also a parody or a composite figure.

The entire book is teasing, sly, elusive in this way; Woolf plays with her audience, refusing to be entirely serious, denying any earnest or subversive intention. As M. C. Bradbrook has written, 'The camouflage in *A Room of One's Own*...prevents Mrs Woolf from committing the indelicacy of putting a case or the possibility of her being accused of waving any kind of banner. The arguments are clearly serious and personal and yet they are dramatized and surrounded with all sorts of disguises to avoid an appearance of argument.'[5] In the opening chapters, this defensiveness leads to a rather unpleasantly Stracheyesque kind of innuendo, as if the Cambridge setting had recalled the style of the Apostles. An example is the appearance of a Manx cat in the Oxbridge luncheon scene. Mary Beton is suddenly convulsed with laughter at the sight of 'that abrupt and truncated animal.... I had to explain my laughter by pointing at the Manx cat, who did look a little absurd, poor beast, without a tail, in the middle of the lawn. Was he really born so, or had he lost his tail in an accident?...It is strange what a difference a tail makes – you know the sort of things one says as a lunch party breaks up and people are finding their coats and hats.'[6] This certainly sounds like a feline swipe at Cantabrigian impotence.

In chapter 3, however, the narrative finally moves beyond this kind of gamesmanship and focuses on the question of women and fiction. Woolf insists that a woman must have an independent income and a room of her own if she is to write fiction, and that the mind of the artist should be androgynous. Apart from the specific question of income, to which Marxists object, these ideas are very nearly as civilized and unabrasive as the style, and it is easy to get caught up in the seductive flow. Who could possibly object to the idea of androgyny? Even clinical psychology confirms that 'the really creative individual combines "masculine" and "feminine" qualities'[7]; indeed, since masculine and feminine personality qualities are stereotypes to begin with, it is virtually a tautology to say that creative people are not limited to one set. Woolf's selection of Shakespeare to exemplify the androgynous artist also provokes little disagreement, especially since we know so little about Shakespeare's life; although there is no obvious connection between her other examples – Keats, Sterne, Cowper, Lamb, and Coleridge – one could probably discover some similarities, perhaps in their attitudes toward fantasy and madness.

Woolf, however, does not supply the connections; nor does she encourage the reader to pursue them very strenuously. If one can see *A Room of One's Own* as a document in the literary history of female aestheticism, and remain detached from its narrative strategies, the concepts of androgyny and the private room are neither as liberating nor as obvious as they first appear. They have a darker side that is the sphere of the exile and the eunuch.

Virginia Woolf was extremely sensitive to the ways in which female experience had made women weak, but she was much less sensitive to the ways in which it had made them strong. Filling in the outlines of her 1918 review, she wrote finely about the problems in the lives of several of her predecessors: their domestic responsibilities, their narrowness of range, and their frustration and anger. 'We feel the influence of fear in it', she wrote of Charlotte Brontë's portrait of Rochester, 'just as we constantly feel an acidity which is the result of oppression, a buried suffering smouldering beneath her passion, a rancour which contracts those books, splendid as they are, with a spasm of pain'.[8] All of these passionate responses she deplored because she thought that they distorted the artist's integrity. She describes with compassion and scornful illustration how women writers were disadvantaged and harassed – an important and fully realized discovery. But in wishing to make women independent of all that dailiness and bitterness, so that they might 'escape a little from the common sitting room and see human beings not always in their relation to each other but in relation to reality',[9] she was advocating a strategic retreat, and not a victory; a denial of feeling, and not a mastery of it.

We can see this withdrawal most plainly in the theory of androgyny presented in the last chapter of the book, which is the psychological and theoretical extension of the material reform implied in the private room. Woolf brings in the discussion of androgyny in a characteristically low-keyed way, as if it were an afterthought; but it is central to her thinking not only in this book but also in her novels. The androgynous vision, in Woolf's terms, is a response to the dilemma of a woman writer embarrassed and alarmed by feelings too hot to handle without risking real rejection by her family, her audience, and her class. A room of one's own is the first step toward her solution; more than an office with a typewriter, it is a symbol of psychic withdrawal, an escape from the demands of other people. Mary Beton or Mary Carmichael would not, in entering that room, be liberated from the fear of what people might say or fortified to express her anger or her pain; instead, she would be encouraged to forget both her grievances and her fellows, and seek an underlying or transcendent meaning. Woolf had faith that the androgynous vision would express itself in uniquely feminine terms, but purely and unconsciously, as femininity's essence distilled in a new supple sentence and open structure, as a pervasive but inoffensive quality of perception, 'that curious sexual quality which comes only when sex is unconscious of itself'.[10] Stripped of its anger, femininity would spread out over fiction to become a smooth and absorbent surface.

In describing androgyny, Woof goes a step further to imagine that the highly developed creative mind needs no such crutch as physical privacy to transcend the burden of sex consciousness. The passage in which she gracefully leads up to the idea intimates unmistakably that feminist awareness is a painful state of mind:

> If one is a woman one is often surprised by a sudden splitting off of consciousness, say in walking down Whitehall, when from being the natural inheritor of that civilisation she becomes, on the contrary, outside of it, alien and critical. Clearly the mind is always altering its focus, and bringing the world into different perspectives. But some of these states of mind seem, even if adopted spontaneously, to be less comfortable than others. In order to keep oneself continuing in them one is unconsciously holding something back, and gradually the repression becomes an effort. But there may be some state of mind in which one could continue without effort because nothing is required to be held back.[11]

Despite a certain fluttering of indefinite pronouns here, I think that the less comfortable states of mind that Woolf refers to are the angry and alienated ones, the feminist ones, and that she would like to possess a more serene and thus more comfortable consciousness.

In Virginia Woolf's case, agitation was the first symptom of mental collapse, and the personal need for equanimity without repression is very close to the surface of these carefully abstract sentences. 'Equanimity', said her physician in 1925, 'practice equanimity'. But how can one, if one is a woman, be serene in the face of injustice? There is an eerie hint that in the androgynous solution Woolf provides there lurks a psychological equivalent of lobotomy. Yet when she actually describes androgyny, Woolf uses a literal sexual imagery of intercourse between the manly and womanly powers of the mind:

> If one is a man, still the woman part of the brain must have effect; and a woman also must have intercourse with the man in her. Coleridge perhaps meant this when he said that a great mind is androgynous. It is

29

when this fusion takes place that the mind is fully fertilised and uses all its faculties. Perhaps a mind that is purely masculine cannot create, any more than a mind that is purely feminine.[12]

The minutely Freudian analogy with biological sexuality here, particularly in the last sentence, continues a few pages later in a passage of almost erotic revery:

Some marriage of opposites has to be consummated. The whole of the mind must lie wide open if we are to get the sense that the writer is communicating his experience with perfect fullness. There must be freedom and there must be peace.... The curtains must be close drawn. The writer, I thought, once his experience is over, must lie back and let his mind celebrate its nuptials in darkness. He must not look or question what is being done.[13]

Obviously Virginia Woolf had not looked at or questioned what she had done in this passage: made the writer male. In a book exquisitely in control of its pronouns, this is not a small thing. It suggests, I think, how unconsciously she had felt the soft, dead hand of the Angel in the House descend upon her shoulder, censoring even this innocent metaphorical fantasy, and transferring it to the mind of a male voyeur. How could any woman writer pretend to be androgynous – indifferent, undivided – in the grip of such inhibition? At some level, Woolf is aware that androgyny is another form of repression or, at best, self-discipline. It is not so much that she recommends androgyny as that she warns against feminist engagement: 'It is fatal for anyone who writes to think of their sex. It is fatal to be a man or woman pure and simple; one must be woman-manly or man-womanly. It is fatal for a woman to lay the least stress on any grievance; to plead even with justice any cause; in any way to speak consciously as a woman. And fatal is no figure of speech; for anything written with that conscious bias is doomed to death. It ceases to be fertilised.'[14] In many respects Woolf is expressing a class-oriented and Bloomsbury-oriented ideal – the separation of politics and art, the fashion of bisexuality. It is only fair to note that she found male writers ruined by exaggerated, or exacerbated, virility. But there is also more than a hint of fear in her warning. She had taken to heart the cautionary tales to be found in the lives of earlier women writers. She had seen the punishment that society could inflict on women who made a nuisance of themselves by behaving in an uncivilized manner. It seems like a rationalization of her own fears that Woolf should have developed a literary theory that made anger and protest flaws in art.

The androgynous mind is, finally, a utopian projection of the ideal artist: calm, stable, unimpeded by consciousness of sex. Woolf meant it to be a luminous and fulfilling idea; but, like other utopian projections, her vision is inhuman. Whatever else one may say of androgyny, it represents an escape from the confrontation with femaleness or maleness. Her ideal artist mystically transcends sex, or has none. One could imagine another approach to androgyny, however, through total immersion in the individual experience, with all its restrictions of sex and anger and fear and chaos. A thorough understanding of what it means, in every respect, to be a woman, could lead the artist to an understanding of what it means to be a man. This revelation would not be realized in any mystical way; it would result from daring to face and express what is unique, even if unpleasant, or taboo, or destructive, in one's own experience, and thus it would speak to the secret heart in all people.

One can see the problem more clearly, I think, in a different context. Woolf disliked partisanship in fiction, and she interpreted it as broadly as possible. In a review of American fiction, she objected to the pervasive sense of national identity and compared it revealingly to the sexual identity of women:

Women writers have to meet many of the same problems that beset Americans. They too are conscious of their own peculiarities as a sex; apt to suspect insolence, quick to avenge grievances, eager to shape an art of their own. In both cases all kinds of consciousness – consciousness of self, of race, of sex, of civilization – which have nothing to do with art, have got between them and the paper, with results that are, on the surface at least, unfortunate.

It is easy enough to see that Mr Anderson, for example, would be a much more perfect artist if he could forget that he is an American; he would write better prose if he could use all words impartially, new or old, English or American; classical or slang.

Nevertheless as we turn from his autobiography to his fiction we are forced to own (as some women writers also make us own) that to come fresh to the world, to turn a new angle to the light, is so great an achievement that for its sake we can pardon the bitterness, the self-consciousness, the angularity which inevitably go with it.[15]

I suspect that few readers will agree that the great flaw in American literature is its national consciousness, its insistence on exploring what is local and special in American culture, or its use of the language which that culture has generated. The sort of perfect artist who can forget where he comes from is a figure more pathetic than heroic. Similarly, the notion that women should transcend any awkwardly unorthodox desire to write about being women comes from timidity and not strength.

Virginia Woolf herself never approached the state of serene indifference she called androgyny; as shown in the quotation above, she was even able to appreciate the excellence of partisan art. She did try, however, to get away from personal identity, from the claims of the self to be expressed. In terms of the female aesthetic, as I have shown, egolessness was associated with the highest form of female perception. Thus James Naremore, writing of the duality of Woolf's vision, says:

> On the one hand is the world of the self, the time-bound, landlocked, everyday world of the masculine ego, of intellect and routine, where people live in fear of death, and where separations imposed by time and space result in agony. On the other hand is a world without a self – watery, emotional, erotic, generally associated with the feminine sensibility – where all of life seems blended together in a kind of halo, where the individual personality is continually being dissolved by intimations of eternity, and where death reminds us of sexual union.[16]

Naremore argues that both of these worlds are equal in Virginia Woolf's writing, except that the second is a little more equal. The chasm between them, however, is never bridged. Indeed, an extended residence in the world without a self is the worst possible preparation for a sojourn in the other world: skills atrophy, courage evaporates, and self-deception becomes habitual. Woolf's books show signs of a progressive technical inability to accommodate the facts and crises of day-to-day experience, even when she wanted to do so.

Woolf did change her ideas over a period of years. In 1928, androgyny, which she had also celebrated in the tedious high camp of *Orlando*, represented her ambivalent solution to the conflict of wishing to describe female experience at the same time that her life presented paralyzing obstacles to such self-expression. The novel, she wrote firmly, should not be 'the dumping-ground for the personal emotions'. Woolf seems to have been echoing the formidable Beatrice Webb, who had told the Woolfs in 1918 that 'marriage was the waste paper basket of the emotions'.[17] But where would female emotions and experiences find an outlet?

In the 1930s Woolf tried to deal with the problem by splitting her writing into 'male' journalism and 'female' fiction. David Daiches has noticed that the mannerisms of her fiction frequently disappeared in her criticism and biography: 'The force and clarity of much of her occasional prose sometimes makes us wonder whether she would not have made a brilliant political pamphleteer. For while in her fiction her prose tends to be subtle and lyrical, elsewhere she can write in a most forthright and virile idiom.'[18] Woolf's most complex and candid analysis of her own inhibitions as a writer is found in the 1931 essay, 'Professions for Women', in which she described the phantom of the Angel in the House, and her own self-censorship:

> I want you to imagine me writing a novel in a state of trance. I want you
> to figure to yourselves a girl sitting with a pen in her hand, which for
> minutes, and indeed for hours, she never dips into the inkpot. The
> image that comes to my mind when I think of this girl is the image of a
> fisherman lying sunk in dreams on the verge of a deep lake with a rod
> held out over the water. She was letting her imagination sweep
> unchecked round every rock and cranny of the world that lies
> submerged in the depth of our subconscious being. Now came the
> experience that I believe to be far commoner with women writers than
> with men. The line raced through the girl's fingers. Her imagination had
> rushed away. It had sought the pools, the depths, the dark places where
> the largest fish slumber. And then there was a smash. There was an
> explosion. There was foam and confusion. The imagination had dashed
> itself against something hard. The girl was roused from her dream.... To
> speak without figure, she had thought of something, something about
> the body, about the passions, which it was unfitting for her as a woman
> to say. Men, her reason told her, would be shocked. The consciousness
> of what men will say of a woman who speaks the truth about her
> passions had roused her from her artist's state of unconsciousness. She
> could write no more.[19]

There is much in this passage worth discussing a length – the shift from the
first to the third person narrative, the 'figure' of fishing as an allegory of
woman's failure to reach orgasm, the significance of the hard explosive
somethings that rouse the girl from her dream, and the projection of
responsibility at the end onto men. Here I wish to emphasize the last part,
the most typical, I think, of the direction of Woolf's thought: it is men who
mysteriously control these fantasies by judging them harshly. The sense of
this judgement is plain enough, and true enough, to a point, but Woolf
wished neither to accuse men nor to look very closely at her own
capitulation and self-repression. On the other hand, she was much too
honest and perceptive not to see the evasion in her own writing; even if she
had not been, there was the composer Ethel Smyth to point it out to her.
Smyth had been a co-performer at the Women's Service League when the
paper was read, and she urged Woolf to try to write about her 'experiences
as a body'. Woolf in turn suggested that Smyth attempt a novel about the
sexual lives of women. At any rate, Woolf began to think in terms of a
nonfictional work, 'a sequel to *A Room of One's Own* – about the sexual life
of women'.[20] The fact that this work eventually turned out to be *Three
Guineas* demonstrated that she was incapable of carrying out her plan.

Furthermore, the decade of the thirties brought Woolf into repeated
contact with death and tragedy; the deaths of Lytton Strachey, Roger Fry,
and her nephew Julian Bell were devastating. Julian's death in the Spanish

Civil War seemed particularly senseless and tragic because of its
associations with the male world of aggression, uniforms, and glory. At
the same time she felt a kind of guilt about it; she could not understand
his intensity and commitment, and she was forced to question her own
attitudes. In a private memoir of her nephew written shortly after his
death, she asked herself, 'What made him do it? I suppose it's a fever in
the blood of the younger generation which we can't possibly understand. I
have never known anyone of my generation have that feeling about a war.
We were all CO's in the Great War. And though I understand that this is a
'cause', can be called the cause of liberty & so on, still my natural reaction
is to fight intellectually: if I were any use, I should write against it: I
should evolve some plan for fighting English tyranny'.[21] Here is the
motive behind *Three Guineas*: an effort to write, for once, a serious, angry
manifesto against war from a feminist viewpoint, partly as a gesture for
Julian, partly as her own way of fighting tyranny.

Finally, throughout the latter part of the thirties Woolf was experiencing
menopause. Still unable to ignore – much less transcend – the claims of
female experience, and also unable to express them in her novels, she
sought to evade them once more in a sexless secession from the male
world. *Three Guineas* (originally called *On Being Despised*) was the book
nobody liked – not even Leonard. Not only did it advocate an almost total
withdrawal from male society, on the lines of *Lysistrata*, but it also refused
steadfastly to be charming. To the question, How shall we prevent war?
Three Guineas replies that women should found an 'Outsiders Society',
honorable, anonymous, indifferent, and self-sufficient, completely
detached from the bloody patriarchy.

Whereas the tone and the repeated allusions to men hiding behind the
curtains in *A Room of One's Own* show a controlled awareness of a male
audience, *Three Guineas* is basically concerned with a female audience, 'the
daughters of educated men'. And here Woolf was betrayed by her own
isolation from the female mainstream. Many people were infuriated by the
class assumptions in the book, as well as by its political naiveté. More
profoundly, however, Woolf was cut off from an understanding of the day-
to-day life of the women whom she wished to inspire; characteristically,
she rebelled against aspects of female experience that she had never
personally known and avoided describing her own experience. Thus for
all its radical zeal in linking war with patriarchy (Engels had made the
same kind of point in *Origins of the Family, Private Property and the State*), its
careful research (there are 123 lengthy footnotes), and its courage, *Three
Guineas* rings false. Its language, all too frequently, is empty sloganeering
and cliché; the stylistic tricks of repetition, exaggeration, and rhetorical
question, so amusing in *A Room of One's Own*, become irritating and
hysterical.

Most of the flaws of *Three Guineas* were exposed in Q. D. Leavis's cruelly accurate *Scrutiny* review. Leavis addressed herself to the question of female experience, making it clear that from her point of view, Woolf knew damn little about it:

> 'Daughters of educated men' [she quoted] 'have always done their thinking from hand to mouth…. They have thought while they stirred the pot, while they rocked the cradle. It was thus that they win us the right', etc. I agree with someone who complained that to judge from the acquaintance with the realities of life displayed in this book there is no reason to suppose Mrs Woolf would know which end of the cradle to stir. Mrs Woolf in fact can hardly claim that she has thus helped us to win the right, etc. I myself, however, have generally had to produce contributions for this review with one hand, while actually stirring the pot, or something of that kind, with the other, and if I have not done my thinking while rocking the cradle it was only because the daughters even of educated men ceased to rock infants at least two generations ago. Well, I feel bound to disagree with Mrs Woolf's assumption that running a household alone and unaided necessarily hinders or weakens thinking. One's own kitchen and nursery, and not the drawing room and dinner table where tired professional men relax among the ladies (thus Mrs Woolf), is the realm where living takes place, and I see no profit in letting our servants live for us. The activities Mrs Woolf wishes to free educated women from as wasteful not only provide a valuable discipline, they serve as a sieve for determining which values are important and genuine and which are conventional and contemptible.[22]

Despite its bias, this view is very persuasive. *Three Guineas* is often indignant, articulate, solid – even powerful – but the metaphor of an Outsiders Society is all too accurate a picture of Woolf's world.

In Georg Lukács' formulation, the ethic of a novelist becomes an aesthetic problem in his writing. Thus it is not surprising to recognize in Virginia Woolf's memorable definition of life: 'a luminous halo, a semitransparent envelope surrounding us from the beginning of consciousness to the end', another metaphor of uterine withdrawal and containment. Woolf's fictional record of the perceptions of this state describes consciousness as passive receptivity; 'The mind receives a myriad impressions…an incessant shower of innumerable atoms.'[23] In one sense, Woolf's female aesthetic is an extension of her view of women's social role: receptivity to the point of self-destruction, creative synthesis to the point of exhaustion and sterility. In *To the Lighthouse*, for example, Mrs Ramsay spends herself in repeated orgasms of sympathy: 'There was scarcely a shell of herself left for her to know herself by; all was so lavished and spent.'[24] Similarly, Woolf herself was drained and spent at the conclusion of each novel.

Yet there is a kind of power in Woolf's fiction, that comes from the occasional intense emotion that resists digestion by the lyric prose. There is also a kind of female sexual power in the *passivity* of her writing: it is insatiable. There is a sexual ecstasy in Mrs Ramsay's exhaustion: 'She seemed to fold herself together, one petal closed in another…while there throbbed through her, like the pulse in a spring which has expanded to its full width and now gently ceases to beat, the rapture of successful creation.'[25] The free-flowing empathy of woman seeks its own ecstatic extinction. For Mrs Ramsay, death is a mode of self-assertion. Refined to its essences, abstracted from its physicality and anger, denied any action, Woolf's vision of womanhood is as deadly as it is disembodied. The ultimate room of one's own is the grave.

Notes

1. *Towards a Recognition of Androgyny*, (New York, 1973), p. 123.

2. Review of Carolyn Heilbrun and Nancy Topping Bazin, *Virginia Woolf and the Androgynous Vision*, *New York Times Book Review* (15 April 1973) p. 10.

3. Moody, *Virginia Woolf*, (London, 1963), p. 41. See also Q. D. Leavis, 'Caterpillars of the World, Unite', *Scrutiny* VII (1938), p. 205.

4. Aunt Caroline Emelia, called 'The Nun' by Virginia and Vanessa, had been jilted by a young man who went out to India. At one point, Virginia wrote a 'comic life' of her aunt, but it has been lost. Bell, *Virginia Woolf*, pp. 6–7, 93.

5. 'Notes on the Style of Mrs Woolf', in *Critics on Virginia Woolf*, ed. Jacqueline E. M. Latham (London, 1970), pp. 24–5.

6. *A Room of One's Own* (New York, 1957), p. 21.

7. Judith Bardwick, *The Psychology of Women*, (New York, 1971), p. 203.

8. *A Room of One's Own*, pp. 127–8.

9. Ibid., p. 198.

10. Ibid., pp. 161–2.

11. Ibid., p. 169.

12. Ibid., p. 170.

13. Ibid., p. 181–2.

14. Ibid., p. 181.

15. 'American Fiction', *Collected Essays*, II, (London, 1966), p. 113.

16. *The World Without a Self*, (New Haven, 1972), p. 245.

17. 'Women and Fiction', *Collected Essays*, II, p. 149. Leonard Woolf quotes Beatrice Webb's remark in *Beginning Again* (London, 1964), p. 117.

18. *Virginia Woolf*, (New York, 1963), pp. 150–151.

19. 'Professions for Women', *Collected Essays*, II, pp. 287–8.

20. *A Writer's Diary*, pp. 158–9.

21. BELL, II, pp. 258–9.

22. 'Caterpillars of the World, Unite', *Scrutiny* (September 1938), 210–11.

23. 'Modern Fiction', *Collected Essays*, II, p. 103.

24. *To the Lighthouse*, (New York, 1955), p. 60.

25. Ibid., pp. 60–1.

TORIL MOI *Sexual/Textual Politics**

Toril Moi's *Sexual/Textual Politics: Feminist Literary Theory*, (1985) was one of the first volumes to survey the development of feminist literary theory from Kate Millett to the present. Moi's brisk and clear explication takes the reader through the major names and texts of both Anglo-American and French feminist perspectives. Her volume is divided into two parts: the first is on 'Anglo-American Feminist Criticism', while the second is on 'French Feminist Theory'. The movement from 'criticism' to 'theory' is noteworthy. Moi views French feminism as theoretically conscious and elaborate, Anglo-American feminism as more concerned with praxis, less alert to theory. Printed here is her introductory chapter to *Sexual/Textual Politics*, 'Who's Afraid of Virginia Woolf? Feminist Readings of Woolf'. Moi uses Woolf as a kind of test case for the success or failure of different modes of feminist analysis. In Moi's assessment, Anglo-American criticism, as exemplified chiefly in Elaine Showalter's chapter on Woolf from *A Literature of Their Own*, is inadequate in comparison with a French reading of Woolf, dependent on the work

---

* An earlier version of 'Who's Afraid of Virginia Woolf? Feminist Readings of Woolf', appeared in *The Canadian Journal of Social and Political Theory*, vol. 9, nos. 1 and 2 (Winter/Spring, 1985). This version reprinted from Toril Moi, *Sexual/Textual Politics: Feminist Literary Theory* (London and New York: Methuen, 1985), pp. 1–18.

of Jacques Derrida and Julia Kristeva. It is French feminism, Moi believes, that can make sense of the deconstructive potential of Woolf's work: Anglo-American feminism, still tied to the values of traditional humanism, can only censure (see Introduction, pp. 7-11).

On a brief survey, the answer to the question posed in the title of this chapter would seem to be: quite a few feminist critics. It is not of course surprising that many male critics have found Woolf a frivolous Bohemian and negligible Bloomsbury aesthete, but the rejection of this great feminist writer by so many of her Anglo-American feminist daughters requires further explanation. A distinguished feminist critic like Elaine Showalter, for example, signals her subtle swerve away from Woolf by taking over, yet changing, Woolf's title. Under Showalter's pen *A Room of One's Own* becomes *A Literature of Their Own*, as if she wished to indicate her problematic distance from the tradition of women writers she lovingly uncovers in her book.

In this chapter I will first examine some negative feminist responses to Woolf, exemplified particularly in Elaine Showalter's long, closely-argued chapter on Woolf in *A Literature of Their Own*. Then I will indicate some points towards a different, more positive feminist reading of Woolf, before finally summing up the salient features of the feminist response to Woolf's writings. The point of this exercise will be to illuminate the relationship between feminist critical readings and the often unconscious theoretical and political assumptions that inform them.

The rejection of Woolf

Elaine Showalter devotes most of her chapter on Woolf to a survey of Woolf's biography and a discussion of *A Room of One's Own*. The title of her chapter, 'Virginia Woolf and the flight into androgyny', is indicative of her treatment of Woolf's texts. She sets out to prove that for Woolf the concept of androgyny, which Showalter defines as 'full balance and command of an emotional range that includes male and female elements'(p. 263)[1] was a 'myth that helped her evade confrontation with her own painful femaleness and enabled her to choke and repress her anger and ambition'. For Showalter, Woolf's greatest sin against feminism is that 'even in the moment of expressing feminist conflict, Woolf wanted to transcend it. Her wish for experience was really a wish to forget experience'(p. 282). Showalter sees Woolf's insistence on the androgynous nature of the great writer as a flight away from a 'troubled feminism' (p. 282) and locates the moment of this flight in *Room*.

In opening her discussion of this essay Showalter claims that:

What is most striking about the book texturally and structurally is its strenuous charm, its playfulness, its conversational surface.... The techniques of *Room* are like those of Woolf's fiction, particularly *Orlando*, which she was writing at the same time: repetition, exaggeration, parody, whimsy, and multiple viewpoint. On the other hand, despite its illusions of spontaneity and intimacy, *A Room of One's Own* is an extremely impersonal and defensive book.

(p. 282).

Showalter gives the impression here that Woolf's use of 'repetition, exaggeration, parody, whimsy, and multiple viewpoint' in *Room* contributes only to creating an impression of 'strenuous charm', and therefore somehow distracts attention from the message Woolf wants to convey in the essay. She goes on to object to the impersonality of *Room*, an impersonality that springs from the fact that Woolf's use of many different personae to voice the narrative 'I' results in frequently recurring shifts and changes of subject position, leaving the critic no single unified position but a multiplicity of perspectives to grapple with. Furthermore, Woolf refuses to reveal her own experience fully and clearly, but insists on disguising or parodying it in the text, obliging Showalter to point out for us that 'Fernham' really *is* Newnham College, that 'Oxbridge' really *is* Cambridge and so on.

The steadily shifting, multiple perspectives built up by these techniques evidently exasperate Showalter, who ends by declaring that 'The entire book is teasing, sly, elusive in this way; Woolf plays with her audience, refusing to be entirely serious, denying any earnest or subversive intention' (p. 284). For Showalter, the only way a feminist can read the book properly is by remaining 'detached from its narrative strategies' (p. 285); and if she manages to do so, she will see that *Room* is in no way a particularly liberating text: 'If one can see *A Room of One's Own* as a document in the literary history of female aestheticism, and remain detached from its narrative strategies, the concepts of androgyny and the private room are neither as liberating nor as obvious as they first appear. They have a darker side that is the sphere of the exile and the eunuch' (p. 285). For Showalter, Woolf's writing continually escapes the critic's perspective, always refusing to be pinned down to one unifying angle of vision. This elusiveness is then interpreted as a denial of authentic feminist states of mind, namely the 'angry and alienated ones' (p. 287), and as a commitment to the Bloomsbury ideal of the 'separation of politics and art' (p. 288). This separation is evident, Showalter thinks, in the fact that Woolf 'avoided describing her own experience' (p. 294). Since this avoidance makes it impossible for Woolf to produce really committed feminist work, Showalter naturally concludes that *Three Guineas* as well as *Room* fail as feminist essays.

My own view is that remaining detached from the narrative strategies of *Room* is equivalent to not reading it at all, and that Showalter's impatience with the essay is motivated much more by its formal and stylistic features than by the ideas she extrapolates as its content. But in order to argue this point more thoroughly, it is necessary first to take a closer look at the theoretical assumptions about the relationship between aesthetics and politics that can be detected in Showalter's chapter.

Showalter's theoretical framework is never made explicit in *A Literature of Their Own*. From what we have seen so far, however, it would be reasonable to assume that she believes that a text should reflect the writer's experience, and that the more authentic the experience is felt to be by the reader, the more valuable the text. Woolf's essays fail to transmit any direct experience to the reader, according to Showalter, largely because as an upper-class woman Woolf lacked the necessary negative experience to qualify as a good feminist writer. This becomes particularly evident in *Three Guineas*, Showalter argues:

> Here Woolf was betrayed by her own isolation from female mainstream. Many people were infuriated by the class assumptions in the book, as well as by its political naiveté. More profoundly, however, Woolf was cut off from an understanding of the day-to-day life of the women whom she wished to inspire; characteristically, she rebelled against aspects of female experience that she had never personally known and avoided describing her own experience.
>
> (p. 294).

So Showalter quotes Q. D. Leavis's 'cruelly accurate *Scrutiny* review' with approval, since 'Leavis addressed herself to the question of female experience, making it clear that from her point of view, Woolf knew damn little about it' (p. 295).

Showalter thus implicitly defines effective feminist writing as work that offers a powerful expression of personal experience in a social framework. According to this definition, Woolf's essays can't be very political either. Showalter's position on this point in fact strongly favours the form of writing commonly known as critical or bourgeois realism, precluding any real recognition of the value of Virginia Woolf's modernism. It is not a coincidence that the only major literary theoretician Showalter alludes to in her chapter on Woolf is the Marxist critic Georg Lukács (p. 296).

Given that Showalter herself can hardly be accused of Marxist leanings, this alliance might strike some readers as curious. But Lukács was a major champion of the realist novel, which he viewed as the supreme culmination of the narrative form. For him, the great realists, like Balzac or Tolstoy, succeeded in representing the totality of human life in its social context, thus representing the fundamental truth of history: the 'unbroken upward evolution of mankind' (Lukács, p. 3)[2]. Proclaiming himself a 'proletarian humanist', Lukács states that 'the object of proletarian humanism is to reconstruct the complete human personality and free it from the distortion and dismemberment to which it has been subjected in class society' (p. 5). He reads the great classical tradition in art as the attempt to sustain this ideal of the total human being even under historical conditions that prevent its realization outside art.

In art the necessary degree of objectivity in the representation of the human subject, both as a private individual and as a public citizen, can be attained only through the representation of *types*. Lukács argues that the type is 'a peculiar synthesis which organically binds together the general and the particular both in characters and situations' (p. 6). He then goes on to insist that 'true great realism' is superior to all other art forms:

> True great realism thus depicts man and society as complete entities, instead of showing merely one or the other of their aspects. Measured by this criterion, artistic trends determined by either exclusive introspection or exclusive extra-version equally impoverish and distort reality. Thus realism means a three-dimensionality, an all-roundness, that endows with independent life characters and human relationships.
>
> (p. 6).

Given this view of art, it follows that for Lukács any art that represents 'the division of the complete human personality into a public and private sector' contributes to the 'mutilation of the essence of man' (p. 9). It is easy to see how this aspect of Lukács's aesthetics might appeal to many feminists. The lack of a totalizing representation of both the private and the working life of women is Patricia Stubbs's main complaint against all novels written by both men and women in the period between 1880 and 1920, and Stubbs echoes Showalter's objection to Woolf's fiction when she claims that in Woolf 'there is no coherent attempt to create new models, new images of women', and that 'this failure to carry her feminism through into her novels seems to stem, at least in part, from her aesthetic theories' (Showalter, p. 231). But this demand for new, realistic images of women takes it for granted that feminist writers should want to use realist fictional forms in the first place. Thus both Stubbs and Showalter object to what they regard as Woolf's tendency to wrap everything in a 'haze of subjective perceptions' (Stubbs, p. 231),[3] perilously echoing in the process Lukács's Stalinist view of the 'reactionary' nature of modernist writing. Modernism, Lukács held, signified an extreme form of the fragmented, subjectivist, individualist psychologism typical of the oppressed and exploited human subject of capitalism.[4] For him, futurism as well as surrealism, Joyce as well as Proust, were decadent, regressive descendants of the great anti-humanist Nietzsche, and their art thus lent itself to exploitation by fascism. Only through a strong, committed belief in humanist values could art become an effective weapon in the struggle against fascism. It was this emphasis on a totalizing, humanist aesthetics that led Lukács to proclaim as late as 1938 that the great writers of the first part of the twentieth century would undoubtedly turn out to be Anatole France, Romain Rolland and Thomas and Heinrich Mann.

Showalter is not of course like Lukács, a *proletarian* humanist. Even so, there is detectable within her literary criticism a strong, unquestioned belief in the values, not of proletarian humanism, but of traditional bourgeois humanism of a liberal-individualist kind. Where Lukács sees the harmonious development of the 'whole person' as stunted and frustrated by the inhuman social conditions imposed by capitalism, Showalter examines the oppression of women's potential by the relentless sexism of patriarchal society. It is certainly true that Lukács nowhere seems to show any interest in the specific problems of *women's* difficulties in developing as whole and harmonious human beings under patriarchy; no doubt he assumed naively that once communism had been constructed everybody, including women, would become free beings. But it is equally true that Showalter in her own criticism takes no interests in the necessity of combatting capitalism and fascism. Her insistence on the need for political art is limited to the struggle against sexism. Thus she gives Virginia Woolf no credit for having elaborated a highly original theory of the relations between sexism and fascism in *Three Guineas*; nor does she appear to approve of Woolf's attempts to link feminism to pacifism in the same essay, of which she merely comments that: '*Three Guineas* rings false. Its language, all too frequently, is empty sloganeering and cliché; the stylistic tricks of repetition, exaggeration, and rhetorical question, so amusing in *A Room of One's Own*, become irritating and hysterical.' (Showalter, p. 295).

Showalter's traditional humanism surfaces clearly enough when she first rejects Woolf for being too subjective, too passive and for wanting to flee her female gender identity by embracing the idea of androgyny, and then goes on to reproach Doris Lessing for merging the 'feminine ego' into a greater collective consciousness in her later books (p. 311). Both writers are similarly flawed: both have in different ways rejected the fundamental need for the individual to adopt a unified, integrated self-identity. Both Woolf and Lessing radically undermine the notion of the unitary self, the central concept of Western male humanism and one crucial to Showalter's feminism.

The Lukácsian case implicitly advocated by Stubbs and Showalter holds that politics is a matter of the right content being represented in the correct realist form. Virginia Woolf is unsuccessful in Stubbs's eyes because she fails to give a 'truthful picture of women', a picture that would include equal emphasis on the private and the public. Showalter for her part deplores Woolf's lack of sensitivity to 'the ways in which (female experience) had made (women) strong' (p. 285). Implicit in such criticism is the assumption that good feminist fiction would present truthful images of strong women with which the reader may identify. Indeed it is this that Marcia Holly recommends in an article entitled 'Consciousness and authenticity: towards a feminist aesthetic'. According to Holly, the new feminist aesthetic may move 'away from formalist criticism and insist that we judge by standards of authenticity'(Holly, p. 4).[5] Holly, again quoting Lukács, also argues that as feminists: 'We are searching for a truly revolutionary art. The content of a given piece need not be feminist, of course, for that piece to be humanist, and therefore revolutionary. Revolutionary art is that which roots out the essentials about the human condition rather than perpetuating false ideologies' (p. 42). For Holly, this kind of universalizing humanist aesthetic leads straight to a search for the representation of strong, powerful women in literature, a search reminiscent of The Soviet Writers' Congress's demand for socialist realism in 1934. Instead of strong, happy tractor drivers and factory workers, we are now, presumably, to demand strong, happy *women* tractor drivers. 'Realism', Holly argues, 'first of all demands a consistent (noncontradictory) perception of those issues (emotions, motivations, conflicts) to which the work has been limited' (p. 42). Once again, we are confronted with a version of Showalter's demand for a unitary vision, with her exasperation at Woolf's use of mobile, pluralist viewpoints, with her refusal to let herself be identified with any of the many 'I's in her text; the argument has come full circle.

What feminists such as Showalter and Holly fail to grasp is that the traditional humanism they represent is in effect part of patriarchal ideology. At its centre is the seamlessly unified self – either individual or collective – which is commonly called 'Man'. As Luce Irigaray or Hélène Cixous would argue, this integrated self is in fact a phallic self, constructed on the model of the self-contained, powerful, phallus. Gloriously autonomous, it banishes from itself all conflict, contradiction and ambiguity. In this humanist ideology the self is the *sole author* of history and of the literary text: the humanist creator is potent, phallic and male – God in relation to his world, the author in relation to his text.[6] History or the text become nothing but the 'expression' of this unique individual: all art becomes autobiography, a mere window on to the self and the world, with no reality of its own. The text is reduced to a passive, 'feminine' reflection of an unproblematically 'given', 'masculine' world or self.

Rescuing Woolf for feminist politics: some points towards an alternative reading

So far we have discussed some aspects of the crypto-Lukácsian perspective

implicit in much contemporary feminist criticism The major drawback of
this approach is surely signalled in the fact that it proves incapable of
appropriating for feminism the work of the greatest British woman writer
of this century, despite the fact that Woolf was not only a novelist of
considerable genius but a declared feminist and dedicated reader of other
women's writings. It is surely arguable that if feminist critics cannot
produce a positive political and literary assessment of Woolf's writing, then
the fault may lie with their own critical and theoretical perspectives rather
than with Woolf's texts. But do feminists have an alternative to this
negative reading of Woolf? Let us see if a different theoretical approach
might rescue Virginia Woolf for feminist politics.[7]

Showalter wants the literary text to yield the reader a certain security, a
firm perspective from which to judge the world. Woolf, on the other hand,
seems to practise what we might now call a 'deconstructive' form of
writing, one that engages with and thereby exposes the duplicitous nature
of discourse. In her own textual practice, Woolf exposes the way in which
language refused to pinned down to an underlying essential meaning.
According to the French philosopher Jacques Derrida, language is
structured as an endless deferral of meaning, and any search for an
essential, absolutely stable meaning must therefore be considered
metaphysical. There is no final element, no fundamental unit, no
transcendental signified that is meaningful *in itself* and thus escapes the
ceaseless interplay of linguistic deferral and difference. The free play of
signifiers will never yield a final, unified meaning that in turn might
ground and explain all the others.[8] It is in the light of such textual and
linguistic theory that we can read Woolf's playful shifts and changes of
perspective, in both her fiction and in *Room*, as something rather more than
a wilful desire to irritate the serious-minded feminist critic. Through her
conscious exploitation of the sportive, sensual nature of language, Woolf
rejects the metaphysical essentialism underlying patriarchal ideology,
which hails God, the Father or the phallus as its transcendental signified.

But Woolf does more than practise a non-essentialist form of writing.
She also reveals a deeply sceptical attitude to the male-humanist concept
of an essential human identity. For what can this self-identical identity be
if all meaning is a ceaseless play of difference, if *absence* as much as
presence is the foundation of meaning? The humanist concept of identity
is also challenged by psychoanalytic theory, which Woolf undoubtedly
knew. The Hogarth Press, founded by Virginia and Leonard Woolf,
published the first English translations of Freud's central works, and when
Freud arrived in London in 1939 Virginia Woolf went to visit him. Freud,
we are tantalizingly informed, gave her a narcissus.

For Woolf, as for Freud, unconscious drives and desires constantly exert
a pressure on our conscious thoughts and actions. For psychoanalysis the
human subject is a complex entity, of which the conscious mind is only a

small part. Once one has accepted this view of the subject, however, it becomes impossible to argue that even our conscious wishes and feelings originate within a unified self, since we can have no knowledge of the possibly unlimited unconscious processes that shape our conscious thought. Conscious thought, then, must be seen as the 'overdetermined' manifestation of a multiplicity of structures that intersect to produce that unstable constellation the liberal humanists call the 'self'. These structures encompass not only unconscious sexual desires, fears and phobias, but also a host of conflicting material, social, political and ideological factors of which we are equally unaware. It is this highly complex network of conflicting structures, the anti-humanist would argue, that produces the subject and its experiences, rather than the other way round. This belief does not of course render the individual's experiences in any sense less real or valuable; but it does mean that such experiences cannot be understood other than through the study of their multiple determinants – determinants of which conscious thought is only one, and a potentially treacherous one at that. If a similar approach is taken to the literary text, it follows that the search for a unified individual self, or gender identity or indeed 'textual identity' in the literary work must be seen as drastically reductive.

It is in this sense that Showalter's recommendation to remain detached from the narrative strategies of the text is equivalent to not reading it all. For it is only through an examination of the detailed strategies of the text on all its levels that we will be able to uncover some of the conflicting, contradictory elements that contribute to make it precisely *this* text, with precisely these words and this configuration. The humanist desire for a unity of vision or thought (or as Holly puts it, 'for a non-contradictory perception of the world') is, in effect, a demand for a sharply reductive reading of literature – a reading that, not least in the case of an experimental writer like Woolf, can have little hope of grasping the central problems posed by pioneering modes of textual production. A 'non-contradictory perception of the world', for Lukács's Marxist opponent Bertolt Brecht, is precisely a reactionary one.

The French feminist philosopher Julia Kristeva has argued that the modernist poetry of Lautréamont, Mallarmé and others constitutes a 'revolutionary' form of writing. The modernist poem, with its abrupt shifts, ellipses, breaks and apparent lack of logical construction is a kind of writing in which the rhythms of the body and the unconscious have managed to break through the strict rational defences of conventional social meaning. Since Kristeva sees such conventional meaning as the structure that sustains the whole of the symbolic order – that is, all human social and cultural institutions – the fragmentation of symbolic language in modernist poetry comes for her to parallel and prefigure a total *social* revolution. For Kristeva, that is to say, there is a *specific practice of writing* that is itself 'revolutionary', analogous to sexual and political transformation, and that by its very existence testifies to the possibility of transforming the symbolic order of orthodox society from the inside.[9] One might argue in this light that Woolf's refusal to commit herself in her essays to a so-called rational or logical form of writing, free from fictional techniques, indicates a similar break with symbolic language, as of course do many of the techniques she deploys in her novels.

Kristeva also argues that many women will be able to let what she calls the 'spasmodic force' of the unconscious disrupt their language because of their strong links with the pre-Oedipal mother-figure. But if these unconscious pulsations were to take over the subject entirely, the subject would fall back into pre-Oedipal or imaginary chaos and develop some form of mental illness. The subject whose language lets such forces disrupt the symbolic order, in other words, is also the subject who runs the greater risk of lapsing into madness. Seen in this context, Woolf's own periodic attacks of mental illness can be linked both to her textual strategies and to her feminism. For the symbolic order is a patriarchal order, ruled by the Law of the Father, and any subject who tries to disrupt it, who lets unconscious forces slip through the symbolic repression, puts her or himself in a position of revolt against this regime. Woolf herself suffered acute patriarchal oppression at the hands of the psychiatric establishment, and *Mrs Dalloway* contains not only a splendidly satirical attack on that profession (as represented by Sir William Bradshaw), but also a superbly perspicacious representation of a mind that succumbs to 'imaginary' chaos in the character of Septimus Smith. Indeed Septimus can be seen as the negative parallel to Clarissa Dalloway, who herself steers clear of the threatening gulf of madness only at the price of repressing her passions and desires, becoming a cold but brilliant woman highly admired in patriarchal society. In this way Woolf discloses the dangers of the invasion of unconscious pulsions as well as the price paid by the subject who successfully preserves her sanity, thus maintaining a precarious balance between an overestimation of so-called 'feminine' madness and a too precipitate rejection of the values of the symbolic order.[10]

It is evident that for Julia Kristeva it is not the biological sex of a person, but the subject position she or he takes up, that determines their revolutionary potential. Her views of feminist politics reflect this refusal of biologism and essentialism. The feminist struggle, she argues, must be seen historically and politically as a three-tiered one, which can be schematically summarized as follows:

(1) Women demand equal access to the symbolic order. Liberal feminism. Equality.
(2) Women reject the male symbolic order in the name of difference. Radical feminism. Femininity extolled.
(3) (This is Kristeva's own position.) Women reject the dichotomy between masculine and feminine as metaphysical.

The third position is one that has deconstructed the opposition between masculinity and femininity, and therefore necessarily challenges the very notion of identity. Kristeva writes: 'In the third attitude, which I strongly advocate – which I imagine? – the very dichotomy man/woman as an opposition between two rival entities may be understood as belonging to *metaphysics*. What can 'identity', even 'sexual identity', mean in a new theoretical and scientific space where the very notion of identity is challenged?' ('Women's time', 33 – 4)[11] The relationship between the second and the third positions here requires some comment. If the defence of the third position implies a total rejection of stage two (which I do not think it does), this would be a grievous political error. For it still remains *politically* essential for feminists to defend women *as* women in order to counteract the patriarchal oppression that precisely despises women *as* women. But an 'undeconstructed' form of 'stage two' feminism, unaware of the metaphysical nature of gender identities, runs the risk of becoming an inverted form of sexism. It does so by uncritically taking over the very metaphysical categories set up by patriarchy in order to keep women in their places, despite attempts to attach new feminist values to these old categories. An adoption of Kristeva's 'deconstructed' form of feminism therefore in one sense leaves everything as it was – our positions in the political struggle have not changed – but in another sense radically transforms our awareness of the nature of that struggle.

Here, I feel, Kristeva's feminism echoes the position taken up by Virginia Woolf some sixty years earlier. Read from this perspective, *To the Lighthouse* illustrates the destructive nature of a metaphysical belief in strong, immutably fixed gender identities – as represented by Mr and Mrs Ramsay – whereas Lily Briscoe (an artist) represents the subject who deconstructs this opposition, perceives its pernicious influence and tries as far as is possible in a still rigidly patriarchal order to live as her own woman, without regard for the crippling definitions of sexual identity to which society would have her conform. It is in this context that we must situate Woolf's crucial concept of androgyny. This is not, as Showalter argues, a flight from fixed gender identities, but a recognition of their falsifying metaphysical nature. Far from fleeing such gender identities because she fears them, Woolf rejects them because she has seen them for what they are. She has understood that the goal of the feminist struggle must precisely be to deconstruct the death-dealing binary oppositions of masculinity and femininity.

In her fascinating book *Toward a Recognition of Androgyny*, published in 1973, Carolyn Heilbrun sets out her own definition of androgyny in similar terms when she describes it as the concept of an 'unbounded and hence fundamentally indefinable nature' (p. xi).[12] When she later finds it necessary to distinguish androgyny from feminism, and therefore implicitly defines Woolf as a non-feminist, her distinction seems to be based on the belief that only the first two stages of Kristeva's three-tiered struggle could count as feminist strategies. She acknowledges that in modern day society it might be difficult to separate the defenders of androgyny from feminists, 'because of the power men now hold, and because of the political weakness of women' (p. xvi–xvii), but refuses to draw the conclusion that feminists can in fact desire androgyny. As opposed to Heilbrun, I would stress with Kristeva that a theory that demands the deconstruction of sexual identity is indeed authentically feminist. In Woolf's case, the question is rather whether or not her remarkably advanced understanding of feminist objectives prevented her from taking up a progressive political position in the feminist struggles of her day. In the light of *Three Guineas* (and of *A Room of One's Own*), the answer to this question is surely 'no'. The Woolf of *Three Guineas* shows an acute awareness of the dangers of both liberal and radical feminism (Kristeva's positions one and two), and argues instead for a 'stage three' position; but despite her objections she ends up firmly in favour of women's right to financial independence, education and entry into the professions – all central issues for feminists of the 1920s and 1930s.

Nancy Topping Bazin reads Woolf's concept of androgyny as the *union* of masculinity and femininity – precisely the opposite, in fact, of viewing it as the deconstruction of the duality. For Bazin, masculinity and femininity in Woolf are concepts that retain their full essential charge of meaning. She thus argues that Lily Briscoe in *To the Lighthouse* must be read as being just as feminine as Mrs Ramsay, and that the androgynous solution of the novel consists in a *balance* of the masculine and the feminine 'approach to truth' (p. 138).[13] Herbert Marder, conversely, advances in his *Feminism and Art* the trite and traditional case that Mrs Ramsay must be seen as an androgynous ideal in herself: 'Mrs Ramsay as wife, mother, hostess, is the androgynous artist in life, creating with the whole of her being' (p. 128).[14] Heilbrun rightly rejects such a reading, claiming that: 'It is only in groping our way through the clouds of sentiment and misplaced biographical information that we are able to discover Mrs Ramsay, far from androgynous and complete, to be as one-sided and life-denying as her husband' (Heilbrun, p. 155). The host of critics who with Marder read Mrs Ramsay and Mrs Dalloway as Woolf's ideal of feminity are thus either betraying their vestigial sexism – the sexes are fundamentally different and should stay that way – or their adherence to what Kristeva would call a 'stage two feminism': women are different from men and it is time they began praising the superiority of their sex. These are both, I believe, misreadings of Woolf's texts, as when Kate Millett writes that: 'Virginia Woolf glorified two housewives, Mrs Dalloway and Mrs Ramsay, recorded the suicidal misery of Rhoda in *The Waves* without ever explaining its causes, and was argumentative yet somehow unsuccessful, perhaps because unconvinced, in conveying the frustrations of the woman artist in Lily Briscoe ' (pp. 139–40).[15]

A combination of Derridean and Kristevan theory, then, would seem to hold considerable promise for future feminist readings of Woolf. But it is important to be aware of the political limitations of Kristeva's arguments. Though her views on the 'politics of the subject' constitute a significant contribution to revolutionary theory, her belief that the revolution within the subject somehow prefigures a later social revolution poses severe problems for any materialist analysis of society. The strength of Kristevan theory lies in its emphasis on the politics of language as a material and social structure, but it takes little or no account of other conflicting ideological and material structures that must be part of any radical social transformation. These and other problems will be discussed in the chapter on Kristeva (pp. 150–73). It should nevertheless be emphasized that the 'solution' to Kristeva's problems lies not in a speedy return to Lukács, but in an integration and transvaluation of her ideas within a larger feminist theory of ideology.

A Marxist-feminist critic like Michèle Barrett has stressed the materialist aspect of Woolf's politics. In her introduction to *Virginia Woolf: Women and Writing*, she argues that: 'Virginia Woolf's critical essays offer us an unparalleled account of the development of women's writing, perceptive discussion of her predecessors and contemporaries, and a pertinent insistence on the material conditions which have structured women's consciousness' (p . 36).[16] Barrett, however, considers Woolf only as essayist and critic, and seems to take the view that when it comes to her fiction, Woolf's aesthetic theory, particularly the concept of an androgynous art, 'continually resists the implications of the materialist position she advances in *A Room of One's Own*' (p. 22). A Kristevan approach to Woolf, as I have argued, would refuse to accept this binary opposition of aesthetics on the one hand and politics on the other, locating the politics of Woolf's writing *precisely in her textual practice*. That practice is of course much more marked in the novels than in most of the essays.

Another group of feminist critics, centred around Jane Marcus, consistently argue for a radical reading of Woolf's work without recourse to either Marxist or post-structuralist theory. Jane Marcus claims Woolf as a 'guerilla fighter in a Victorian skirt' (p. 1), and sees in her a champion of both socialism and feminism. Marcus's article 'Thinking back through our mothers', however, makes it abundantly clear that it is exceptionally difficult to argue this case convincingly. Her article opens with this assertion: 'Writing, for Virginia Woolf, was a revolutionary act. Her alienation from British patriarchal culture and its capitalist and imperialist forms and values, was so intense that she was filled with terror and determination as she wrote. A guerilla fighter in a Victorian skirt, she trembled with fear as she prepared her attacks, her raids on the enemy' (p. 1).[17] Are we to believe that there is a causal link between the first and the following sentences – that writing was a revolutionary act for Woolf *because* she could be seen to tremble as she wrote? Or should the passage be read as an extended metaphor, as an image of the fears of *any* woman writing under patriarchy? In which case it no longer tells us anything specific about Woolf's particular writing practices. Or again, perhaps the first sentence is the claim that the following sentences are meant to corroborate? If this is the case, the argument also fails. For Marcus here unproblematically evokes biographical evidence to sustain her thesis about the nature of Woolf's writing: the reader is to be convinced by appeals to biographical circumstances rather than to the texts. But does it really matter whether or not Woolf was in the habit of trembling at her desk? Surely what matters is what she wrote? This kind of emotionalist argument surfaces again in Marcus's extensive discussion of the alleged parallels between Woolf and the German Marxist critic Walter Benjamin ('Both Woolf and Benjamin chose suicide rather than exile before the tyranny of fascism', p. 7). But surely Benjamin's suicide at the Spanish frontier, where as an exiled German Jew fleeing the Nazi occupation of France he feared being handed over to the Gestapo, must be considered in a rather different light from Woolf's suicide in her own back garden in unoccupied England, however political we might wish her private life to be? Marcus's biographical analogies strive to establish Woolf as a remarkable individual, and so fall back into the old-style historical-biographical criticism much in vogue before the American New Critics entered the scene in the 1930s. How far a radical feminist approach can simply take over such traditional methods untransformed is surely debatable.

We have seen that current Anglo-American feminist criticism tends to read Woolf through traditional aesthetic categories, relying largely on a liberal – humanist version of the Lukácsian aesthetics, against which Brecht so effectively polemicized. The anti-humanist reading I have advocated as yielding a better understanding of the political nature of Woolf's aesthetics has yet to be written. The only study of Woolf to have integrated some of the theoretical advances of post-structuralist thought is written by a man, Perry Meisel, and though it is by no means an anti-feminist or even an unfeminist work, it is nevertheless primarily concerned with the influence on Woolf of Walter Pater. Meisel is the only critic of my acquaintance to have grasped the radically deconstructed character of Woolf's texts: 'With 'difference' the reigning principle in Woolf as well as Pater, there can be no natural or inherent characteristics of any kind, even between the sexes, because all character, all language, even the language of sexuality, emerges by means of a difference from itself'(p. 234).[18] Meisel also shrewdly points out that this principle of difference makes it impossible to select any one of Woolf's works as more representative, more essentially 'Woolfian' than any other, since the notable divergence among her texts 'forbids us to believe any moment in Woolf's career to be more conclusive than another' (p. 242).

It is a mistake, Meisel concludes, to 'insist on the coherence of self and author in the face of a discourse that dislocates or decentres them both, that skews the very categories to which our remarks properly refer' (p. 242).

The paradoxical conclusion of our investigations into the feminist reception of Woolf is therefore that she has yet to be adequately welcomed and acclaimed by her feminist daughters in England and America . To date she has either been rejected by them as insufficiently feminist, or praised on grounds that seem to exclude her fiction. By their more or less unwitting subscription to the humanist aesthetic categories of the traditional male academic hierarchy, feminist critics have seriously undermined the impact of their challenge to that very institution. The only difference between a feminist and a non-feminist critic in this tradition then becomes the formal political perspective of the critic. The feminist critic thus unwittingly puts herself in a position from which it becomes impossible to read Virginia Woolf as the progressive, feminist writer of genius she undoubtedly was. A feminist criticism that would do both justice and homage to its great mother and sister: this, surely, should be our goal.

Notes and References

1. ELAINE SHOWALTER, *A Literature of Their Own: British Women Novelists from Brontë to Lessing* (New Jersey: Princeton University Press, 1977).

2. GEORG LUKÁCS, 'Preface' in *Studies in European Realism: A Sociological Survey of the Writings of Balzac, Stendhal, Zola, Tolstoy, Gorki and others* (London: Merlin Press, 1979).

3. PATRICIA STUBBS, *Women and Fiction: Feminism and the Novel 1880–1920* (Brighton: Harvester Press, 1979).

4. ANNA COOMBES'S readings of *The Waves* show a true Lukácsian distaste for the fragmented and subjective web of modernism, as when she writes that 'My problem in writing this paper has been to attempt to politicize a discourse which obstinate (sic) seeks to exclude the political and the historical, and where this is no longer possible, then tries to aestheticize glibly what it cannot 'realistically' incorporate' (p. 238).

5. MARCIA HOLLY, 'Consciousness and Authenticity: Towards a Feminist Aesthetic', in Josephine Donovan (ed.), *Feminist Literary Criticism: Explorations in Theory* (Lexington: University Press of Kentucky, 1975).

6. For further discussion of this point, see the section on Gilbert and Gubar (pp. 37–69).

7. The term 'Anglo-American' must be taken as an indication of a specific approach to literature, not as an empirical description of the critic's nationality. The British critic Gillian Beer, in her essay 'Beyond determinism: George Eliot and Virginia Woolf', raises the same kind of objections to Showalter's reading of Woolf as I have done in this paper. In her 1984 essay, 'Subject and object and the nature of reality: Hume and elegy in *To the Lighthouse*', Beer develops this

approach in a more philosophical context.

8. For an introduction to Derrida's thought and to other forms of deconstruction see Norris.

9. My presentation of Kristeva's position here is based on her *La Révolution du langage poétique.*

10. One feminist critic, Barbara Hill Rigney, has tried to show that in *Mrs Dalloway* 'madness becomes a kind of refuge for the self rather than its loss', (p. 52). This argument in my view finds little support in the text and seems to depend more on the critic's desire to preserve her Laingian categories than on a responsive reading of Woolf's text.

11. JULIA KRISTEVA 'Women's Time', trans. Alice Jardine and Harry Blake, *Signs*, vol. 7, no. 1, (1981), pp. 13–35.

12. CAROLYN HEILBRUN, *Toward Androgyny: Aspects of Male and Female in Literature* (London: Victor Gollancz, 1973).

13. NANCY TOPPING BAZIN, *Virginia Woolf and Androgynous Vision* (New Jersey: Rutgers University Press, 1973).

14. HERBERT MARDER, *Feminism and Art: A Study of Virginia Woolf* (Chicago: University of Chicago Press, 1968).

15. KATE MILLETT, *Sexual Politics* (London: Virago Press, 1977).

16. MICHÈLE BARRETT (ed.), *Virginia Woolf: Women and Writing* (London: Women's Press, 1979).

17. JANE MARCUS, 'Thinking Back Through Our Mothers', in Jane Marcus (ed.), *New Feminist Essays on Virginia Woolf* (London: Macmillan, 1981), pp. 1–30.

18. PERRY MEISEL, *The Absent Father: Virginia Woolf and Walter Pater* (New Haven: Yale University Press, 1980).

2 Peggy Kamuf and Nancy K. Miller

PEGGY KAMUF *Replacing Feminist Criticism**

The problem Peggy Kamuf faces is to answer her opening question concerning the place of feminist criticism within the university, without reproducing the categories of inclusion and exclusion which feminism, at its best, has tried to deconstruct. Kamuf believes that much of what has passed for feminist criticism hitherto – studying a tradition of women's writing, for example – replicates a discredited humanist endeavour. To isolate an object of study (even if that object is woman instead of man), to search for the essential truth about that object, may maintain existing power structures rather than undermine them. Kamuf recognizes that there are political situations where one is locked in to an oppositional relationship, and that these situations will occur in the university as often as elsewhere. However, her ideal feminist practice remains fluid, refusing the fixities of objects of study, unified identity, binary opposition. (See Introduction, pp. 12–13).

What is the place of feminist critical practice in the institution, in particular, the university? Like many invitations to debate, this question seems destined to elicit answers in the form of paired oppositions. It can function, that is, to define potential relative positions as in formal argument. And for this reason, it is unlikely that this particular inquiry will ever lead beyond the limits of its own form and toward a response that is not already constrained by those limits. How can a question be posed here without reverting to the very terms of opposition which feminist theory has sought to undo?

In one sense, the remarks which follow attempt to unravel the logic of relative positions. If there is an answer to the question with which I began,

---

* Peggy Kamuf, 'Replacing Feminist Criticism' originally formed part of an exchange with Nancy K. Miller at a Symposium on Feminist Criticism, held at Cornell University, October 1981. It was subsequently published in *Diacritics*, 12, no. 2 (summer, 1982), pp. 42–7.

it will not be found in some theoretical stand called for here but rather in the erosion of the very ground on which to take a stand. In another sense, by going over again, so as to erode, some old ground, I hope to leave open the possibility of reframing another question in the necessary terms of a feminist critique of institutions. This other question attempts to articulate the object with the place of critical activity.[1]

In a recent article which argues that feminist scholars cannot continue to study exclusively literature by women, the author suggests as one reason the increased pressures to streamline university curricula, thereby possibly endangering any activity which locates itself too singularly in the margins of a central academic tradition (Judith Spector, 'Gender Studies: New Directions for Feminist Criticism', *College English*, April 1981, p. 376). This view would seem to be part of a growing consensus among those involved in women's studies in general, that they must prepare to respond to an imminent re-centralization of the university. I refer you, for another example, to the debate about 'mainstreaming' women's studies in *Women's Studies Quarterly* (Spring, Summer 1981).

In very general terms, such proposals to resituate feminist critical activity appear to rest on a number of unexamined political or theoretical judgments. For example, one finds there is a surprising degree of assent to the notion that a recentralized university economy is the inevitable solution to an academic recession, even though this view may also entail subscribing to the principle – which has a certain currency right now – that whatever is good for business is good for the rest of social institutions. This uncritical acceptance of the principle of centrality would relocate at the center of the human enterprise a feminist criticism which has been redefined to reflect, as this same critic writes, 'something more in line with what life is really like' (Spector, ibid). In this fashion, humanist metaphors of centrality work to coordinate a model of the efficient (i.e. cost-effective) institution with the notion of literature as mimetic representation. What I want to outline briefly is how a recentering of feminist theory can be seen to derive from a dominant pattern of ideological assumptions. I will be suggesting that by delimiting as the object of criticism literature by but also about, for and against women, this central form of feminist theory has already made certain assumptions about the place of critical activity within socio-political structures and their institutions. As one consequence, the attempt to redefine that object and relocate that activity may not be able to acknowledge how it risks getting misplaced.

The feminist critique of cultural institutions (including literature) has, in large part, proceeded from the evidence of woman's traditional exclusion and has therefore implied either that those institutions must be expanded to include what has been excluded (for example, by 'mainstreaming' women's literature) or that they must be abandoned in favor of distinctly feminine-centered cultural models. These opposing strategies, in other words, both rest on the same analysis of phallocentrism's most readily evident feature – the order of women's exclusion – and proceed in practice to attempt to correct or reverse that feature at the same level at which it appears. What is thus left intact, perhaps, are the regions where the logic of exclusion disguises its operations more completely. One result may have been a feminist theory that accepts a determination of its place within the larger structure that anchors phallocentrism in culture. I take as an example of this limitation a feminist theory which accepts the place assigned to it by the disciplinary traditions of humanism; in this I am following up to a certain point, a road which has already been mapped by Michel Foucault in his analysis of humanistic thought and its institutions. I will be looking for the possible extensions that could lead us beyond a too-narrowly defined field of feminist practice. To do so, however, may mean to invite a question about that 'us' just offered, the pronoun which signals a common and thus, in a sense, singular subject – or object – of feminist theory.

There are two axes to Foucault's critique of what, in a French institutional context, are called the human sciences, or less formally but perhaps more accurately, the sciences of man, which include both humanities and social sciences. The first axis concerns the object of humanistic inquiry – what it is that is studied – and the second concerns the aim – what it is that is gained (or simply produced) by that study. Briefly, this critique sets out from the commonplace notion that the human sciences take as their object 'man', considered from the several angles of the conditions of his existence and his symbolic capacities. Yet, whereas traditional (i.e., humanistic) history of science tends to extend this model of inquiry back to the renaissance (and even before) as well as forward indefinitely into the future, Foucault's archaeology contends that the objectification of 'man' – its appearance within the field of knowable objects – has a much more recent history, only since about the end of the eighteenth century in Europe. It is, then, as a rather novel epistemological invention that 'man' – in his social, psychological, and linguistic manifestation – occupies the center stage of inquiry. This view is eccentric in the sense that it does not take up the humanistic assumption of a trans-historical and universal center of thought and, as such, it can theorize about what may lie outside the self-reflecting circle of that thought. In historical terms, for example, Foucault is able to posit both (1) that the human sciences and their object displaced another epistemological domain in which 'man' stood at the limit of the represented field, organizing its procedures but not himself interrogated; and (2) that the modern epistemological construct may itself have been brought to the brink of another displacement that would efface 'man' as either the hidden or the all-too-visible center of thought. On the last page of *Les*

Mots et les choses (The Order of Things), one reads: 'Man is an invention which the archaeology of our thought can easily show to be of recent date. And perhaps to be nearing its end' (my translation). This process of ending has begun when thought moves beyond the limits of what has made it possible to think 'man' as an autonomous whole, a circumscribable object, and into those regions surrounding the humanistic homeland, what one might call the no-man's land of the unconscious, the autonomous structures of language and the dynamics of history.

Although this particular evaluation of 'man-centered' tradition has only been sketched here in its most general outline, it may be possible at least to conjecture along what lines it could intersect with a reflection about an effective feminist practice of criticism. One might conclude, for example, that Foucault's careful excavation of the consolidated image of man on the face of modern Western society's knowledge of itself confirms the exclusion which is a hidden consequence of the identification of human with masculine. Isn't it precisely this exclusion which feminist scholars in all the disciplines of the human sciences have set up to expose and to rectify? Foucault's own conclusion, however, about the necessary displacement of a man-centered or (in less exclusive terms) human-centered epistemology might also give feminist scholars reason to pause and to wonder to what extent their efforts must remain caught as a reflection of the same form of nineteenth-century humanism from which we have inherited our pervasively androcentric modes of thought. In other words, if one can accept the major part of this analysis of how and why Western thought about human forms has taken the shape it has, then can one also conclude that modifying that shape to include its feminine contours will result in something fundamentally different? If, on the other hand, the empirical rectification of an empirical error can only result in yet another form of that error which is the possibility of a totalizing reference to an object – whether masculine, feminine or somehow both – then what is put in question here is perhaps the idea that feminist criticism can seek to define its object and still practise an effective critique of power structures. To put it yet another way: if feminist theory lets itself be guided by questions such as what is women's language, literature, style or experience from where does it get its faith in the form of these questions to get at truth, if not from the same central store that supplies humanism with its faith in the universal truth of man? And what if notions such as 'getting-at-the-truth-of-the-object' represented a principal means by which the power of power structures are sustained and even extended?

This, in effect, is the question which Foucault has been asking in *Surveiller et punir (Discipline and Punish)* and *La Volonté de savoir (The Will to Knowledge)*. Reviewing the institutional development of the human sciences in the nineteenth century, he discerns behind the codified procedures for increasing knowledge about 'man' in all his many aspects a growing technology of control and a proliferation of instruments of power. It is not so much that the human sciences do not produce knowledge, but rather that the codification of human experience and the investigation of human interaction, at the same time as they extend the empirical base of a given discipline, also open up new and previously uncharted regions for the control (or the *discipline* in another, less ivory-tower sense) of that experience and that interaction. This, together with the fact that the empirical human sciences necessarily operate with the concept of a norm rather than physical or *a priori* law, goes a long way towards explaining why these disciplines have historically been active partners in institutions which execute social norms by means of exclusion and internment – asylums, prisons, juvenile homes, hospitals and, not least, schools.

Once again, this is hardly an adequate summary of consistently intricate analyses, but it will suffice if it indicates what must interest feminist theory in those analyses: to wit: that power has pursued its aim of social control through proliferating institutions and that these institutions may be understood in many cases as the spatial realizations of the principles of humanistic knowledge. To put it more simply and with still less justice to Foucault's analyses; power and knowledge maintain highly ambiguous relations which get articulated in institutions.

Returning now to the question of the place of feminist criticism, which is also the question of its relation to an institution, one might at least hesitate before replying that the criticism should aim to rectify an omission from the institutional mainstream, producing a knowledge about women which has been excluded there by a masculine-dominated ideology disguised as universal humanism. To expose and dismantle this disguise, in order to reach, as one feminist critic has described it, the authentic and essential human (as opposed to masculine) truths of literature (Marcia Holly, 'Consciousness and Authenticity: Toward a Feminist Aesthetic' in *Feminist Literary Criticism: Explorations in Theory*, Donovan, (ed.) Lexington: The University Press of Kentucky, 1975, p. 42) may have an appeal as a theoretical program precisely because it replicates the familiar dream of humanism: a single center of truth to which all representation refers. In its articulation with and within an institution, what is to prevent such a program from taking the form which that articulation has historically assumed, in Foucault's estimate at least – a centrally defined space of power? If feminist theory can be content to propose cosmetic modifications on the face of humanism and its institutions, will it have done anything more than reproduce the structure of woman's exclusion in the same code which has been extended to include her?

This would seem to be one of the primary limitations of an assumption guiding much current feminist scholarship: an unshaken faith in the ultimate arrival at essential truth through the empirical method of accumulation of knowledge, knowledge about women. Consider for example the following passage from an anthology of essays on feminist literary theory in which the author proposes a revision of aesthetic models to include specifically feminine components:

> Through information gleaned from research in women's studies, I see a gradual falling together of truth and probabilities about women – their experience, their history, their wisdom, their culture – and this constellation will provide the basis for a feminine aesthetic...Until we have had a chance to study women's art, history, and culture more extensively, so as to begin to codify the patterns of consciousness delineated therein, I believe we will be unable to develop a more substantial feminine aesthetic.
> (JOSEPHINE DONOVAN, 'Afterword: Critical Revision' in Donovan, *op. cit,.* pp. 77.– 8;).

What is striking about this passage, I think, is first the combined appeal to a specific 'we' and to a certain method of defining who that 'we' is. The 'we', in other words, is constituted by a shared faith in its eventual consolidation at the end of an empirical process which will have codified its patterns of consciousness. Secondly, there is an implicit assumption in such programs that this knowledge about women can be produced in and of itself without seeking any support within those very structures of power which – or so it is implied – have prevented knowledge of the feminine in the past . Yet what is it about those structures which could have succeeded until now in excluding such knowledge if it is not a similar appeal to a 'we' that has had a similar faith in its own eventual constitution as a delimited and totalizable object?

I earlier pointed to two contrary feminist strategies which share a humanist determination of woman's exclusion: on the one hand an expansion of institutions to include at their center what has been historically excluded: on the other hand, the installing of a counter-institution based on feminine-centered cultural models. By way of indicating another, yet-to-be-determined level of feminist critical practice, I am going to conclude by a strategic shift within the outlines of Foucault's archaeology. That analysis, you recall, ends with the end of man as the central object of thought. What I have suggested above is that to the extent that feminist thought assumes the limits of humanism, it may be reproducing itself as but an extension of those limits and reinventing the institutional structures that it set out to dismantle. By stepping back now from the field which opposes a certain feminist centrality to Foucauldian eccentricity, it may be possible to imagine for a moment that when one or the other speaks of the end of man in Western thought, they are referring *essentially* to the same thing. What one may too easily overlook is the odd relation that can pertain between a discourse which, like most feminist discourse, situates itself at the center of the humanist enterprise and perhaps supplies a new impetus for the totalizing quest of that enterprise, and a discourse which, like Foucault's, situates itself frankly outside this center from where it may envision the approaching end of humanistic goals. What one and the other position may be said to share is the fixity of their situation in relation to an enclosing limit. Each discourse may be seeking to consolidate, by accumulating evidence, its right to speak on one side or the other of this limit. Thus whether one speaks from inside about an end of man and the beginning of *authentic* non-sexist humanism, or from outside about the end of humanism and the beginning of humanity's unthinkable other, it is finally the metaphor of inside and outside which dominates in one direction and the other. And it is at least questionable whether this opposition can ever be simply separated from the long and potent series of other oppositions which it organizes and commands, including inclusion and exclusion, the same and the different, self and other, 'us' and 'them'.[2] That this list underwrites and is underwritten by gender opposition no doubt needs no further elaboration here. Having understood that, however, can a feminist practice on this cultural text stop there, leaving oppositional logic in place and in the place it has always occupied as the unquestioned ground and limit of thought?

One will, of course, continue to find oneself engaged on this ground by a political-social distribution of effects that shapes our institutions and that itself remains an oppressive application of oppositional determinations. Yet through the practice of literature one can understand how every meaning structure attempts to conceal its own contradiction, how logical oppositions rest on an aporia, on undecidability. Thus an engagement of patriarchal meaning structures which does not keep in view its own contradictory disengagement of that meaning can have little interest, finally, for feminist theory. That theory has more to learn from the shifts that affects a discourse on women and fiction which also situates itself in the institutional context. For example, the author of *A Room of One's Own* (the text of lectures read to two newly-founded women's colleges) can read the history of woman's silence as a patriarchal invention, can acknowledge many of the structures which must be overcome to undo that silence and yet can still write that 'it is fatal for any one who writes to think of their sex ...It is fatal for a woman...in any way to speak consciously as a woman' (New York: Harcourt, Brace and World, 1957, p. 108). In the more than fifty years since Virginia Woolf gave her lectures, the institutional organization of woman's silence has changed its face. What still remains, however, is that lever of contradiction with which to disengage meaning from patterns of sexual opposition.

That feminist thought has yet to decide where to situate itself on the map of the known world's division – either in a canonical mainstream with its centers of learning and culture, or in an outlying and unexplored region – may be the clue that such generic distinctions cannot contain it. To pursue this analogy still further (and at the risk of leaving even further behind or below the solid ground of a more quotidian tread), what feminist thought can and has put in question is the capacity of any map to represent more than a fiction of the world's contours. The line traced along the eastern edge of North America, for example, the line following the extreme border of an American context, for all its inlets and protrusions, its islands and peninsulas, still can only demarcate with the fiction of an arbitrarily traced line the point at which land moves out to sea and the ground slips from beneath us.

At these limits, traced and then retraced, always in view of a greater accuracy of representation, a feminist practice can have its greatest force if, at the same time as it shifts the sands of an historical sedimentation, it leaves its own undecidable margins of indeterminacy visible, readable on the surface of the newly-contoured landscape. That is, its own inevitable inaccuracy and lack of finality which must always show up wherever lines are drawn for the purpose of theoretical argument or for the more solid purpose of re-mapping an institution. It is tempting, of course, to assume that, once drawn, the lines of a representation can resist the eroding movement of a fluid element, and can keep the sea of fictions from wetting feet planted firmly in the ground. But that would be to deny a necessary plurivocality and plurilocality which even here, for example, press on the edge of these remarks. I am left, then, with room enough only to conclude from necessity: the necessity of replacing this discourse with another and of finding always another place from which to begin again.

Notes

1. It is here that these remarks will reflect what they owe to Elaine Marks, director of the Women's Studies Research Center at the University of Wisconsin-Madison.

2. A critique of the project to put an end to 'man' has been outlined by Jacques Derrida in *Les Fins de l'Homme* ('The Ends of Man'), *Marges de la philosophie* (Paris, Minuit, 1972) where he writes: 'What is difficult to think today is an end of man which is not organized by a dialectic of truth and negativity, an end of man which is not a teleology in the first person plural' (p. 144).

NANCY K. MILLER *'The Text's Heroine: A Feminist Critic and Her Fictions'**

Nancy Miller agrees with Peggy Kamuf on the difficulty – impossibilty, even – of finding an 'effective feminist practice of criticism', but on many other issues she disagrees with her. For instance, Miller believes that feminists do need to struggle for women's place in the academy and do need to study women writers. To fail to undertake these projects is to reinforce the silence and invisibility of women in patriarchal society. The difference between Miller's emphasis on the importance of the female signature against Kamuf's interest in inscriptions of femininity can be illustrated by their contrary responses to the anonymous, seventeenth-century text, *The Portuguese Letters*. For Miller, a feminist reading concentrates on the author 'as sexually gendered subject': for Kamuf, a feminist reading lies in 'looking behind the mask of the proper name'.** The historical and political examples that Miller mentions at the end of her article point to the need to retain the female signature. Equally aware of the significance of Kamuf's arguments and of the demands of the present political moment, Miller's stratagem is to combine a post-structuralist analysis with a female-centred politics (see Introduction, pp. 12–13).

Je risquerai même cette hypothèse, que le sexe même du destinateur attend de l'autre sa détermination. C'est l'autre qui décidera peut-être qui je suis, homme ou femme. Et cela ne se décide pas une fois: cela peut se décider comme ça une autre fois.

(JACQUES DERRIDA in *L'Oreille de l'autre*)

(I will even risk affirming, this hypothesis, that the very sex of the addressor receives its determination from the other. I mean that it is the other who will perhaps decide who I am, man or woman. And is it not the case that it is decided once and for all; but it can be decided like that some other time.)

L'homme a . . . été élevé pour fonctionner, pour s'adresser au monde comme un texte destiné à trouver des lecteurs, tandis que la femme

---

* Nancy K. Miller, 'The Text's Heroine: A Feminist Critic and Her Fictions' originally formed part of an exchange with Peggy Kamuf at a Symposium on Feminist Criticism held at Cornell University, October 1981. Reprinted from *Diacritics*, 12. no. 2 (Summer, 1982, pp. 48–53.
** Peggy Kamuf 'Writing Like a Woman', in *Women and Language in Literature and Society*, eds. Sally McConnell-Ginet, Ruth Borker, Nelly Furman (New York: Praeger Publishers, 1980) p. 286.

l' était pour constituer un ailleurs métaphorique, un repos de la pensée
qui s'écarte pour réver un instant.

(CLAUDINE HERRMANN, Les Voleuses de langue)

(Man has been raised in order to function, in order to address the world
like a text destined to find its readers, while woman was elected to
constitute a metaphorical other-world, a repose of thought which steps
aside in order to dream for an instant.)

When the feminist critic institutionalizes the woman writer, what story
authorizes her to do so? As I begin to answer that question, I will be
locating myself in a discursively polemical (but personally irenic) relation
to Peggy Kamuf's questions about what might constitute an 'effective
feminist practice of criticism' (p. 44), particularly in relation to the
epistemological mapping and Foucauldian paradigms she so elegantly
outlines. I want to say at the start, however, that I foresee no real
agreement on this matter here or elsewhere, because I think that the
question of an effective feminist practice is *insoluble*. Or rather, while there
indeed exist effective practices – written documents or strategies which by
their analyses and accounts move, persuade, even transform – I do not
believe it is possible to theorize, to *think aloud*, the grounds of such a
practice in a way that transcends powerful internal contradiction. (This
may always be the case when practice and its demands precede theory,
which historically has been the case with feminism.)

Before addressing the question of the woman writer – the woman who
signs 'woman' and the feminist critic who places her in the institution – I
want to sketch out the territory of the dilemma. It is characterized by the
polarities of what might be thought of as metonymies as opposed to
metaphors: psychohistorical needs as opposed to articulate, epistemological
claims; material contingencies as opposed to theoretical urgencies. Those
oppositions have also been named by Elaine Marks – in a presentation she
described as existing in a zone somewhere between a working paper and a
position paper at a Barnard College Women's Issues Luncheon last spring –
as the American empirical and social science model of Women's Studies vs
the French ludic endeavour emerging from the more speculative operations
of 'les sciences de l'homme' engaged in by decentered subjects of the
'feminine' (rather than 'feminist') persuasion. This is also a problematic that
can be understood in relation to *shoes*: as in the sturdy, sensible sort worn by
American feminists, and the more elegant sort worn by Cixous herself. (This
is a Cixousian exemplum. In the course of an informal presentation, also at
Barnard, in the Fall of 1979, Hélène Cixous figured the same paradigm in
shoes in order to make a point about difference and recuperation: the
danger of a feminist identification too readily perceived; and the distinction
as well between lesbian and 'homosexuelle'.)

I think that these polarizations are unfortunate, if all too accurate, when they separate *effectively* women who (ideally) might otherwise collaborate within a single institution or (more realistically) within the larger project of feminist scholarship, but they do not seem about to go away. And they are not going away, I think, because of a larger problem in the women's movement itself, a problem currently reflected in the debates on the proper place of Women's Studies – in the margins or in the mainstream – that Kamuf alludes to in her paper. The problem has everything to do with sexual identity and the ways in which those two terms should be understood, separately and conjoined. For the purposes of argument, but also because of the scene of my enunciation, I will align myself with those on the side of what Peggy Kamuf in these pages calls 'correction' with those who wish to 'rectify' or reverse women's exclusion without – apparently – taking the proper measure of the *epistemological* dangers implicit in such a position.

I will speak as one who believes that 'we women' must continue to work for the woman who has been writing, because not to do so will reauthorize our oblivion. Perhaps I can expand upon my conviction that it matters who writes and *signs* woman by an example that in many ways works against me. It is the case of the *Portuguese Letters*. These are five letters published anonymously in Paris, in 1669, as being the translation of letters written in Portuguese. They were enormously popular, and for some the debate over their origins and authenticity is not over. (Indeed, in a recent edition of the *Letters* (*Lettres de la religieuse portugaise*, Paris: Librairie Générale Française, 1979), Yves Florenne rehearses the 'evidence' yet again, arguing for the true sound of 'a woman's voice' (p. 77), the pained cries of a woman in love; or at least for the possibility that anonymous was a woman.) I believe – as ultimately Kamuf seems to – that the letters were probably written by a man, a Frenchman and literary type (a hack, some say) named Guilleragues, though thought for centuries (by some) to have been written by a *real* Portuguese nun.

Why bother with this slight text, written, in the (perhaps) final analysis, by a man? It serves in the French history of the novel not as *the* first novel, as opposed to other forms of prose fiction – for that place is occupied by the anonymously published *Princesse de Clèves* – but literarily as its pre-text. It prefigures – one might also say, it engenders or at least generates – the production of an epistolary fiction whose fundamental trope, I have argued elsewhere, is that of a *'penultimate* masochism, the always renewable figure of feminine suffering' ('I's in Drag: The Sex of Recollection', *The Eighteenth Century*, 22, No 1, 1981,pp. 45–47; p. 56). The nun's last words in the face of her fickle lover's persistent silence are these. 'But I wish nothing more of you; I am mad to repeat the same things so often: I must give you up and think no more of you; I even think I must no longer write to you. Must I give you an exact account of everything I do? (Letter V, *my translation*) The 'original' or authorizing intertext here is Virgilian, via an Ovidian rewriting. Ovid feminizes the epic model of female suffering by scaling it down, casting it in elegiac verses, the *Heroides*: the imagined love letters primarily of abandoned women, of which the exemplary case is Dido – who made the fatal error of believing the man would stay and respect her in the morning.

It matters to me that the letters from a 'Portguese nun' – as the case in point – situate their line of descent in a patrilineal fashion, because I think that the textualization – hence glamorization – of female suffering around the male is an important issue for women, though less simple than some feminists want to imagine – before and after the epistemological rupture Foucault diagnoses. Indeed, society did not wait for the invention of man to repress 'woman' or oppress women and the 'end of man' in no way precludes the reinscription of woman as Other. What bothers me about the metalogically 'correct' position is what I take to be its necessary implications for practice: that by glossing 'woman' as an archaic signifier, it glosses over the *referential* suffering of women. Moreover, and implicitly, to code as 'cosmetic', and to foreclose as untimely discussions of the author as sexually gendered subject in a socially gendered exchange – who produced, for example, *this* masochistic discourse and for whose benefit? – is to be too confident that non-discursive practices will respond correctly to the correct theory of discursive practice. It may also be the case that having been killed off along with 'man', the author can now be rethought *beyond* traditional notions of biography; now that through feminist rewritings of literary history the security of a masculine identity, the hegemony of homogeneity, has been radically problematized.

In her troubling and provocative essay, 'Writing Like a Woman', in what we might call the Cornell volume, *Women and Language in Literature and Society* (ed. Sally McConnell-Ginet, Ruth Borker and Nelly Furman (New York: Praeger, 1980), pp. 284–99), Peggy Kamuf, preparing to review the language and logic of the debate over origins and authorship of the *Portuguese Letters*, written by a man or by a woman – writes (arguing with Patricia Meyer Spacks in *The Female Imagination*):

> If the inaugural gesture of this feminist criticism is the reduction of the literary work to its signature and to the tautological assumption that the feminine 'identity' is one which signs itself with a feminine name, then it will be able to produce only tautological statements of dubious value: women's writing is writing signed by women…. If these…are the gounds of a practice of feminist criticism, then that practice must be prepared to ally itself with the fundamental assumptions of patriarchy which relies on the same principles. If, on the other hand, by 'feminist' one understands a way of reading texts that points to the masks of truth with which phallocentrism hides its fictions, then one place to begin

such a reading is by looking behind the mask of the proper name, the sign that secures our patriarchal heritage: the father's name and the index of sexual identity.

(pp. 285-6)

And she concludes, after applying deconstructive pressures to the terms of the debate, that by refusing the tautological and empirical definition of identity (writing as a woman is to be a woman writing) in favor of an attention to the figuration of resemblance (writing as a woman) one has at least opened the door, or the book, to another kind of *reading*. This would be a reading that by refusing the metaphors of unproblematized paternity – the signature – allows for the emergence of a less stable rhetoric of maternity. What this means in my translation is that like Kristeva, whose interest in a female practice is related primarily to a more general concern with an avant-garde, dissident and marginal work in language, Kamuf would prefer to see 'feminist' criticism address itself not to the productions signed by biological women alone, but to all productions that put the 'feminine' into play – the feminine then being a modality or process accessible to both men and women. (This might also be said to be the case of Cixous in 'The Laugh of the Medusa' where in one of her famous footnotes she lists Genet along with Colette and Marguerite Duras as examples of those who have produced French inscriptions of femininity. Elsewhere in that essay, and more recently, of course, she has insisted upon a writerly female specificity attached to a female libido and body.)

More locally, Kamuf doesn't care whether the *Portuguese Letters* were written by a woman or by a man, and I do. Just as I care if *The Story of O* was written by 'Pauline Réage'or Jean Paulhan, which is in fact the same example, though for me the pornography of female submission is no more than – surely no worse than – the embodiment of sentimental masochism. I *prefer* to think that this *positioning* of woman is the writing of a masculine desire attached to the male body. Just as I like to know that the Brontean writing of a female anger, desire and selfhood issues from a female pen. (This preference is not without its vulnerabilities, as I indicated earlier. It could, I suppose, one day be proven definitively that the heroines of the *Letters* and *The Story of O* were female creations, after all. I would then have to start over again. But it would be a different (not obverse) story, since the story of the woman who writes is *always* another story.) It is Catharine Stimpsom who has, I think, most accurately analyzed the political fallout of these bodily identities:

...male writers – a Genet – can appropriate the feminine as a stance for the male through which to express receptive subordination before God or a god-like phallus.... Still other male writers, like a Henry James, write about women, particularly lovely victims. Self-consciously empathetic, they speak of and for the feminine.

Each of these strategies is limited, if only because of the obvious anatomical differences.... A male writer may speak of, for, to and from the feminine. He cannot speak, except fictively, of, for, to and from the female. This inability hardly has the dignity of a tragic fact, but it does have the grittiness of simple fact.

('Ad/d Feminam: Women, Literature and Society', *Selected Papers from the English Institute, Literature & Society*, edited with a preface BY EDWARD W. SAID, Baltimore and London; (The Johns Hopkins Press, 1978), p. 179)

This 'grittiness of simple fact' has everything to do with the ways in which the signature of women has functioned historically; in terms of the body, the sexual ideologies that define it; in terms of civil status, the legal restrictions that construct it. I want to invoke briefly Virginia Woolf's speculation about Judith Shakespeare:

And undoubtedly...her work would have gone unsigned. That refuge she would have sought certainly. It was the relic of the sense of chastity that dictated anonymity to women even so late as the nineteenth century. Currer Bell, George Eliot, George Sand, all the victims of inner strife as their writings prove , sought ineffectively to veil themselves by using the name of a man.... Anonymity runs in their blood. The desire to be veiled still possesses them.

(*A Room of One's Own* (New York: Harcourt, Brace & World, 1957), p. 52.)

The desire to be veiled that unveils the anxiety of a genderized and sexualized body, I would argue, is *not* what runs in the blood of the 'Portuguese nun'. What is at work there instead, I think, is a male (at least masculine) desire to paper over an anxiety about destination and reception: a sense of powerlessness about writing in a new genre addressed to an unknown 'destinataire' that takes the abandoned woman's body – the next best thing to a female corpse – as its pretext. The woman-in-love figured here is the masochist Simone de Beauvoir analyzed in *The Second Sex*, whose passion turns to self-mutilation when it turns out that 'no man really is God' (trans. H. M. Parshley, (New York: Bantam Books, 1970), p. 612).

In other words, what I read in the *Portuguese Letters* is an ideology of desire that allows woman to become a subject only upon the condition of her 'subordination before...a god-like Phallus'. Just as we read of O:

O was happy that René had had her whipped and had prostituted her, because her impassioned submission would furnish her lover with the proof that she belonged to him, but also because the pain and shame of the lash, and the outrage inflicted on her by those who compelled her to pleasure when they took her, and at the same time delighted in their own without paving the slightest heed to hers, seemed to be the very redemption of her sins.

(PAULINE RÉAGE, *The Story of O*, Trans. Sabine d'Estrée (New York: Grove Press, 1967), p. 93).

'Mariane' the 'nun', writes in her third letter: 'I saw you leave. I can't hope to ever see you return and yet I'm still alive: I've betrayed you, I beg your forgiveness. But don't grant it! Treat me severely! Don't judge that my feelings are violent enough! Be more difficult to satisfy! Tell me that you want me to die of love for you! And I beg you to give me this help so that I can overcome the weakness of my sex...' (*Lettres de la Réligieuse Portugaise*, pp. 28–29; translation mine). (If 'dying of love is a trope', as Kamuf nicely commented during the round table, what is it a trope of?) Kate Millett has interrogated the psycho-logics of these feminine investments in pain: 'It is ingenious', she writes of Freud's 'Femininity', to describe masochism and suffering as inherently feminine... [I]t justifies any conceivable domination or humiliation forced upon the female as mere food for her nature. To carry such a notion to its logical conclusion, abuse is not only good for woman but the very thing she craved.' (*Sexual Politics* (New York: Doubleday, 1970), pp. 194–5).

However, here is where I come to the end of my 'American' posture. For the next step in that agenda typically is to establish reading lists that reflect 'correct' feminist positions, and to call for the production of literature with positive role models. (This position is clearly laid out in Cheri Register's 'American Feminist Literary Criticism: A Bibliographical Introduction', in *Feminist Literary Criticism*, ed. Josephine Donovan, (Lexington: University Press of Kentucky, 1975), pp. 1–28 especially 11–28). To be fair, this prescriptive aesthetic represents only one strain of criticism; it does not tell the whole story. Nevertheless, hortatory formulations of this sort, 'But women's literature must go beyond the scenarios of compromise, madness and death. Although the reclamation of suffering is the beginning, its purpose is to discover the new world', threaten to erase the ambiguities of the feminist project, unless they are at the same time re-problematized as is the case with Elaine Showalter who goes on, in her tough-minded update of feminist tropologies, to cite literature that has 'gone beyond reclaiming suffering to its *re-investment*'[1] ('Toward a Feminist Poetics,' *Women Writing and Writing about Women*, ed. Mary Jacobus (London: Croom Helm, 1979), p. 32; emphasis mine). Nor would I argue that reading works by women because of the signature is an activity *ethically* superior – *because marginal* – to that of reading works by men; or works by women alongside those of men (though I myself *feel* it

to be an absolutely compelling project). Indeed I think that
'intersextuality,' to borrow a coinage from Naomi Schor, has much to teach
us ('"L' intersextualité": Superposition dans "Lorenzaccio"', paper
delivered at the Third International Colloquium on Poetics, November,
1979, Columbia University). See also 'La pèrodie: Superposition dans
"Lorenzaccio"', *Michigan Romance Studies*, (forthcoming). Sand's reading
and rewriting of Rousseau is as important as her reading Mme de Staël;
and what would James have done without Eliot? Nevertheless, I do
believe in books and courses based on the signature even if, as in the case
of the *Portuguese Letters, The Story of O,* and the novels of the Brontës the
signature was not at the time of reception a reliable index of sexual
identity. The exceptions in the final analysis only point to the rules. Even
though such lists and such courses may betray a naive faith in origins,
humanism, and centrality, because they also make visible the marginality,
eccentricity and vulnerability of women, they concretely challenge the
confidence of humanistic discourse as *universality.*

Let us turn to Foucault before closing; to Foucault at the end of 'What is
an Author?' (Michel Foucault, in *Language, Counter-Memory, Practice*, ed.
Donald F. Bouchard (Ithaca: Cornell, 1980), pp. 113–38). He imagines what
would happen in a society 'without any need for an author.':

> No longer the tiresome repetitions:
> 'Who is the real author?'
> 'Have we proof of his authenticity and originality?'
> 'What has he revealed of his most profound self in his language?'
> New questions will be heard:
> 'What are the modes of existence of this discourse?'
> 'Where does it come from; how is it circulated; who controls it?'
> 'What placements are determined for possible subjects?'
> 'Who can fulfill these diverse functions of the subject?'
> Behind all these questions we would hear little more than the murmur
> of indifference:
> 'What matter who's speaking?'
>
> (p.138)

This sovereign indifference, I would argue, is one of the masks...behind
which phallocentrism hides its fictions: the authorizing function of its own
discourse authorizes the 'end of woman' without consulting her. What
matter who's speaking? I would answer it matters, for example, to women
who have lost and still routinely lose their proper name in marriage, and
whose signature – not merely their voice – has not been worth the paper it
was written on : women for whom the signature – by virtue of its power in
the world of circulation – is not immaterial. Only those who have it can
play with not having it. We might want to remind ourselves of the status

of women's signatures in France before the law of 1965: '...[S]ince 1965, a woman can exercise any profession without her husband's permission. She can alone establish a contract which concerns the maintenance of the home and open a personal bank account. Hereafter dual consent is necessary in order to buy, sell, mortgage a building...finalize a commercial lease...or make purchases on credit' (Maïté Albistur and Daniel Armogathe, *Histoire du Féminisme français* (Paris: des femmes, 1977), Vol. II, pp. 642–43: translation mine).

In the place of proper closure, and in the face of insolubility: let us retain a 'modern', post-humanistic reading of 'literature' that has indeed begun to rethink the very locations of the center and periphery, and within that fragile topology, the stability of the subject. But at the same time, we must live out (the hortatory always returns) a practical politics within the institution grounded in regional specificities. This is to call for, then, a decentered vision (*theoria*) but a centered action that will not result in a renewed invisibility. If feminists decide that the signature is a matter of indifference, if women's studies becomes gender studies, the real end of women in the institution will not be far off. The text's heroine will become again no more than a fiction.

What we might wish for instead, perhaps, is a female materialism attentive to the needs of the body as well as the luxuries of the mind. Can we imagine, or should we, a position that speaks in tropes and walks in sensible shoes?

Notes

1. In a more recent overview, Showalter takes an altogether a-meliorist position which is much closer to my own: 'feminist critics', she concludes, must address themselves 'to what women actually write, not in relation to a theoretical, political, metaphoric, or visionary ideal of what women ought to write' ('Feminist Criticism in the Wilderness', *Critical Inquiry*, 8. No. 2 (Winter 1981), p. 205).

3 Julia Kristeva and Gayatri Chakravorty Spivak

JULIA KRISTEVA *About Chinese Women**

About Chinese Women (1977) is the product of a trip by Julia Kristeva to China in 1974. Rapidly written, it was published that same year in France. The account is not intended as a comprehensive evaluation of Chinese society but, Kristeva tells us, as 'analytical sketches, bits of information, fleeting impressions'. The two-part structure of the work, 'From this Side' and 'Chinese Women', embodies the division between West and East. The first extract included here is the opening chapter to the first section, where Kristeva confronts the 'otherness' of Chinese culture and demolishes the innocence of the traveller who believes she is 'just' looking or 'just' visiting. If Kristeva is to move across this gulf between West and East it is her own situation as a Western woman that she must address. In so doing, concepts of identity, notions of universalism, glib transpositions of Western categories to an Eastern context are all called into question. The chapter includes a section which many commentators have found anti-feminist. Kristeva investigates the difference between 'women' as a biological and political group, working collectively on questions of women's rights and needs, and the 'feminine' as that force which escapes the repressive monotheism of our culture. In this latter sense men too 'have been the "women" of the community'. The second extract is from the opening chapter of the second section where Kristeva discusses the history of Chinese family structures and the importance of the matrilineal model of the family. Kristeva links the family structure to the functions of language and writing and finds, in certain linguistic forms, 'an echo of the pre-Oedipal, the pre-symbolic, the Mother'. In the bodies, looks, voices of Chinese women today, Kristeva continues her search for traces of feminine *jouissance*. Post Tiananmen Square, readers

---

* Reprinted from Julia Kristeva, *About Chinese Women* (London: Marion Boyars, 1977), pp. 11–16, 55–65, trans. Anita Barrows; renumbered from the original.

of Kristeva will feel that this search has become even more urgent (See Introduction, pp. 14–16).

Sitting here in front of the typewriter, trying to write about my experience in China, I am haunted by one scene in particular. It makes me hesitate at each touch of the keyboard; but it excites me as well. Not to lose sight of it; to make it transparent on every page: such are the stakes in the course that follows.

Forty kilometers from the former Chinese capital of Xi'an (the first capital of China after it was unified under the emperor Quin Shi Huangdi in the second century BC, and the great capital of the T'ang Dynasty (618–906)) is Huxian, the chief village of an agricultural region. The road we travel to get there is hot; the sun beats down on peasants in broad bamboo hats, on unsupervised children skipping about in quiet games, on a hearse drawn by some men while others, in two parallel lines alongside it, surround it with thin parallel poles carried across their shoulders. Everyone from the village is in the square where we are supposed to attend an exhibit of peasant painting in one of the nearby buildings. An enormous crowd is sitting in the sun: they wait for us wordlessly, perfectly still. Calm eyes, not even curious, but slightly amused or anxious: in any case, piercing, and certain of belonging to a community with which we will never have anything to do. They don't distinguish among us man or woman, blonde or brunette, this or that feature of face or body. As though they were discovering some weird and peculiar animals, harmless but insane. Unaggressive, but on the far side of the abyss of time and space. 'A species – what they see in us is a different species', says one of our group. 'You are the first foreigners to visit the village', says the interpreter, always sensitive to the least of our tropisms. I don't feel like a foreigner, the way I do in Baghdad or New York. I feel like an ape, a martian, an *other*. Three hours later, when the gates of the exhibit are opened to let our cars pass through, they are still there, sitting in the sun – amused, or anxious – calm, distant, piercing, silent, gently releasing us into our 'strangeness'.

Field anthropologists have certainly had such shocks: 'You are a different species'. But in China, the feeling of alienation seems to me even more important, because it is addressed to us by a society which has nothing exotic about it, no relation whatsoever to any 'primitive mentality'. On the contrary, it comes from what is called a 'modern nation', a nation with 'modern problems', in which even something that we may find irritating or archaic is easily identified: something not all that far from us, the regimes of Eastern Europe. So nothing disorienting there; even less so for me, who recognized my own pioneer komsomol childhood in the little red guards, and who owe my cheekbones to some Asian ancestor. The strangeness persists, then, through a highly developed civilization which

71

enters without complexes into the modern world, and yet preserves a logic unique to itself that no exoticism can account for.

I think that one of the functions – if not the most important – of the Chinese Revolution today is to introduce this breach ('there are others') into our universalist conceptions of man and history. It's not worth the trouble to go to China if one insists on closing one's eyes to this breach. Obviously there are those who find a solution: they try to fill the abyss by rewriting a China for 'our people' (who may have some revolutionary or revisionist or liberal cause which will be strengthened by proving that the Chinese are *like* us, *against* us, or *to be ignored*); or else by creating a China *against* 'them' (against those who are deforming China by making it conform to 'their' ideology rather than 'ours'). To write 'for' or 'against': the old trick of a militant committed to maintaining his position. It can help, it can stifle: what is lost is the chance that the discovery of 'the other' may make us question ourselves about what, here and now, is new, scarcely audible, disturbing.

It is not my goal – and it is perhaps useless to try – to discover all those things which, in modern Chinese culture and society, determine the indefinable stare of the peasants of Huxian, who, in fact, did nothing but return the look I gave them without letting them see it, moulded as I am by universalist humanism, proletarian brotherhood, and (why not?) false colonial civility. I want to put into relief here one single aspect of that which creates the abyss between us and the villagers of Huxian: Chinese women, the Chinese family, their tradition, their present revolution. I make this choice for two reasons.

First, because the studies of specialists, my own impressions, and the most recent developments in the cultural revolution prove that, in ancient history but also throughout the history of Chinese socialism and up to the present, the role of women and, consequently, that of the family, have a particular quality in China which is unknown in the monotheistic West. To observe that particular aspect of China is, therefore, to try to understand what makes China unique: a focus which seeks to measure the distance that separates me from Huxian. No way at all to understand China if one is not sensitive to the women, to their condition, to their difference. Without that, there's no point even in being interested in China: one will know everything beforehand, and won't even hear the silence in Huxian Square; or, at best, if one hears it, one will be petrified by it, sickened, annoyed, separated forever from them; one will feel like forgetting them in order to forget at the same time the whole of China, or to understand it in one blow: easy.

Second, and perhaps especially, I make this choice because the *otherness* of China is invisible if the man or woman who speaks here, in the West, doesn't position him/herself some place where our capitalist monotheistic fabric is shredding, crumbling, decaying. But where? The class warfare, the new ideological and political mechanisms that have arisen since May '68 come to mind. Yes, certainly, especially when they don't mimic the reasoning of the capitalist system or the classical parties they believe they're fighting. But do you know many who don't? We're left with the 'underground' – those who aren't yet organized, who in their impossible utopian 'dadaist' approach to politics provoke only laughter. And if the otherness, and therefore the novelty, of China were not visible except from there, because this underground, itself 'out of order' in our world, is its repressed content, the symptom of all that monotheistic capitalism has crushed in order to make itself everywhere identical and impermeable to crisis? The 'underground': women, young people, those who speak differently – artists, poets.... It is still essential that their anguish in the present community be more than just a disillusioned travesty of social bonds, or a sullen demand for a new social order. Living in the political system on the planet today, they must discover here and elsewhere that which is involved in an entirely different 'change of the tide' – an end to pre-history, dream and reality henceforth in continuous flux.

Women. We have the luck to be able to take advantage of a biological peculiarity to give a name to that which, in monotheistic capitalism, remains on this side of the threshold of repression, voice stilled, body mute, always foreign to the social order. A well-deserved luck, for, in fact, in the entire history of patrilineal or class-stratified societies, it is the lot of the feminine to assume the role of *waste*, or of the hidden work-force in the relationships of production and the language which defines them. But a *limited luck*, because others, men, since at least the end of the nineteenth century and in ever-increasing numbers in our time, realize that they have been the 'women' of the community: a misunderstanding perhaps, that confuses the demands of the female sex (if you like), but which prevents a feminist 'we' from becoming a homogeneous 'secret society of females' and disseminates among others our own unnameable anxiety before all that escapes social restraint. A *luck* that will prove to have been *co-opted* if, after an initial phase – no doubt necessary – of searching for our identity, we lock ourselves up inside it: militant romantics of the final 'cause' to be thus revived, theologians of an inverted humanism rather than its iconoclasts.

Who is speaking, then, before the stare of the peasants at Huxian? Whoever on this side is fed up with being a 'dead woman' – Jewish mother, Christian virgin, Beatrice beautiful because defunct, voice without body, body without voice, silent anguish choking on the rhythms of words, the tones of sounds, the colours of images, but without words, without sounds, without images; outside time, outside knowledge, cut-off forever from the rhythmic, colourful violent changes that streak sleep, skin, viscerals: socialized, even revolutionary, but at the cost of the body; body crying, infatuating, but at the cost of time; cut-off, swallowed up; on

73

the one hand, the aphasic pleasure of childbirth that imagines itself a participant in the cosmic cycles; on the other, *jouissance*[1] under the symbolic weight of a law (paternal, familial, social, divine) of which she is the sacrificed support, bursting with glory on the condition that she submit to the denial, if not the murder, of the body....

To relieve her of this weight, to x-ray it, to analyze it, is equivalent to a second Renaissance. Erasmus today would not write a praise of folly, but a critique of this negative term of the social entente, this eternal satire of the community, that is woman. If such is not the perspective, the women's movement is only good for establishing a ministry of women's affairs, i.e. an accelerated rationalization of capitalism. Which is not *nothing*; but even so.... in this world, will China be our Greece?

A few themes, then, a few names, chosen by accident of mood or desire, but dictated as well by the questions that my trip to China provoked in me: the sexual difference; the identification of the daughter with the paternal law; the atemporal and therefore apolitical appeal of polymorphic sexuality; suicide; the sacrifice of the other sex in a paternally dominated family where woman is 'the other race'; the totalitarianism which is the inevitable result of the denial of this difference. Questions that the awakening of woman asks of our western society, questions that have a double interest for us, here.

First, in that they show that *woman as such* does not exist. Either the term dissolves into as many individual cases, and, since the post-romantics already knew it (Rilke, for instance: 'Is it possible to say "women", "children", "boys", and not suspect, for all one's culture, that for a long time now these words have had no plural, but rather an infinity of singulars?'), it's useless to cling to our belief in the latest community except to obtain the right to abortion and the pill. Or, the problems of women have no interest except inasmuch as they bring to an impasse the most serious problems of our type of society; how to live not only without God, but without man?

Secondly, to approach these problems beforehand will avoid dealing with them once we sense that we are encountering them in China; and we will have plenty of opportunities, when we see these girls who brandish pistols and paintbrushes, who liberate themselves from their husbands and fathers under the portrait of Mao, and leave their children, their calligraphy, their exploits in the field of production, science, or the current ideological campaign, as the sole evidence of their *jouissance*. It is more than the necessity to be brief that makes us avoid analyzing all this in China. Rather, it is a vigilance, call it ethical, that keeps us on our guard not to project onto the women of China thoughts which they may evoke but which, in fact, are the products of western experience and concern that alone. It's easy to ascribe innumerable reflections on the 'war between the sexes', the 'virgins of the word', 'timelessness' or 'suicide' to the silences that will occur throughout this journey in China and especially in the 'interviews' at the end: it will be a western vision. Nothing is less certain than 'the truth' about China according to some Viennese professor, or anyone else here in the West.

Refusing, therefore, to know more than they do; and refusing, as well, to endow them with a knowledge that would hold the answer to our own problems – let us first try to question a tradition that has defined us here for at least two thousand years. A quick sketch, a questionnaire, left open-ended.

The other essential characteristic of the Chinese universe is the system of writing, designed for a tonal language. This system of communication is certainly the first thing in China to strike the foreigner's ear and eye, and attract his attention. Linguists know that Chinese functions like any other language, that it is capable of transmitting messages without ambiguity. Modern theoreticians of transformational grammar are trying with some success to formulate the rules of Chinese grammar by making them conform to those of universal reason. Let's not even consider classical Chinese and the various poetic genres that scramble the message, weaving it into numerous ellipses and condensations. In everyday language itself, the 'white language' (*bai hua*) used today, the first thing one is aware of is the role that tonalities play in differentiating meanings. The same thing happens in the all tonal languages, and supports the discoveries of certain psycholinguists, i.e. that tonal variations and intonations are the first elements of the acoustic world that children are able to grasp and reproduce. They are quickly forgotten in a milieu where the language is not based on tones; but children surrounded by tonal speech do retain them, and quite early on. Thus, Chinese children begin taking part in the code of social communication that is language at a much younger age (five or six months) than children in other cultures, since they are capable so early of distinguishing the fundamental trait of their language. And, as the dependency on the mother's body is so great at that age, it is thus the psycho-corporeal imprint of the mother that shapes tonal expression and transmits it without obliterating it, as the underlying but active stratum of communication. The grammatical system, on the other hand, will be a secondary acquisition, more 'socializing' because it ensures the transmission of a message composed of meanings (and not only tonal impulses) to people other than the mother. Does the Chinese language preserve, then, thanks to its tones, a pre-Oedipal, pre-syntactic, pre-symbolic (symbol and syntax being concomitant) register, even if it is evident that the tonal system is not fully realized except in syntax (like the phonological system in French, for example)?

The same question may be asked with regard to the writing. It is, at least in part – and at its origin – an imagistic writing; but it has become increasingly stylized, ideogrammatic, abstract. Nevertheless, it maintains its 'character', which is evocative both visually (in that it resembles an object or objects underlying an idea) and physically (because, to one who writes in Chinese, a memory for movement is more important than a memory for meaning). May we consider these visual and physical components to be manifestations of a psychic stratum more archaic even than those of sense and meaning, let alone logical and syntactical abstraction? As products of the vast unconscious storehouse from which the individual, thus, would never be cut off? It is accepted knowledge among modern historians and archaelogists that the great systems of writing (Egyptian, Babylonian, and Mayan, among others) were invented by the great 'despots'; as a means of centralizing power, perpetuating severe forms of slavery, carrying out great 'projects of state' (principally hydraulic), and developing a bureaucracy of religious or secular castes. If such, according to research, is the nature of productive relations in the great civilizations, we still know very little about the reproductive relations. The logic of Chinese writing (a visual presentation, the mark of a gesture, a signifying arrangement of symbols, logic, and certain syntax) presupposes, at its base, a speaking writing individual for whom what seems to us today a pre-Oedipal phase – dependency on the maternal, socio-natural continuum, absence of clear-cut divisions between the order of things and the order of symbols, predominance of the unconscious impulses – must have been extremely important. Ideogrammic or ideographic writing uses the characteristics of this phase for the ends of national, political, and symbolic power, *without censuring them*. A despotic power that has not forgotten what it owes to the mother and the matrilinear family that has certainly preceded it, though not by long. Hypothesis? Fantasy? – In any case, this would supplement an explanation of the disappearance of the great writing cultures in the face of the rise of monotheism and under its tread. After Egypt, Babylon and the Mayans, only China (and its followers in Japan and southeast Asia) continues to 'write'. The structure of this system of social communication can perhaps be added to the list of historic and geographic accidents responsible for this fact. Not only has Chinese writing maintained the memory of matrilinear pre-history (collective and individual) in its architectonic of image, gesture, and sound; it has been able as well to integrate it into a logico-symbolic code capable of ensuring the most direct, 'reasonable', legislating – even the most bureaucratic – communication: all the qualities that the West believes itself unique in honouring, and that it attributes to the Father. We will return to these feudal and imperial acquisitions later on. Let us say simply here that the imposition of the 'symbolic instance' – *logical* in what concerns language, *despotic* when it comes to social and political matters – has never succeeded in eliminating the (logically) earlier stratum.

But the tones and the writing are not the only evidence that this stratum actively persists: a sort of reticence in metalanguage, in the great metaphysical and/or philosophical theoretical systems, testifies to it as well. This reticence is responsible, perhaps, in another way, for something in the way that ancient and modern Chinese have of explaining their problems, which often is disconcerting to us. Rather than proceeding to an explanation which, for us, is the only logical one – which seeks the causes, makes the deductions, specifies the motivations, appearances, and essences, and at the same time foresees the consequences of an event – an operation which derives from the principle of a logical metaphysical causality – the Chinese give us a 'structuralist' or 'warring' (contradictory) portrait. Behind the event itself there appears a combinatorium or an association that bears the seed of the overthrow of the previous order; a battle between good and evil; two-faced people; persecutions, conspiracies, sensational turns of event. As if the causal, deterministic metaphysical logic had crumbled before the traumatic occurrence whose advent we question; but without losing the symbolic level, the Chinese-speaking individual describes this event as if he were speaking of a game, a war, a combinatorium. We must add that the dramatic combinatorium that replaces the *principio reddendae rationis* is rife with allusions (which, of course, are beyond our comprehension) to historic or literary events familiar to any Chinese, without his necessarily being a scholar. So that it suffices to establish a structural analogy between the present circumstance and one in antiquity, which will eliminate the need to ask if and when the present event actually occurred: certainly it occurred, since it is being made analogous to an event that is certified by literature and tradition. Such an 'aesthetic' mode of reasoning may make us uneasy; but it has a certain symbolic effectiveness. By eliminating straight away the problem of an 'objective truth' (which it would be impossible to do in the political world burdened with power relationships), it shifts people to a symbolic situation in literature or in the past, selected according to the influence it continues to exert in the present. And it is there, in that symbolic, archetypal situation, that the dramas of passion, ideology, and politics that underlie the present traumatic event which concerns us and which we seek to understand (in our own terms) are called into play and begin to unravel, as in a psychodrama, a pre-psychoanalytic 'happening'; as in the sort of theatre Sade introduced for the inmates at Charenton.

A revival of archaic, pre-Oedipal modes of operation? A consonance with the very latest methods of logic and psychology? In any case, it is also, perhaps, this kind of thinking that ties ancient to modern China, the old semi-feudal society to communism. It is also, perhaps, what separates us from any Chinese man or woman with whom we enter into dialogue …across Huxian Square.

I went to the Pampo Museum of pre-history, near Xi'an. The excavations begun in 1953 have unearthed a village that modern Chinese archeologists consider to have been organized as a primitive matriarchal commune, prior to the appearance of patriarchy, private property, and class distinctions. In 1958, the findings were placed in a museum which, by a state decree of 1961, is under the auspices of the State Council. A woman of about thirty, who looked like a suntanned schoolgirl, told us about ancient times. Chang Shufang, mother of two, did not study history at the University. She began by teaching herself in whatever time she had left over from her more or less technical duties as museum guide, and she is presently continuing her studies in night classes, where university professors come to teach museum employees. Chang Shufang among the ruins of Pampo: a veritable dramatic setting of Engels' *On the Origin of the Family, Private Property, and The State*. The ruins of this 8,000 year-old village are spread over a territory of about 16 acres: the relics in the museum come from the two and a half acres that have been explored to date. Three distinct zones arise on this soil, whitened by time and limestone, creating before my eyes the distant life which Mme Chang attempts to explain with the help of Engels.

There are two types of habitation: round ones above ground, and square ones slightly below the surface. Do they indicate a separation of sexes (men, women)? Different practical uses (homes, silos)? Or different historical periods? Seed fossils – millet, colza, wild plants – suggest a certain level of agricultural development: 'It was the women who gathered the wild plants; by cultivating them around the house, women invented agriculture, which allowed them to play a major social – and even political – role', explains Mme Chang. 'Men devoted themselves to hunting and fishing, and, later on, to breeding animals.' The village, along the banks of the River Zhanhe, abounded in fish. The fish was a totem, and is represented in pottery paintings. At the centre of the village was the house of the Great Ancestress, surrounded by hearths where men and women belonging to the two divisions of the economy (farmers and hunters) gathered together at night. Outside the village, separated by a sort of moat were the two other areas, burial grounds and pottery works, side by side. There are round vessels made of terra cotta, of variable size (from five to thirty cm), widening at the mouth, with or without a spout. Some have inscriptions – the precursors of writing – tracings, runes, auguries. Others are covered with elegant designs in black and red-brown: fish, pairs of fish, or simply squares, circles, and triangles which, according to Chang Shufang, are earlier representations of fish. But there are also wild birds, elephants, giraffes, who don't seem to have lived in the region: are they the fruit of some imagination, or the memories of migrants? In any case, one finds the impressions of women's fingernails on the pottery. Women not only cultivated the grain, but made the pottery and did the cooking. Some of the pottery is hand-cast, some seems to have been thrown on a wheel. A pot made for drawing water demonstrates a certain empirical knowledge of the laws of gravity. One pot uses steam for cooking. All are evidence, according to Chang Shufang, of the development of production in the primitive commune.

We know that it was matriarchal essentially from the burial grounds. The women's graves contain more funerary objects – pottery, bracelets, bone hairpins, whistles, etc. – than the men's. Children are buried with the women (only babies are not admitted to the burial ground; their bodies are placed in urns not far from the houses). Here, there are common graves: men are buried with men, and women with women. But in this same region of Xi'an, another excavation has revealed the existence of burial grounds where the Mother occupies the central position, and is surrounded by the skeletons of the other members of the 'family' (doubtless a two-part funeral rite: first the two sexes are buried in separate graves, then the family is placed around the grandmother). Sacrifical rites do not appear to have been among the customs of this period, and, therefore, of the matriarchal commune: none of the skeletons bears evidence of a violent death. Finally, according to Mme Chang, the central house, the Great Ancestress' house, seems to have been also the central meeting place, where the political affairs of this society without paternal domination or private property were collectively decided. Recent paintings illustrate the conclusions of Chang Shufang. One sees the Great Ancestress, whose youthful features seem more Ukranian than Chinese, directing the groups of hunters, potters, and farmers. In a recent speech, Mao himself seems deeply persuaded of her existence:

> (In the primitive society) there was not yet the practice of burying women with their dead husbands, but they were obliged to subject themselves to men. First men were subject to women, and then things moved towards their opposite, and women were subject to men. This stage in history has not yet been clarified, although it has been going on for a million years and more. Class society has not yet lasted 5,000 years. Cultures such as that of Lung Shan and Yang Shao at the end of the primitive era had coloured pottery. In a word, one devours another, one overthrows another...[2]

A fantasy projection of some Golden Age? An accidental coincidence of Engels' theories and the Chinese past? A superficial interpretation of archeological facts? Perhaps. But the enigma persists: a mother of the centre.

Is it an echo of this central role of the tribal mother that we hear in the sexual treatises and erotic rites of feudal China? What is certain is that all the manuals of the 'Art of the Bedchamber' – which date back to the first century AD – depict the woman as the principal initiator of love-making, since it is she who knows not only its technique, but also its secret (alchemical) meaning and its benefits to the body (longevity).

Furthermore, she is portrayed as the party whose right to *jouissance* is incontestable. Thus, the three female figures who, in the form of a dialogue that is anything but platonic, teach the arcane meanings of sex to the Emperor: Shunü (Daughter of Candour), Xuannü (Daughter with Jade Hair), and Carnü (Chosen Daughter), quite obviously know a great deal more than the males who come to consult them – before the 'masters' of later treatises come along and cloak amorous advice in military terminology. But whether it is divulged by a woman or an expert 'master', the advice about love-making is principally concerned with the pleasure of the woman. Foreplay is extensively discussed, and the goal of the act itself, each time, is the orgasm of the woman, who is thought to have an inexhaustible *yin* essence, whereas the man, on the other hand, the delicate artisan of this *jouissance*, is supposed to withhold his own orgasm in order to achieve health and longevity, if not immortality. One can imagine social reasons for such practices: polygamy required a certain order in the relationships among the various wives, and demanded that they be satisfied at least at regular intervals so that peace reigned in the harem; obviously, the one available male had to spare his strength. Whatever the reasons, though, the psychosomatic result of this kind of *jouissance* is that the woman does not consider herself as 'inferior', 'devalued', and desirable only at that price – which is the case in sexual economies dominated by the phallus. Furthermore, because the man is neither the master nor the active, inducing principle of the orgasm, but rather one of two who are each two in themselves (each partner being both *male* and *female*, the difference between them being a matter of degree), the sexual act becomes a mutual exchange: what is missing in the one is offered by the other. Without being an 'egalitariansim' – since it maintains the differences – this kind of sexual practice is essentially genital: the sexual treatises are designed for married life. They impress us with their positivity, their attitude toward sex as 'normal': nothing is sinful in this refined quest for pleasure. What we think of as perversion seems to integrate itself easily into these customs: female homosexuality in particular. A vestige of the 'matriarchy' or the *modus vivendi* of the polygamous family? Female sexuality and masturbation are not merely 'tolerated' – they are taken for granted and considered to be perfectly 'natural'. Sexual treatises provide detailed descriptions of lesbian and mastubatory techniques, some of them extraordinarily sophisticated. What is problematic is the woman who cheats: the one who tries to pass for a man, who perverts the *yin/yang* duality by acting as a rather brutal, domineering male seducer. Male homosexuality seems more problematic, even though during certain periods (the earlier Han, who reigned in the early centuries BC, and also, particularly, the southern Song Dynasty, 1127–1279; but also the Ming – 1368–1644) it was practised quite openly, and underlay what were called the 'great intellectual friendships' under the

Tang (618–906). But, without being isolated as a 'special case', a
'deviation', or a 'sexual peculiarity', homosexuality seems about as diffuse
in the vast current of genital eroticism as sadism and masochism. Van
Gulik[3] emphasizes that cases of 'perversion' are rare in China. It might be
more accurate to say that they are rare as such, in isolation; but the so-
called 'perverted' act is incorporated into an erotic practice where
whatever is pleasurable is considered 'normal', provided that the pleasure
includes, at one point or another in the process, *both sexes*. One can *engage*
in homosexual, sadistic or masochistic practices; one *is not defined as* a
sadist, a masochist, a homosexual.

Such an economy, based on the *jouissance* of the woman without
sacrificing that of the man, proceeds from the idea that the sexual
relationship is not a relationship of identification, absorption of the one by
the other, negation of the differences. In other words, nothing in the
sexual–psychological relationship here corresponds to the western
medieval concept of love. The explosive, blossoming, sane and
inexhaustible *jouissance* of the woman is perhaps precisely that permanent
flight which precludes two individuals, two psychic entities, from coming
together to gaze narcissistically into each other's eyes. But this feminine
jouissance, that could become the support of the mystery, the ultimate
source of God, the Absolute, does not do so in China; for it is constantly
counterbalanced by the other, the *yang*, which certainly takes for itself and
gives of itself, but not every time. The *yang* represents the limit of
jouissance, the prohibition that may be ephemeral, may be overridden –
but is nonetheless present. It is precisely this difference, this *otherness*,
which is brought back into balance after the act of love; and precisely
because the two terms are well separated, without possibility of confusion.
Some praise it, others regret it. A melancholy regret, that draws strength
from the fact that women, high priestesses of carnal love, are excluded
from social relationships and become alienated in a feudal society whose
hierarchical order depends on forgetting the bedchamber.

> They who were first as form and shadow
> Now they are distant as Chinese and Huns.
> Even Chinese and Huns meet now and then,
> While husband and wife are as different as Lucifer and Orion.

writes Fu Xian in the third century AD. But praise is heard from others,
because if men and women are two separate races and even two separate
universes, their conflict is an aspect of the perpetual cosmic and social
movement. This permanent flux has no 'unity' save that of *conception*,
which has nothing immaculate or universally stable about it, but rather
takes place during a complex strategy between two sexes. Such a strategy
cannot be defined; it can only be suggested by metaphor: the alchemical

crucible, or war. 'On the incarnation of the Tao, the true Oneness (i.e. conception) is difficult to represent. After this transmutation, the couple separates, and each one returns again to his or her own side.'[4] Much emphasis has been placed on the influence of Chinese sexual theory and practice on the development of the sexual mystique of Tantric Buddhism. There is one essential difference, however, between the Chinese universe and the Buddhist universe in this regard: in China, the two sexes harmonize, but generally do not fuse. The erotic-alchemical dyad of Taoism is not a hermaphrodite; never does the one absorb the other to the point that its existence is made superfluous. The Tantra, on the other hand, says: 'Why should I need another woman? I have a woman within myself.' Taoism nourishes this concept of sexual life that underlies Chinese society, and remains permanently in the shadow of family life, even when Confucianism reigns supreme over the political scene from at least the Song period on. Taoist sects, and, afterward, Taoist institutions (like Buddhist monasteries) are reputed to have given refuge to sexual practices where women played the major role, when such practices were condemned by Confucian propaganda. Later on, we shall see the extent to which women were despised in some forms of Confucianism; but even these never had the idea of 'carnal sin', and certain Taoist precepts were integrated into the system during the Confucian revival of the eleventh century. However, without proscribing eroticism, Confucianism began by subordinating it to the goal of procreation. Like some of our contemporary anthropologists, the Confucians were interested only in those aspects of sexual practice that would ensure procreation. They would later embark on an all-out attack on the sex manuals of the Han and the Tang, and would prohibit any demonstration of heterosexual relationship. Finally, during the Ming dynasty (1368–1644), they would plunge into an embittered puritanism where eroticism became a deviation, a transgression, reserved for bordellos and for what henceforth would be known as pornographic literature.

What's left today of the 'Art of the Bedchamber' and its feminine *jouissance*? What's left of the treatises of the Han and the Tang after Confucian puritanism and the modern importation of bourgeois morality?

A secret sect, practising group sex according to Taoist rules, was dissolved in 1950.

A more or less Confucian 'modesty' is still in evidence. Is this a result of the effort at sublimation required to build the new society? Or is it simply distrust of strangers? It is impossible to get the Chinese to talk about it today. But one can watch these relaxed feminine bodies floating lightly along the streets of Peking, among the tufts of willow moss. One can glimpse the quick, hot, laughing glances, or the clever, furtive smiles of these girls, walking arm-in-arm through the park. Or one can listen to these women's voices, which don't stick in the throat, but rather vibrate, rhythmic and melodious, with the whole body, down to the tiniest cell, free of guilt or provocation. An empty centre, around which the society of men revolves without ever speaking of it. So…one can think what one pleases, before these people. Beginning with oneself.

Notes

1. This word, for which there is no suitable English equivalent, is used in psychoanalytic contexts to mean the simultaneously organic and symbolic sexual pleasure of the speaking (human) subject.

2. 'Discourse on Philosophical Problems, August 18, 1964', in Mao Tse-tung, *Unrehearsed Talks and Letters: 1956–74*, ed. Stuart Schram, (Pelican Books, 1974), p. 226.

3. *La vie sexuelle dans la Chine ancienne*, Gallimard, 1971.

4. According to the Taoist treatise on alchemy: *The Pact of the Triple Equation*, quoted by Van Gulik, p. 115.

GAYATRI CHAKRAVORTY SPIVAK *'French Feminism in an International Frame'**

Gayatri Chakravorty Spivak describes herself as a Marxist, feminist, deconstructivist. Born in India, educated in the States, conversant with French thought – for example, in her translation of Jacques Derrida's *Of Grammatology* (1976) – she has the advantage of a diverse cultural and intellectual experience. All these influences are brought to bear in this fruitful and complex essay. How to link the First-World academic feminist and the Third-World impoverished woman is a problem from Spivak's own history and one she sees in contemporary feminist thinking. Her appraisal of Julia Kristeva's *About Chinese Women* (1977) leads her to conclude that intelligence and sympathy are not enough. Rather than applying French feminism to a very different cultural and political situation, it may be more productive,

* Gayatri Chakravorty Spivak, 'French Feminism in an International Frame' appeared originally in *Yale French Studies*, no. 62 (1981). Reprinted from *In Other Worlds: Essays in Cultural Politics* (New York and London: Methuen, 1987), pp. 134–53.

Spivak believes, to reverse the coin and consider how 'International Feminism is defined within a Western European context'. 'America', 'English', 'French' will be the first terms to be investigated. Elsewhere, Spivak has been highly critical of Anglo-American feminism; here she turns a severe eye to French feminism. Using Elaine Marks and Isabelle de Courtivron's *New French Feminisms: An Anthology* (1981) as her reference, she questions French feminism's confidence in the revolutionary potential of a literary and philosophical avant-garde. She also discusses various forms of anti-feminism – where feminism is considered as a reformulation of humanism, or as a deviation from the class struggle, or as synonymous with essentialism and biologism. Ultimately though, Spivak decides that the application of French feminism's double programme – against sexism and for feminism – to concerns of female pleasure is, indeed, a possible link between First-and Third-World women (see Introduction, pp. 14–16).

A young Sudanese woman in the Faculty of Sociology at a Saudi Arabian University said to me, surprisingly: 'I have written a structural functionalist dissertation on female circumcision in the Sudan.' I was ready to forgive the sexist term 'female circumcision'. We have learned to say 'clitoridectomy' because others more acute than we have pointed out our mistake.

But Structural Functionalism? Where 'integration' is 'social control [which] defines and *enforces...a degree of solidarity*'? Where 'interaction, seen from the side of the economy', is defined as 'consist[ing] of the supply of income and wealth applied to purposes strengthening the persistence of cultural patterns?'[1] Structural functionalism takes a 'disinterested' stance on society as functioning structure. Its implicit interest is to applaud a system – in this case sexual – because it functions. A description such as the one below makes it difficult to credit that this young Sudanese woman had taken such an approach to clitoridectomy:

In Egypt it is only the clitoris which is amputated, and usually not completely. But in the Sudan, the operation consists in the complete removal of all the external genital organs. They cut off the clitoris, the two major outer lips (*labia majora*) and the two minor inner lips (*labia minora*). Then the wound is repaired. The outer opening of the vagina is the only portion left intact, not however without having ensured that, during the process of repairing, some narrowing of the opening is carried out with a few extra stitches. The result is that on the marriage night it is necessary to widen the external opening by slitting one or both ends with a sharp scalpel or razor so that the male organ can be introduced.[2]

In my Sudanese colleague's research I found an allegory of my own ideological victimage:

The 'choice' of English Honors by an upper-class young woman in the Calcutta of the fifties was itself highly overdetermined. Becoming a professor of English in the US fitted in with the 'brain drain'. In due course, a commitment to feminism was the best of a collection of accessible scenarios. The morphology of a feminist theoretical practice came clear through Jacques Derrida's critique of phallocentrism and Luce Irigaray's reading of Freud. (The stumbling 'choice' of French avant-garde criticism by an undistinguished Ivy League Ph.D working in the Midwest is itself not without ideology-critical interest.) Predictably, I began by identifying the 'female academic' and feminism as such. Gradually I found that there was indeed an area of feminist scholarship in the US that was called 'International Feminism': the arena usually defined as feminism in England, France, West Germany, Italy, and that part of the Third World most easily accessible to American interests: Latin America. When one attempted to think of so-called Third women in a broader scope, one found oneself caught, as my Sudanese colleague was caught and held by Structural Functionalism, in a web of information retrieval inspired at best by: 'what can I do *for* them?'

I sensed obscurely that this articulation was part of the problem. I re-articulated the question: What is the constituency of an international feminism? The following fragmentary and anecdotal pages approach the question. The complicity of a few French texts in that attempt could be part both of the problem – the 'West' out to 'know' the 'East' determining a 'westernized Easterner's symptomatic attempt to 'know her own world'; or of something like a solution – reversing and displacing (if only by juxtaposing 'some French texts' and a 'certain Calcutta') the ironclad opposition of West and East. As soon as I write this, it seems a hopelessly idealistic restatement of the problem. I am not in a position of choice in this dilemma.

To begin with, an obstinate childhood memory.

I am walking alone in my grandfather's estate on the Bihar-Bengal border one winter afternoon in 1949. Two ancient washerwomen are washing clothes in the river, beating the clothes on the stones. One accuses the other of poaching on her part of the river. I can still hear the cracked derisive voice of the one accused: 'You fool! Is this your river? The river belongs to the Company!' – the East India Company, from whom India passed to England by the Act for the Better Government of India (1858); England had transferred its charge to an Indian Governor-General in 1947. India would become an independent republic in 1950. For these withered women, the land as soil and water to be used rather than a map to be learned still belonged, as it did one hundred and nineteen years before that date, to the East India Company.

I was precocious enough to know that the remark was incorrect. It has taken me thirty-one years and the experience of confronting a nearly inarticulable question to apprehend that their facts were wrong but the fact was right. The Company does still own the land.

I should not consequently patronize and romanticize these women, nor yet entertain a nostalgia for being as they are. The academic feminist must learn to learn from them, to speak to them, to suspect that their access to the political and sexual scene is not merely to be *corrected* by our superior theory and enlightened compassion. Is our insistence upon the especial beauty of the old necessarily to be preferred to a careless acknowledgment of the mutability of sexuality? What of the fact that my distance from those two was, however micrologically you defined class, class-determined and determining?

How, then, can one learn from and speak to the millions of illiterate rural and urban Indian women who live 'in the pores of' capitalism, inaccessible to the capitalist dynamics that allow us our shared channels of communication, the definition of common enemies? The pioneering books that bring First World feminists news from the Third World are written by privileged informants and can only be deciphered by a trained readership. The distance between 'the informant's world', her 'own sense of the world she writes about', and that of the non-specialist feminist is so great that, paradoxically, *pace* the subtleties of reader-response theories, here the distinctions might easily be missed.

This is not the tired nationalist claim that only a native can know the scene. The point that I am trying to make is that, in order to learn enough about Third World women and to develop a different readership, the immense heterogeneity of the field must be appreciated, and the First World feminist must learn to stop feeling privileged *as a woman*.

These concerns were well articulated in my approach to feminism when I came across Julia Kristeva's *About Chinese Women*.[3] Here again I found a link with my own ideological victimage, 'naturalization' transformed into privilege.

French theorists such as Derrida, Lyotard, Deleuze and the like, have at one time or another been interested in reaching out to all that is not the West, because they have, in one way or another, questioned the millennially cherished excellences of Western metaphysics: the sovereignty of the subject's intention, the power of predication and so on. There is a more or less vaguely articulated conviction that these characteristics had something like a relationship with the morphology of capital. The French feminist theory that makes its way to us comes to a readership more or less familiar with this enclave.

During the 1970s, the prestigious journal *Tel Quel* – Kristeva is on the editorial committee – pursued an assiduous if somewhat eclectic interest in the matter of China.[4] Before I consider that interest as it is deployed in

About Chinese Women, let us look briefly at the solution Kristeva offers Frenchwomen in the first part of her book:

> We cannot gain access to the temporal scene, i.e., to political affairs, except by identifying with the values considered to be masculine (dominance, superego, the *endorsed communicative word* that institutes stable social exchange)…[We must] achieve this identification in order to escape a smug polymorphism where it is so easy and comfortable for a woman here to remain; and by this identification [we must] gain entry to social experience. [We must] be wary from the first of the premium on narcissism that such an integration may carry with it: to reject the validity of homologous woman, finally virile: and to act, on the socio-politico-historical stage, as her negative: that is, to act first with all those who 'swim against the tide', all those who refuse…But neither to take the role of revolutionary (male or female): to refuse all roles…to summon this timeless 'truth' – formless, neither true or false, echo of our pleasure, of our madness, of our pregnancies – *into the order of speech* and *social symbolism*. But how? By listening; by recognizing the unspoken in speech, even revolutionary speech; by calling attention at all times to whatever remains unsatisfied, repressed, new, eccentric, incomprehensible, disturbing to the *status quo*.
>
> (p. 38; italics mine)

This is a set of directives for class- and race-privileged literary women who can ignore the seductive effects of identifying with the values of the other side while rejecting their validity,[5] and, by identifying the political with the temporal and linguistic, ignore as well the micrology of political economy. To act with individualistic rather than systematic subverters in order to summon timeless 'truths' resembles the task of the literary critic who explicates the secrets of the avant-garde artist of western Europe; the program of 'symptomatic and semiotic reading' – here called 'listening' – adds more detail to that literary-critical task.[6] The end of this chapter reveals another line of thought active in the group I mention above: to bring together Marx and Freud: 'An analyst conscious of history and politics? A politician tuned into the unconscious? A woman perhaps…' (p. 38).

Kristeva is certainly aware that such a solution cannot be offered to the nameless women of the Third World. Here is her opening descriptions of some women in Huxian Square: 'An enormous crowd is sitting in the sun: they wait for us wordlessly, perfectly still. Calm eyes, not even curious, but slightly amused or anxious: in any case, piercing, and certain of belonging to a community with which we will never have anything to do' (p. 11). Her question, in the face of those silent women, is about her *own* identity rather than theirs: 'Who is speaking, then, before the stare of the peasants at Huxian?' (p. 15). This too might be a characteristic of the group of thinkers to whom I have, most generally, attached her. In spite of their occasional interest in touching the *other* of the West, of metaphysics, of capitalism, their repeated question is obsessively self-centered: if we are not what official history and philosophy say we are, who then are we (not), how are we (not)?

It is therefore not surprising that, even as she leaves the incredibly detailed terrain of the problem of knowing who she herself is exactly – the speaking, reading, listening 'I' at his particular *moment* – she begins to compute the reality of who 'they' are in terms of *millennia*: 'One thing is certain: a revolution in the rules of kinship took place in China, and can be traced to sometime around BC 1000' (p. 46).

The sweeping historiographical scope is not internally consistent. Speaking of modern China, Kristeva asserts drastic socio-sexual structural changes through legislation in a brisk reportorial tone that does not allow for irony (p. 118; p. 128). Yet, speaking of ancient China, she finds traces of an older matrilineal and matrilocal society (evidence for which is gleaned from two books by Marcel Granet, dating from the twenties and thirties, and based on 'folk dance and legend', (p. 47) – and Lévi-Strauss's general book on elementary structures of kinship) lingering through the fierce Confucian tradition to this very day because, at first, it seems to be speculatively the more elegant argument (p. 68). In ten pages this speculative assumption has taken on psychological causality (p. 78).

In another seventy-odd pages, and always with no encroachment of archival evidence, speculation has become historical fact: 'The influence of the powerful system of matrilinear descent, and the Confucianism that is so strongly affected by it, can hardly be discounted' (p. 151). Should such a vigorous conclusion not call into question the authority of the following remark, used, it seems, because at that point the author needs a way of valorizing the women of the countryside today over the women of the cities: 'An intense life-experience has thrust them from *a patriarchal world which hadn't moved for millennia* into a modern universe where they are called upon to command' (p. 193; italics mine)? Where then are those matrilocal vestiges that kept up women's strength all through those centuries?[7]

It is this wishful use of history that brings Kristeva close to the eighteenth-century Sinophiles whom she criticizes because 'they deformed those systems in order to assimilate them into their own' (p. 53). In the very next page, 'the essential problem' of the interpretation of Chinese thought, defined (under cover of the self-deprecatory question) as a species of differential semiotics: 'The heterogeneity of this Li [form and content at once] defies symbolism, and is actualized only by derivation, through a combination of opposing signs (+ and –, earth and sky, etc.), all of which are of equal value. In other words, there is no single isolatable symbolic principle to oppose itself and assert itself as transcendent law.' Even as the Western-trained Third-World feminist deplores the absence of the usual kind of textual analysis and demonstration, she is treated to the most stupendous generalizations about Chinese writing, a topos of that very eighteenth century that Kristeva scorns: 'Not only has Chinese writing maintained the memory of matrilinear pre-history (collective and individual) in its architectonic of image, gesture, and sound; it has been able as well to integrate it into a logico-symbolic code capable of ensuring the most direct, 'reasonable', legislating – even the most bureaucratic – communication: all the qualities that the West believes itself unique in honouring and that it attributes to the Father' (p. 57). Kristeva's text seems to authorize, here and elsewhere, the definition of the essentially feminine and the essentially masculine as non-logical and logical. At any rate, this particular movement ends with the conclusion that 'the Chinese give us a "structuralist" or "warring" (contradictory) portrait' (p. 57).

Kristeva prefers this misty past to the present. Most of her account of the latter is dates, legislations, important people, important places. There is no transition between the two accounts. Reflecting a broader Western cultural practice, the 'classical' East is studied with primitivistic reverence, even as the 'contemporary' East is treated with realpolitikal contempt.

On the basis of evidence gleaned from lives of great women included in translated anthologies and theses of the *troisième cycle* (I take it that is what 'third form thesis', p. 91, indicates) and no primary research; and an unquestioning acceptance of Freud's conclusions about the 'pre-oedipal' stage, and no *analytic* experience of Chinese women, Kristeva makes this prediction: 'If the question [of finding a channel for sexual energy in a socialist society through various forms of sublimation outside the family] should be asked one day, and if the analysis of Chinese tradition that the *Pi Lin Pi Kong* [against Lin and Kong] Campaign seems to have undertaken is not interrupted, it's not altogether impossible that China may approach it with much less prudishness and fetishistic neurosis than the Christian West has managed while clamouring for "sexual freedom"' (p. 90). Whether or not the 'Christian West' as a whole has been clamouring for sexual freedom, the prediction about China is of course a benevolent one; my point is that its provenance is symptomatic of a colonialist benevolence.

The most troubling feature of *About Chinese Women* is that, in the context of China, Kristeva seems to blunt the fine edge of her approach to literature. She draws many conclusions about 'the mother at the centre' in ancient China from 'all the manuals of the "Art of the Bedchamber" – which date back to the first century AD' and 'a novel of the Qing Dynasty…*The Dream of the Red Pavilion*' (p. 61, 79). Let us forget that there is no attempt at textual analysis, not even in translation. We must still ask, are these manuals representative or marginal, 'normal' or 'perverse', have they a class fix? Further, is the relationship between 'literature and life' so unproblematic as to permit *The Dream* to be described as 'an accurate portrait of noble families' because it 'is currently studied in China as evidence of the insoluble link between class struggle and intra/inter-familial attitudes' (pp. 78–9)? How may it differ when a Chinese person with a 'Chinese experience' studies it in Chinese, apparently in this way? Is it only the West that can afford its protracted debate over the representationality of realism? Similar questions haunt the reader as Kristeva launches into a running summary of the female literati of China since 150 AD, in terms of dominant themes. She offers this impressionistic comment on a poet who, we are told, is 'among the greatest, not only in China, but in the literature of the entire world' (p. 50): 'Li Qingzhao breathes into these universal traits of Chinese poetry a musicality rarely attained by other poets: the brilliantly inter-twined rhythms and alliterations, the shape of the characters themselves, create a language where the least aural or visual element becomes the bearer of this symbiosis between body, world, and sense, a language that one cannot label 'music' or 'meaning' because it is both at once.' The poem is then 'quoted' twice – first in English transcription and literal translation, and next in 'a translation (from a French version by Philippe Sollers)'. What would happen to Louise Labé in such a quick Chinese treatment for a Chinese audience with a vestigial sense of European culture as a whole? What is one to make of the gap between the last lines of the two translations: 'This time/how a single world/sadness is enough' and 'this time one/word death won't be enough?' What would happen to 'Absent thee from felicity awhile' in a correspondingly 'free' Chinese version?

As we come to the literatures of modern China, all the careful apologies of the opening of the book seem forgotten: 'Let us examine the findings of a few researchers on family psychology or its representation in modern fiction, as a means of understanding the forms these feudal/Confucian mores take in Chinese culture today' (p. 95). As far as I can tell, the author's source of literary information – a few simple statistics – is a single article by Ai-Li S. Chin, 'Family Relations in Modern Chinese Fiction', in M. Freedman, ed., *Family and Kinship in Chinese Society*.[8] It seems startling, then, that it can be said with apparent ease: 'Are these [mother-daughter] problems intensified by those passionate and archaic rivalries between women which, in the West, produce our Electras, who usurp their mothers' roles by murdering them in the names of their fathers? *Chinese literature is not explicit here*' (p. 146; italics mine).

This brings us to a certain principled 'anti-feminism' in Kristeva's book which may be related to what has been called 'the New Philosophy' in France.[9] 'The Electras – deprived forever of their hymens – militants in the cause of their fathers, frigid with exaltation – are dramatic figures where the social consensus corners any woman who wants to escape her condition:

nuns, "revolutionaries", "feminists"' (p. 32). I think such a sentiment rests upon certain unexamined questions: What is the relationship between myth (the story of Electra), the socio-literary formulation of myths (*Aeschylus's Oresteia*, written for a civic competition with choruses, owned by rich citizens, playing with freelance troupes) and 'the immutable structures' of human behaviour? What hidden agenda does Freud's use of Greek myth to fix the father-daughter relationship – especially at the end of 'Analysis Terminable and Interminable' – contain? Although Kristeva sometimes speaks in a tone reminiscent of *Anti-Oedipus*, she does not broach these questions, which are the basis of that book.[10]

This principled 'anti-feminism', which puts its trust in the individualistic critical avant-garde rather than anything that might call itself a revolutionary collectivity is part of a general intellectual backlash – represented, for instance, by *Tel Quel's* espousal of the Chinese past after the disappointment with the Communist Party of France during the events of May 1968 and the movement toward a Left Coalition through the early 1970s.

The question of how to speak to the 'faceless' women of China cannot be asked within such a partisan conflict. The question, even, of who speaks in front of the mute and uncomprehending women in Huxian Square must now be articulated in sweeping macrological terms. The real differences between 'our Indo-European, monotheistic world...still obviously in the lead' (p. 195) and the Chinese situation must be presented as the fact that the 'Chinese women whose ancestresses knew the secrets of the bedchamber better than anyone...are similar to the men' (p. 198). Thus, when Chinese Communism attacks the tendencies – 'pragmatic, materialistic, psychological' – that 'are considered "feminine" by patriarchal society', it does not really do so; because in China the pre-patriarchal society has always lingered on, giving women access to real rather than representative power. I have indicated above my reasons for thinking that the evidence for this lingering maternal power, at least as offered in this book, is extremely dubious. Yet that is, indeed, Kristeva 's 'reason' for suggesting that in China the Party's suppression of the feminine is not really a suppression of the 'feminine': 'By addressing itself thus to women, (the Party) appeals to their capacity to assume the symbolic function (the structural constraint, the law of the society): a capacity which itself has a basis in tradition, since it includes *the world prior to and behind the scenes of Confucianism*' (p. 199; italics mine).

My final question about this macrological nostalgia for the pre-history of the East is plaintive and predictable: what about us? The 'Indo-European' world whose 'monotheism' supports the argument of the difference between China and the West is not altogether monotheistic. The splendid, decadent, multiple, oppressive, and more than millennial polytheistic tradition of India has to be written out of the *Indo*-European picture in order that this difference may stand.

The fact that Kristeva thus speaks for a generalized West is the 'naturalization transformed into privilege' that I compared to my own ideological victimage. As she investigates the pre-Confucian text of the modern Chinese woman, her own pre-history in Bulgaria is not even a shadow under the harsh light of the Parisian voice. I hold on to a solitary passage:

> For me – having been educated in a 'popular democracy', having benefited from its advantages and been subjected to its censorship, having left it inasmuch as it is possible to leave the world of one's childhood, and probably not without bearing its 'birthmarks' – for me what seems to be 'missing' in the system is, indeed, the stubborn refusal to admit anything is missing.
>
> (p. 156)

Who is speaking here? An effort to answer that question might have revealed more about the mute women of Huxian Square, looking with qualified envy at 'the incursion of the West'.

I am suggesting, then, that a *deliberate* application of the doctrines of French High 'Feminism' to a different situation of political specificity might misfire. If, however, International Feminism is defined within a Western European context, the heterogeneity becomes manageable. In our own situation as academic feminists, we can begin thinking of planning a class. What one does not know can be worked up. There are experts in the field. We can work by the practical assumption that there is no serious communication barrier between them and us. No anguish over uncharted continents, no superstitious dread of making false starts, no questions to which answers may not at least be entertained.

Within such a context, after initial weeks attempting to define and name an 'American' and an 'English' feminism, one would get down to the question of what is specific about French feminism. We shall consider the fact that the most accessible strand of French feminism is governed by a philosophy that argues the impossibility of answering such a question.

We now have the indispensable textbook for this segment of the course: *New French Feminisms: An Anthology*, edited by Elaine Marks and Isabelle de Courtivron.[11] In the United States, French feminism or, more specifically, French feminist theory, has so far been of interest to a 'radical' fringe in French and Comparative Literature departments rather than to the feminists in the field. A book such as this has an interdisciplinary accessibility. This is somewhat unlike the case in England, where Marxist feminism has used mainstream (or masculist) French 'theory' – at least Althusser and Lacan – to explain the constitution of the subject (of ideology or sexuality) – to produce a more specifically 'feminist' critique of Marx's theories of ideology and reproduction.[12]

Because of a predominantly 'literary' interest, the question in French feminist texts that seems most relevant and urgent is that of a specifically feminine discourse. At the crossroads of sexuality and ideology, woman stands constituted (if that is the word) as object. As subject, woman must learn to 'speak "otherwise,"' or *make audible* [what]...suffers silently in *the holes of* discourse' (Xavière Gauthier, p. 163).

The relationship between this project of 'speaking' (writing) and Kristeva's project of 'listening' (reading) is clear. Such a writing is generally though not invariably attempted in feminist fiction or familiar-essay-cum-prose-poem such as Cixous's *Préparatifs de noces au delà de l'abîme* or Monique Wittig's *Lesbian Body*.[13] As such it has strong ties to the 'evocative magic' of the prose poem endorsed by Baudelaire – the power of indeterminate suggestion rather than determinate reference that could overwhelm and sabotage the signifying conventions. Baudelaire is not often invoked by the French theorists of feminist or revolutionary discourse. Is it because his practice remains caught within the gestures of an embarrassingly masculist decadence (linked to 'high capitalism' by Walter Benjamin, *A Lyric Poet in the Era of High Capitalism*)?[14]

The important figures for these theorists remain Mallarmé and Joyce. Julia Kristeva and Hélène Cixous, the two feminists discourse-theorists who are most heard in the US, do not disavow this. Kristeva seems to suggest that if women can accede to the avant-garde in general, they will fulfill the possibilities of their discourse (p. 166). Cixous privileges poetry (for 'the novelists [are] allies of representation', p. 250) and suggests that a Kleist or a Rimbaud can speak as women do. Older feminist writers like Duras ('the rhetoric of women, one that is anchored in the organism, in the body' (p. 238) – rather than the mind, the place of the subject) or Sarraute are therefore related to the mainstream avant-garde phenomenon of the *nouveau roman.*

In a certain sense the definitive characteristic of the French feminist project of founding a woman's discourse reflects a coalition with the continuing tradition of the French avant-garde. It can be referred to the debate about the political potential of the avant-garde, between Expressionism and Realism.[15]

It is also an activity that is more politically significant for the producer/writer than the consumer/reader. It is for the writer rather than the reader that Herbert Marcuse's words may have some validity: 'There is the inner link between dialectical thought and the effort of avant-garde literature: the effort to break the power of facts over the word, and to speak a language which is not the language of those who establish, enforce and benefit from the facts.'[16] As even a quick glance at the longest

entries for the late nineteenth and twentieth centuries in the PMLA
bibliographies will testify, the 'political' energy of avant-garde production,
contained within the present academic system, leads to little more than the
stockpiling of exegeses, restoring those texts back to propositional
discourse. In fact, given this situation, the power of a *Les Guérillères* or a
Tell Me a Riddle (to mention a non-French text) – distinguishing them from
the 'liberated texts' supposedly subverting the traditional components of
discourse', but in fact sharing 'all the components of the most classic
pornographic literature' (Benoîte Groult, p. 72) – is what they talk *about*,
their *substantive* revision of, rather than their apparent *formal* allegiance to,
the European avant-garde. This differential will stubbornly remain in the
most 'deconstructive' of readings.

The search for a discourse of woman is related not merely to a literary
but also the philosophical avant-garde which I mentioned with reference
to *About Chinese Women*. The itinerary of this group is set out in Jacques
Derrida's 'The Ends of Man'.[17] Louis Althusser launched a challenge
against Sartre's theory of humanistic practice and his anthropologistic
reading of Marx with his own 'Feuerbach's "Philosophical Manifesto"' in
1960.[18] Althusser's position was *scientific* anti-humanism. The challenge in
French philosophy described by Derrida in his essay (which makes a point
of being written in 1968), again largely in terms of Sartre and his
anthropologistic reading of Heidegger, can be called an *anti-scientific* anti-
humanism. (Sartre does not remain the butt of the attack for long. An echo
of the importance of Sartre as the chief philosopher of French humanism,
however, is heard in Michèle Le Doeuff's 'Simone de Beauvoir and
Existentialism', presented on the occasion of the thirtieth anniversary of
The Second Sex in New York.[19] Le Doeuff's essay reminds us that, just as
the current anti-humanist move in French philosophy was 'post-Sartrean'
as well as 'post-structuralist', so also the discourse-theorists in French
feminism marked a rupture, precisely, from Simone de Beauvoir.)

In 'Ends of Man', Derrida is describing a trend in contemporary French
philosophy rather than specifically his own thoughts, though he does hint
how his own approach is distinct from the others. 'Man' in this piece is
neither distinguished from woman nor specifically inclusive of her. 'Man'
is simply the hero of philosophy: 'There is (in existentialism) no
interruption in a metaphysical familiarity which so naturally relates the *we*
of the philosopher to 'we-men', the total horizon of humanity. Although
the theme of history is eminently present...the history of the concept of
man is never questioned. Everything takes place as though the sign 'man'
had no origin, no historical, cultural, linguistic limit' (p. 35).

Any extended consideration of Derrida's description would locate the
landmark texts. Here suffice it to point at Jean-François Lyotard's *Economie
libidinale*, since it establishes an affinity with the French feminist use of
Marx.[20]

For Lyotard, the Freudian pluralization of 'the grounds of man' is still no more than 'political economy', plotted as it is in terms of investments (German *Besetzung*, English 'cathexis', French *investissement* – providing a convenient analogy) of the libido. In terms of a 'libidinal' economy as such, when the 'libidinal Marx' is taken within this 'libidinal cartography' (p. 117) what emerges is a powerful 'literary-critical' exegesis under the governing allegory of the libido, cross-hatched with analogies between 'a philosophy of alienation and a psychoanalysis of the signifier' (p. 158), or 'capitalist society' and 'prostitution' (p. 169) which has, admittedly, very little to do with the micrological and shifting specificities of the class-struggle and its complicity with the economic text of the world-market.[21]

I have already spoken of the 'New Philosophical' reaction to the possibility of a Left Coalition in 1978. Within this capsule summary such a reaction can be called anti-humanist (against the privileged subject), anti-scientific (against psychoanalysis and Marxism as specific or 'regional' practices) and anti-revolutionary (against collectivities).

It is within this context of the deconstruction of the general sign of 'man' as it exists within the 'metaphysical' tradition (a deconstruction that can 'produce' – Derrida commenting on Blanchot – 'a"female element", which does not signify female person')[22] that the following statements by Kristeva about the specific sign 'woman' should be read:

> On a deeper level (than advertisements or slogans for our demands), however, a woman cannot 'be', it is something which does not even belong in the order of *being*. It follows that a feminist practice can only be negative, at odds with what already exists…. In 'woman' I see something that cannot be represented, something above and beyond nomenclatures and ideologies…. Certain feminist demands revive a kind of naive romanticism, a belief in identity (the reverse of phallocentrism), if we compare them to the experience of both poles of sexual difference as is found in the economy of Joycean or Artaudian prose…. I pay close attention to the particular aspect of the work of the avant-garde which dissolves identity, even sexual identities; and in my theoretical formulations I try to go against metaphysical theories that censure what I just labeled a 'woman' – that is what, I think, makes my research that of a woman.
>
> (pp. 137–8)

I have already expressed my dissatisfaction with the presupposition of the *necessarily* revolutionary potential of the avant-garde, literary or philosophical. There is something even faintly comical about Joyce rising above sexual identities and bequeathing the proper mind-set to the women's movement. The point might be to remark how, even if one knows how to undo identities, one does not necessarily escape the historical determinations of sexism.[23] Yet it must also be acknowledged that there is in Kristeva's text an implicit double program for women which we encounter in the best of French feminism: *against* sexism, where women unite as a biologically oppressed caste; and *for* feminism, where human beings train to prepare for a transformation of consciousness.

Within this group of male anti-humanist avant-garde philosophers, Derrida has most overtly investigated the possibilities of 'the name of woman' as a corollary to the project of charging 'the ends of man'. In *Of Grammatology* he relates the privileging of the sovereign subject not only with phonocentrism (primacy of voice-consciousness) and logocentrism (primacy of the word as law), but also with phallocentrism (primacy of the phallus as arbiter of (legal) identity).[24] In texts such as 'La double séance'[25] (the figure of the hymen as both inside and outside), *Glas* (the project of philosophy as desire for the mother), *Eperons* (woman as affirmative deconstruction), 'The Law of Genre' (the female element as double affirmation) and 'Living On: Border Lines' (double invagination as textual effect) a certain textuality of woman is established.

Hélène Cixous is most directly aware of this line of thought in Derrida. She mentions Derrida's work with approval in her influential 'Laugh of the Medusa' (p. 258) and 'Sorties' (p. 91). Especially in the latter, she uses the Derridean methodology of reversing and displacing hierarchized binary oppositions. The text begins with a series of these oppositions and Cixous says of women: 'she does not enter into the oppositions, she is not coupled with the father (who is coupled with the son)'. Later, Cixous deploys the Derridean notion of *restance* (remains) or minimal idealization, giving to woman a dispersed and differential identity: 'She does not exist, she may be nonexistent; but there must be something of her' (p. 92).[26] She relates man to his particular 'torment, his desire to be (at) the origin' (p. 92). She uses the theme of socio-political and ideological 'textuality' with a sureness of touch that places her within the Derridean-Foucauldian problematic: 'men and women are caught in a network of millennial cultural determinations of a complexity that is practically unanalyzable: we can no more talk about "woman" than about "man" without being caught within an ideological theater where the multiplication of representations, images, reflections, myths, identifications constantly transforms, deforms, alters each person's imaginary order and in advance, renders all conceptualization null and void' (p. 96).[27] 'We can no more talk about "woman" than about "man".' This sentiment is matched by the passage from Kristeva I quote above – to make my point that the decision *not* to search for a woman's identity but to speculate about a woman's discourse by way of the negative is related to the deconstruction – of man's insistence upon his own identity as betrayed by existing models of discourse – launched upon mainstream French anti-humanism.

Cixous relates the idea of this over-determined ideological theatre to the impossible heterogeneity of 'each person's imaginary order'. She is referring here to the Lacanian notion of the 'irremediably deceptive' Imaginary, a 'basically narcissistic relation of the subject to his [sic] ego'; a relationship to other subjects as my 'counterparts'; a relationship to the world by way of ideological reflexes; a relationship to meaning in terms of resemblance and unity.[28] To change the stock of Imaginary counterparts which provides the material for sublation into the symbolic dimension is an important part of the project for a woman's discourse: 'Assuming the *real* subjective position that corresponds to this discourse is another matter. One would cut through all the heavy layers of ideology that have borne down since the beginnings of the family and private property: that can be done only in the imagination. And that is precisely what feminist action is all about: to change the imaginary in order to be able to act on the real, to change the very forms of language which by its structure and history has been subject to a law that is patrilinear, therefore masculine' (Catherine Clément, pp. 130–1).[29] In the following remark by Antoinette Fouque, the space between the 'ideological' and the 'symbolic' is marked by the Imaginary order: 'Women cannot allow themselves to deal with political problems while at the same time blotting out the unconscious. If they do, they become, at best, feminists capable of attacking patriarchy on the ideological level but not on a symbolic level' (p. 117).

Now Cixous, as the most Derridean of the French 'anti-feminist' feminists, knows that the re-inscription of the Imaginary cannot be a project launched by a sovereign subject; just as she knows that 'it is impossible to *define* a feminine practice of writing, and this is an impossibility that will remain' (p. 253). Therefore, in Cixous the Imaginary remains subjected to persistent alteration and the concept's grasp upon it remains always deferred. This is a classic argument within the French anti-humanist deconstruction of the sovereignty of the subject. It takes off from Freud's suggestion that the I (ego) constitutes itself in obligatory pursuit of the it (id): 'I am' must be read as an anaseme of 'where it was there shall I become' (*wo es war soll ich werden*). Most obviously, of course, it relates to Lacan's admonition that the Symbolic order's grasp upon the stuff of the Imaginary is random and pointillist: like buttons in upholstery (*points de capiton*). Yet, as Cixous begins the peroration of 'The Laugh of Medusa' she does take on Lacan. She questions the practice of deciphering every code as referring to the Name-of-the-Father or its alias, the mother-who-has-the-phallus: 'And what about the libido? Haven't I read [Lacan's] the "Signification of the Phallus"....[30] If the New Women, arriving now, dare to create outside the theoretical, they're called in by the cops of the Signifier, fingerprinted, remonstrated, and brought into the line of order that they are supposed to know; assigned by force of trickery to a precise place in the chain that's always formed for the benefit of a privileged "signifier". We are re-membered to the string that leads back, if not to the Name-of-the Father, then, for a new twist, to the place of the phallic mother' (pp. 262–3).[31] As she exposes the phallus to be the 'privileged signifier', she takes her place with Derrida's critique of the Lacanian phallus as the 'transcendental signifier' in 'The Purveyor of Truth', and with his articulation of the phallic mother as the limit of man's enterprise in *Glas*.[32] I believe she is not speaking only of orthodox or neo-Freudian psychoanalysis when she writes: 'Don't remain within the psychoanalytic enclosure' (p. 263). Indeed, the choice of the Medusa as her logo is a derisive takeoff on the notion that woman as object of knowledge or desire does not relate to the *subject*-object but to the *eye*-object dialectic. When she writes: 'You only have to look at the Medusa straight on to see her' (p. 255), I believe she is rewriting the arrogance of 'you only have to go and look at the Bernini statue in Rome to understand immediately she (St Teresa) is coming'.[33] For the passage is followed by an invocation of the male member in splendid isolation: 'It's the jitters that give them a hard-on! for themselves! They need to be afraid of us. Look at the trembling Perseuses moving backward toward us, clad in apotropes'.

The distance between a Cixous, sympathetic to the deconstructive morphology in particular and therefore critical of Lacan's phallocentrism and a Kristeva, sympathetic to French anti-humanism in general, may be measured, only half fancifully, by a juxtaposition like the following. Kristeva: 'In "woman" I see something that cannot be represented'; Cixous: 'Men say there are two unrepresentable things: death and the feminine sex' (p. 255).

(In fact, Kristeva's association with Derridean thought dates back to the sixties. Derrida was a regular contributor to the early *Tel Quel*. Her project, however, has been, not to *deconstruct* the origin, but rather to *recuperate*, archeologically and formulaically, what she locates as the potential originary space *before* the sign. Over the years, this space has acquired names and inhabitants related to specific ideological sets: geno-text, Mallarmean avant-garde, ancient Asiatic linguistics, the Platonic *chora*; and now the European High Art of Renaissance and Baroque, Christian theology through the ages, and personal experience, as they cope with the mystery of pregnancy-infancy).[34]

Like Kristeva, Cixous also seems not to ask what it means to say some 'men', especially of the avant-garde, can be 'women' in this special sense. In this respect, and in much of her argument for 'bisexuality', she is sometimes reminiscent of the Freud who silenced female psychoanalysts by calling them as good as men.[35] The question of the political or historical and indeed ideological differential that irreducibly separates the male from the female critic of phallocentrism is not asked.[36] And, occasionally the point of Derrida's insistence that deconstruction is not a negative metaphysics and that one cannot practise free play is lost sight of: 'To admit', Cixous writes, 'that to write is precisely to work (in) the between, questioning the process of the same *and* of the other without which nothing lives, undoing the work of death – is first to want the two (*le deux*) and both, the ensemble of the one and the other not congealed in sequences of struggle and expulsion or some other form of death, but dynamized to infinity by an incessant process of exchange from one into the other different subject' (p. 254). Much of Derrida's critique of humanism-phallocentrism is concerned with a reminder of the limits of deconstructive power *as well as* with the impossibility of remaining in the in-between. Unless one is aware that one cannot avoid taking a stand, unwitting stands get taken. Further, 'writing' in Derrida is not simply identical with the production of prose and verse. It is the name of 'structure' which operates and fractures knowing (epistemology), being (ontology), doing (practice), history, politics, economics, institutions as such. It is a 'structure' whose 'origin' and 'end' are necessarily provisional and absent. 'The essential predicates in a minimal determination of the classical concept of writing' are presented and contrasted to Derrida's use of 'writing' in 'Signature Event Context'.[37] Because Cixous seems often to identify the Derridean mode of writing about writing with merely the production of prose and verse, a statement like…'women are body. More body, hence more writing' (p. 258) remains confusing.

In a course on International Feminism, the question of Cixous's faithfulness to, or unquestioning acceptance of, Derrida, becomes quickly irrelevant. It suffices here to point out that the sort of anti-feminism that has its ties to anti-humanism understood as a critique of the name of man or of phallocentrism is to be distinguished from the other kinds of French anti-feminism, some of which the editors of *New French Feminism* mention on p. 32. Of the many varieties, I would mention the party-line anti-feminism with which Communist Parties associate themselves: 'The "new feminism" is currently developing the thesis that no society, socialist or capitalist, is capable of favorably responding to the aspirations of women…. If we direct against men the action necessary for women's progress, we condemn the great hopes of women to a dead end' (p. 128). Here the lesson of a double approach – against sexism and for feminism – is suppressed. I feel some sympathy with Christine Delphy's remark, even as she calls for 'a materialist analysis of the oppression of women', that 'the existence of this Marxist line had the practical consequence of being a brake on the [women's] movement, and this fact is obviously not accidental'.[38]

Another variety of anti-'feminism' that should be yet further distinguished: 'The social mode of being of men and women and of women is *in no way* linked with their nature as males and females nor with the shape of their sex organs' (p. 215; italics mine). These are the 'radical feminists' who are interested in shaping a feminist materialism and who are not programmatically or methodologically influenced by the critique of humanism. Unlike them, I certainly would not reject the search for a woman's discourse out of hand. But I have, just as certainly, attended to the critique of such a search as expressed by the 'radical feminists': 'The so-called explored language extolled by some women writers seems to be linked, if not in its content at least by its style, to a trend propagated by literary schools governed by its male masters…. To advocate a direct language of the body is…not subversive because it is equivalent to denying the reality and the strength of social mediations…that oppress us in our bodies' (p. 219). It would be a mistake (at least for those of us not directly embroiled in the French field) to ignore these astute warnings, although we should, of course, point out that the radical feminists' credo – 'I will be neither a woman nor a man in the present historical meaning: I shall be some Person in the body of a woman' (p. 226) – can, if the wonderful deconstructive potential of *personne* in French (*some*one and, at the same time no *one*) is not attended to, lead to the sort of obsession with one's proper identity as property that is both the self-duping and the oppressive power of humanism. This is particularly so because, neither in France nor in the US, apart from the curious example of Derrida, has mainstream academic anti-humanism had much to do with the practical critique of phallocentrism at all. In the US the issue seems to be the indeterminacy of meaning and linguistic determination, in France the critique of identity and varieties of micrological and genealogical analyses of the structures of power.

We should also be vigilant, it seems to me, against the sort of Gallic attitudinizing that has been a trend in Anglo-American literary criticism since the turn of the century. An American-style, 'French' feminist, eager to insert herself/himself into a Star Chamber, can at worst remind one of the tone of *The Symbolist Movement in Literature* by Arthur Symons.[39] It can emphasize our own tendency to offer grandiose solutions with little political specificity, couched in the strategic form of rhetorical questions.[40]

I can do no better than quote here part of the final exchange between Catherine Clément and Hélène Cixous in *La jeune née*, an exchange that is often forgotten:

> H. The class struggle is this sort of enormous machine whose system is described by Marx and which therefore functions today. But its rhythm is not always the same, it is a rhythm that is sometimes most attenuated.

One can sense the frustration in Clément's response, which could be directed equally well at a Lyotard or all of the 'poetic revolutionaries':

> C. It can *appear* attenuated, especially if one is bludgeoned into thinking so. But there is a considerable lag between the reality of the class

struggle and the way in which it is lived mythically, especially by intellectuals for whom is hard to measure the reality of struggles directly, because they are in a position where work on language and the imaginary has a primordial importance and can put blinkers on them (pp. 292, 294–5).

Cixous answers with a vague charge against the denial of poetry by advanced capitalism.

In the long run, the most useful thing that a training in French feminism can give us is politicized and critical examples of 'symptomatic reading' not always following the reversal-displacement technique of a deconstructive reading. The method that seemed recuperative when used to applaud the avant-garde is productively conflictual when used to expose the ruling discourse.

There are essays on Plato and Descartes in Irigaray's *Speculum de l'autre femme*, where the analysis brillliantly deploys the deconstructive *themes* of indeterminacy, critique of identity, and the absence of a totalizable analytic foothold, from a feminist point of view.[41] There are also the analyses of mainly eighteenth century philosophical texts associated with work in progress at the feminist philosophy study group at the women's *École Normale* at Fontenay-aux-Roses. There is the long running commentary, especially on Greek mythemes – marked by an absence of questioning the history of the sign 'myth' an absence, as I have argued in the case of *About Chinese Women*, which in its turn marks a historico-geographic boundary – to be found in *La jeune née*. The readings of Marx, generally incidental to other topics, suffer, as I have suggested above, from a lack of detailed awareness of the Marxian text. The best readings are of Freud. This is because Freud is at once the most powerful contemporary male philosopher of female sexuality, and the inaugurator, in *The Interpretation of Dreams*, of the technique of 'symptomatic reading'. Irigaray's 'La Tâche aveugle d'un vieux rêve de symétrie' (*Speculum*) has justifiably become a classic. More detailed, more scholarly, more sophisticated in its methodology, and perhaps more perceptive is Sarah Kofman's *L'énigme de la femme: la femme dans les textes de Freud*.[42]

This book exposes, even if it does not theorize upon, the possibility of being a deconstructor of the metaphysics of identity, and yet remaining caught within a masculist ideology; an awareness that I have found lacking in Kristeva and Cixous. Kofman comments on Freud's ideological betrayal of his own sympathy for women's mutism. She reveals the curious itinerary of Freud's progress towards his final thoughts upon female sexuality: three moments of the discovery of woman as the stronger sex – three subsequent long movements to sublate that strength into its unrecognizable contrary: the demonstration that woman is indeed the weaker sex. She deconstructs the 'fact' of penis-envy through an analysis of the self-contradictory versions of the pre-oedipal stage. How is a sex possible that is despised by both sexes? This is the masculist enigma to which Freud, like Oedipus, sought a solution. Like Oedipus's mask of blindness, biology, reduced to penis-envy, is Freud's screen solution.

Using Freud's own method of oneirocritique to show its ideological limits, isolating seemingly marginal moments to demonstrate the ethico-political agenda in Freud's attempts at normalization, *L'énigme de la femme* is a fine example of French feminist critical practice of 'symptomatic' – in this case deconstructive – reading. If we can move beyond the texts so far favoured by the French feminists and relate the morphology of this critique with the 'specificity' of other discourses that spell out and establish the power of the patriarchy, we will indeed have gained an excellent strategy for undermining the masculist vanguard.[43] This is no doubt a benefit for female academics, women who, by comparison with the world's women at large, are already infinitely privileged. And yet, since today the discourse of the world's privileged societies dictates the configuration of the rest, this is not an inconsiderable gift, even in a classroom.

As soon as one steps out of the classroom, if indeed a 'teacher' ever fully can, the dangers rather than the benefits of academic feminism, French or otherwise, become more insistent. Institutional changes against sexism here or in France may mean nothing or, indirectly, further harm for women in the Third World.[44] This discontinuity ought to be recognized and worked at. Otherwise, the focus remains defined by the investigator as subject. To bring us back to my initial concerns, let me insist that here, the difference between 'French' and 'Anglo-American' feminism is superficial. However unfeasible and inefficient it may sound, I see no way to avoid insisting that there has to be a simultaneous other focus: not merely who am I? but who is the other woman? How am I naming her? How does she name me? Is this part of the problematic I discuss? Indeed, it is the absence of such unfeasible but crucial questions that makes the 'colonized woman' as 'subject' see the investigators as sweet and sympathetic creatures from another planet who are free to come and go; or, depending on her own socialization in the colonizing cultures, see 'feminism' as having a vanguardist class fix, the liberties it fights for as luxuries, finally identifiable with 'free sex' of one kind or another. Wrong, of course. My point has been that there is something equally wrong in our most sophisticated research, our most benevolent impulses.

'One of the areas of greatest verbal concentration among French feminists is the description of women's pleasure' (*New French Feminisms*, p. 37). Paradoxically enough, it is in this seemingly esoteric area of concern that I find a way of reaffirming the historically discontinuous yet common 'object'-ification of the sexed subject as woman.

If it is indeed true that the best of French feminism encourages us to think of a double effort (*against* sexism and *for* feminism, with the lines forever shifting), that double vision is needed in the consideration of women's reproductive freedom, as well. For to see women's liberation as identical with reproductive liberation is to make countersexism an end in itself, to see the establishment of women's subject-status as an unquestioned good and indeed not to heed the best lessons of French anti-humanism, which disclosed the historical dangers of a subjectivist normativity; and it is also to legitimate the view of culture as a general exchange of women, constitutive of kinship structures where women's object-status is clearly seen as identified with her reproductive function.[45]

The double vision that would affirm feminism as well as undo sexism suspects a pre-comprehended move *before* the reproductive coupling of man and woman, *before* the closing of the circle whose only productive excess is the child, and whose 'outside' is the man's 'active' life in society. It recognizes that 'nature had programmed female sexual pleasure independently from the needs of production' (Evelyne Sullerot, p. 155).

Male and female sexuality are asymmetrical. Male orgasmic pleasure 'normally' entails the male reproductive act – semination. Female orgasmic pleasure (it is not, of course, the 'same' pleasure, only called by the same name) does not entail any one component of the heterogeneous female reproductive scenario: ovulation, fertilization, conception, gestation, birthing. The clitoris escapes reproductive framing. In legally defining woman as object of exchange, passage, or possession in terms of reproduction, it is not only the womb that is literally 'appropriated'; it is the clitoris as the signifier of the sexed subject that is effaced. All historical and theoretical investigation into the definition of woman as legal *object* – in or out of marriage; or as politico-economic passageway for property and legitimacy would fall within the investigation of the varieties of the effacement of the clitoris.

Psychological investigation in this area cannot only confine itself to the effect of clitoridectomy on women. It would also ask why and show how, since an at least symbolic clitoridectomy has always been the 'normal' accession to womanhood and the unacknowledged name of motherhood, it might be necessary to plot out the entire geography of female sexuality in terms of the imagined possibility of the dismemberment of the phallus. The arena of research here is not merely remote and primitive societies; the (sex) objectification of women by the elaborate attention to their skin and façade as represented by the immense complexity of the cosmetics, underwear, clothes, advertisement, women's magazine and pornography networks, the double standard in the criteria of men's and women's ageing; the public versus private dimensions of menopause as opposed to impotence, are all questions within this circuit. The pre-comprehended suppression or effacement of the clitoris relates to every move to define woman as sex object, or as means or agent of reproduction – with no

103

recourse to a subject-function except in terms of those definitions or as 'imitators' of men.

The woman's voice as Mother or Lover or Androgyne has sometimes been caught by great male writers.The theme of woman's *norm* as clitorally ex-centric from the reproductive orbit is being developed at present in our esoteric French group and in the literature of the gay movement. There is a certain melancholy exhilaration in working out the patriarchal intricacy of Tiresias's standing as a prophet – master of ceremonies at the Oedipal scene – in terms of the theme of the feminine norm as the suppression of the clitoris: 'Being asked by Zeus and Hera to settle a dispute as to which sex had more pleasure of love, he decided for the female; Hera was very angry and blinded him, but Zeus recompensed him by giving him long life and power of prophecy' (*Oxford Classical Dictionary*).[46]

Although French feminism has not elaborated these possibilities, there is some sense of them in women as unlike as Irigaray and the *Questions féministes* group. Irigaray: 'In order for woman to arrive at the point where she can enjoy her pleasure as a woman, a long detour by the analysis of the various systems of oppression which affect her is certainly necessary. By claiming to resort to pleasure alone as the solution to her problem, she runs the risk of missing the reconsideration of a social practice upon which her pleasure depends' (p. 105). *Questions féministes*: 'What we must answer is – not the false problem…which consists in measuring the "role" of biological factors and the "role" of social factors in the behavior of sexed individuals – but rather the following [questions]: in what way is the biological political? In other words, what is the political function of the biological?' (p. 227).

If an analysis of the suppression of the clitoris in general as the suppression of woman-in-excess is lifted from the limitations of the 'French' context and pursued in all its 'historical', 'political' and 'social' dimensions, then *Questions féministes* would not need to make a binary opposition such as the following: 'It is legitimate to expose the oppression, the mutilation, the 'functionalization' and the 'objectivation' of the female body, but it is also dangerous to put the female body at the center of a search for female identity' (p. 218). It would be possible to suggest that the typology of the subtraction or excision of the clitoris in order to determine a biologico-political female identity is opposed, in discontinuous and indefinitely context-determined ways, by both the points of view above. It would also not be necessary, in order to share a detailed and ecstatic analysis of motherhood as 'ultimate guarantee of sociality', to attack feminist collective commitments virulently: 'A true feminine innovation…is not possible before maternity is clarified…. To bring that about, however, we must stop making feminism a new religion, an enterprise or a sect.'[47]

The double vision is not merely to work against sexism and for feminism. It is also to recognize that, even as we reclaim the excess of the clitoris, we cannot fully escape the symmetry of the reproductive definition. One cannot write-off what may be called a uterine social organization (the arrangement of the world in terms of the reproduction of future generations, where the uterus is the chief agent and means of production) *in favor of* a clitoral. The uterine social organization should, rather, be 'situated' through the understanding that it has so far been established by excluding a clitoral social organization. (The restoration of a continuous bond between mother and daughter even *after* the 'facts' of gestation, birthing, and suckling is, indeed, of great importance as a persistent effort against the sexism of millennia, an effort of repairing psychological damage through questioning norms that are supposedly self-evident and descriptive. Yet, for the sake of an affirmative feminism, this too should be 'situated': to establish *historical* continuity by sublating a *natural* or *physiological* link as an end in itself is the idealistic subtext of the patriarchal project.) Investigation of the effacement of the clitoris – where clitoridectomy is a metonym for women's definition as 'legal object as subject of reproduction' – would persistently seek to de-normalize uterine social organization. At the moment, the fact that the entire complex network of advanced capitalist economy hinges on home-buying, and that the philosophy of home-ownership is intimately linked to the sanctity of the nuclear family, shows how encompassingly the uterine norm of womanhood supports the phallic norm of capitalism. At the other end of the spectrum, it is this ideologico-material repression of the clitoris as the signifier of the sexed subject that operates the specific oppression of women, as the lowest level of the cheap labor that the multi-national corporations employ by remote control in the extraction of absolute surplus-value in the less developed countries. Whether the 'social relations of patriarchy can be mapped into the social relations characteristic of a mode of production' or whether it is a 'relatively autonomous structure written into family relations'; whether the family is a place of the production of socialization or the constitution of the subject of ideology; what such a heterogeneous sex-analysis would disclose is that the repression of the clitoris in the general or the narrow sense (the difference cannot be absolute) is presupposed by both patriarchy and family.[48]

I emphasize discontinuity, heterogeneity and typology as I speak of such a sex-analysis, because this work cannot by itself obliterate the problems of race and class. It will not necessarily escape the inbuilt colonialism of First-World feminism toward the Third. It might, one hopes, promote a sense of our common yet history-specific lot. It ties together the terrified child held down by her grandmother as the blood runs down her groin and the 'liberated' heterosexual woman who, in spite of Mary Jane Sherfey and the famous p. 53 of *Our Bodies Ourselves*, in bed with a casual lover – engaged, in other words, in the 'freest' of 'free' activities – confronts, at worst, the 'shame' of admitting to the 'abnormality' of her orgasm: at best, the acceptance of such a 'special' need; and the radical feminist who, setting herself apart from the circle of reproduction systematically discloses the beauty of the lesbian body; the dowried bride – a body for burning – and the female wage-slave – a body for maximum exploitation.[49] There can be other lists; and each one will straddle and undo the ideological-material opposition. For me it is the best gift of French feminism, that it cannot itself fully acknowledge, and that we must work at; here is a theme that can liberate my colleague from Sudan, and a theme the old washerwomen by the river would understand

Notes

1. BERT F. HOSELITZ, 'Development and the Theory of Social Systems', in M. Stanley, (ed.), *Social Development* (New York: Basic Books, 1972), pp. 45 and *passim*. I am grateful to Professor Michael Ryan for drawing my attention to this article.

2. NAWAL EL SAADAWI, *The Hidden Face of Eve*: *Women in the Arab World* (London: Zed Press, 1980), p. 5.

3. JULIA KRISTEVA, *About Chinese Women*, trans. Anita Barrows (London: Marion Boyars, 1977).

4. As is indicated by Philippe Sollers, 'On n'a encore rien vu', *Tel Quel*, 85, Autumn 1980, this interest has now been superseded.

5. For an astute summary and analysis of this problem in terms of electoral Communism and Social Democracy, see Adam Przeworski, 'Social Democracy as a Historical Phenomenon', *New Left Review*, 122, July – August 1980.

6. For Kristeva's argument that the literary intellectual is the fulcrum of dissent see 'Un nouveau type d'intellectuel: le dissident', *Tel Quel*, 74, Winter 1977.

7. Joseph Needham's attitudes toward the curious fact of feminine symbolism in Taoism, as expressed in *The Grand Titration*: *Science and Society in East and West* (Toronto: University of Toronto Press, 1969), are altogether tentative.

8. Stanford University Press, 1970. See *Chinese Women*, p. 98n, p. 145 note.

9. For a somewhat dated and dogmatic view of this movement, see Michael Ryan and Spivak, 'Anarchism Revisited: A New Philosophy?' *Diacritics*, 8, no. 2, Summer 1978.

10. *The Standard Edition of the Psychological Works of Sigmund Freud* (London: Hogarth Press, 1964) vol. 23; Gilles Deleuze and Félix Guattari, *Anti-Oedipus: Capitalism and Schizophrenia*, vol. 1, trans. Robert Hurley et al. (New York: Viking Press, 1972).

11. Amherst: University of Massachusetts Press, 1980. In this part of my essay, I have quoted liberally from *New French Feminisms*, giving the name of the author of the particular piece and the page number.

12. I hope to present a discussion of such an appropriation in a forthcoming book on deconstruction, feminism, and Marxism.

13. IRIGARAY, *This Sex Which Is Not One*, trans. Catherine Porter (Ithaca: Cornell University Press, 1985); Cixous, *Préparatifs de noces au delà de l'abîme* (Paris: des femmes, 1978); Wittig, *Lesbian Body*, trans, David Le Vay (New York: William Morrow, 1975).

14. London: New Left Books, 1973.

15. Cf. ERNST BLOCH, ET AL, *Aesthetics and Politics*, trans. Ronald Taylor (London: New Left Books, 1977).

16. *Reason and Revolution: Hegel and the Rise of Social Theory* (Boston: Beacon Press, 1960), p.x.

17. Trans. EDOUARD MOROT-SIR, ET AL., *Philosophy and Phenomenological Research*, 30, no. 1, September 1969.

18. In *For Marx*, trans. Ben Brewster (New York: Vintage, 1970).

19. Trans. COLIN GORDON, *Feminist Studies*, 6, no. 2, Summer 1980.

20. (Paris: Minuit), 1974, p. 10.

21. For a discussion of the lack of specificity in the privileged metaphorics of political economy, especially in some texts of Derrida, see Spivak, 'Il faut s'y prendre en s'en prenant à elles', in *Les fins de l'homme* (Paris: Galilée, 1981).

22. 'The Law of Genre', *Glyph* 7, 1980, p. 225.

23. Percy Shelley's treatment of Harriet and Mary is a case in point; a 'life' is not necessarily 'outside the text'. I have discussed the question in greater detail in 'Finding Feminist Readings: Dante-Yeats' (see pp. 15–29 above) and 'Displacement and the Discourse of Woman' in Mark Krupnick, ed. *Displacement: Derrida and After* (Bloomington: Indiana University Press, 1983), pp. 169–95.

24. DERRIDA, *Of Grammatology*, trans. Spivak (Baltimore: Johns Hopkins University Press, 1976).

25. 'La double séance', *La dissémination* (Paris: Seuil, 1972); *Glas* (Paris: Galilée, 1976); 'The Law of Genre' (op. cit); 'Living On: Border Lines', in Harold Bloom, et al., *Deconstruction & Criticism* (New York: Seabury Press, 1979).

26. For a discussion of the importance of *restance* or minimal idealization in Derrida, see Spivak, 'Revolutions that as Yet Have No Model: Derrida's *Limited Inc.*'

27. Cf. CLÉMENT, 'La Coupable', in *La jeune née* (Paris: Union Générale d'Editions, 1975), p. 15. This network-web-*tissu*-text is the untotalizable yet always grasped 'subject' of 'textuality'. In Barthes it is the 'writable', where we are written into this fuller text. Derrida speaks of it most compellingly in 'Ja, ou le faux-bond', *Digraphes*, 11 March 1977. It is in these terms that Foucault's notion of the microphysics of power should be understood. It is a mistake to think of such a thematic of textuality as a mere reduction of history to language.

28. J. LAPLANCHE AND J. B. PONTALIS, *The Language of Psycho-Analysis*, trans. Donald Nicholson-Smith (New York: Norton, 1973), p. 210. The gap between this distilled definition and its use in the feminist context reminds us yet once again that the use of a dictionary has its own attendant dangers.

29. Clément's use of 'imaginary' and 'symbolic' here inclines towards the colloquial, perhaps because of situational reasons. Clément is addressing irate feminists who are disaffected from what they see as Marxist-feminist theoreticism.

30. LACAN, *Ecrits*, trans. Alan Sheridan (New York: Norton, 1977).

31. Cixous is referring to the two axes of the male subject: the Oedipal norm (discovering the Name-of-the-Father) and the fetishist deviation (fetishizing the Mother as possessing a fantasmatic phallus).

32. 'The Purveyor of Truth', trans. Willis Domingo, et al., *Yale French Studies*, 52, 1975.

33. LACAN, 'God and the Jouissance of the Woman', in *Feminine Sexuality: Jacques Lacan and the école freudienne*, trans, Juliet Mitchell and Jacqueline Rose (London: Routledge & Kegan Paul, 1982). Also cited in Stephen Heath's excellent essay 'Difference', *Screen* 19, no. 8, Autumn, 1978.

34. 'L'engendrement de la formule', *Tel Quel* 37, 38, Spring and Summer, 1969; *Révolution du langage poétique* (Paris: Seuil, 1974); 'Motherhood According to Bellini', *Desire in Language: A Semiotic Approach to Literature and Art*, trans, Thomas Gora, et al. (New York: Columbia University Press, 1980); 'Héréthique de l'amour', *Tel Quel* 74, Winter, 1977; and *passim*.

35. Cf. *La jeune née*, p. 160. 'Femininity', *Standard Edition*, 22, pp. 116–17.

36. I attempt to discuss this question in detail in 'Displacement and the Discourse of Woman' (see n. 23).

37. Trans. SAMUEL WEBER AND JEFFREY MEHLMAN, *Glyph*, I, 1977, p. 181.

38. 'The Main Enemy', *Feminist Issues* I, no. 1(1980), pp. 24–5.

39. London: Heinemann, 1899.

40. As revealed in *Chinese Women*, pp. 200 -1, or the juxtaposition of Cixous, *To Live the Orange* (Paris: Des femmes, 1979), pp. 32–4 and p. 94.

41. *Speculum* (Paris: Minuit, 1974).

42. Paris: Galilée, 1980. A portion of this book has been published as 'The Narcissistic Woman: Freud and Girard' in *Diacritics*, 10 no. 3, Fall 1980.

43. I have attempted to develop the implications of such a strategy in "Displacement and the Discourse of Woman" (see n. 23, 36). As the reader may have surmised, that piece is in many ways a companion to this one.

44. To take the simplest possible American examples, even such innocent triumphs as the hiring of more tenured women or adding feminist sessions at a Convention might mislead, since most US universities have dubious investments, and most Conventions hotels use Third-World female labor in a most oppressive way to the increasing proletarianization of the women of the less developed countries.

45. CLAUDE LÉVI-STRAUSS, 'Structural Study of Myth', in *Myth: A Symposium*, ed. Thomas A. Sebeok (Bloomington: Indiana University Press, 1958), p. 103. The classic defense to be found in *Structuralist Anthropology*, trans. Claire Jacobson and Brooke Grundfest Schoepf (New York: Basic Books, 1963), vol. 1, pp. 61–62, against the feminist realization that this was yet another elaboration of the objectification of women, seems curiously disingenuous. For if women had indeed been symbolized, on that level of generality, as *users* of signs rather than

as signs, the binary opposition of exchanger and exchanged, founding structures of kinship, would collapse.

46. For further ironies of the prohibitions associated with Hera's pleasure, see C. Kerényi, *Zeus and Hera: Archetypal Image of Father, Husband and Wife*, trans. Christopher Holme (Princeton: Princeton University Press, 1975), pp. 97, 113.

47. 'Un nouveau type d'intellectuel: le dissident', p. 71.

48. *Feminism and Materialism: Women and Modes of Production*, ed. Annette Kuhn and AnnMarie Wolpe (London: Routledge & Kegan Paul, 1978), pp. 49, 51. For an eloquent reverie on the ethic of penetration as it denies the clitoris see Irigaray, *New French Feminisms*, p. 100. In 'Displacement', I suggest that such a gesture of penetrative appropriation is not absent from Derrida's reach for the 'name of woman'.

49. SHERFEY, *The Nature and Evolution of Female Sexuality* (New York: Vintage, 1973); *Our Bodies, Ourselves: A Book by and for Women* (New York: Simon and Schuster, 2nd ed., 1971).

4   Hélène Cixous and Catherine Clément

HÉLÈNE CIXOUS AND CATHERINE CLÉMENT *The Newly Born Woman**

This dialogue is the final section of a text jointly written by Hélène Cixous and Catherine Clément. The first section of the book, 'The Guilty One' by Clément, explores the cultural meanings of the sorceress and the hysteric, using a variety of texts and figures from medieval witches to Freud's patients. In the second section, 'Sorties', Hélène Cixous seeks to uncover the *feminine* and to provide women with escape routes from a negative and marginal historical position. The creative and revolutionary possibilities in linking the female body and *feminine writing* is central to Cixous' philosophy. The final 'Exchange' illustrates the shared interests and the different interpretations of Cixous and Clément. They discuss the consequences for femininity of using a master-discourse; the connections between knowledge, power and mastery; the case of Dora and the importance of the hysteric; the political effectiveness of the marginal; the place of language and desire; the relation of sexual politics to the class struggle. The dialogue is enhanced by a series of appropriate quotations which interrelate with the comments of Cixous and Clément (see Introduction, pp. 14–15).

A Woman Mistress

If the position of mastery culturally
comes back to men, what will become of
(our) femininity when we find ourselves
in this position?
    When we use a master-discourse?

---

* HÉLÈNE CIXOUS and CATHERINE CLÉMENT, *The Newly Born Woman* (Manchester: University of Manchester Press, 1985), pp. 136–60; trans. Betsy Wing. Every attempt has been made to replicate the layout of the French original, but the match is not exact.

Mastery-knowledge, mastery-power:
ideas demanding an explanation from us.
Other discourses?

C: Let's start out with the difference between our discourses. Yours is a writing halfway between theory and fiction. Whereas my discourse is, or tries to be, more demonstrative and discursive, following the most traditional method of rhetorical demonstration. That doesn't bother me; I accept that method: it is the method of teaching and of transmitting ideas. We see there can be two women in the same space who are *differently* engaged, speaking of almost exactly the *same things*, investing in two or three different kinds of discourse and going from one to the other and then on to the spoken exchange.

H: I distrust the identification of a subject with a single discourse. First, there is the discourse that suits the occasion. I use rhetorical discourse, the discourse of mastery, orally, for example, with my students, and obviously I do it on purpose; it is a refusal on my part to leave organized discourse entirely in men's power. I never fell for that sort of bait.

C: There is no reason at all not to steal that discourse from men... Besides, that doesn't mean anything; we don't steal anything at all – we are within the same cultural system. Granted it is a phallocentric cultural system but trying to make another in advance is unfounded; perhaps we can think that, hypothetically, one day there might be another system but to will that it suddenly be there – at any minute – is utopian.

H: There will not be *one* feminine discourse, there will be thousands of different kinds of feminine words, and then there will be the code for general communication, philosophical discourse, rhetoric like now but with a great number of subversive discourses in addition that are somewhere else entirely. That is what is going to happen. Until now women were not speaking out loud, were not writing, not creating their tongues – plural, but they will create them, which doesn't mean that the others (either men or tongues) are going to die off.

C: In any case, there is no reason for women not to assume the transmission of knowledge. The term causing a problem is the word *mastery* in the phrase 'discourse of mastery'. If inspired by Lacan, it refers to a relationship between mastery and university, which is such that the master's discourse – from the point of view of its political and economic power – is transferred onto and shapes any discourse dealing with knowledge to be transmitted.

H: I think one has a hard time escaping the discourse of mastery when using for example, as a teacher, discourse I'll call 'objective', by that I mean a discourse that does not involve an easily located subject of

111

enunciation, that speaks at that particular moment not just in the name of but as universal knowledge itself.

The law does not exist

H: In the little chapter 'The Dawn of Phallocentrism', I took, on the one hand, a text by Freud on the origin of patriarchy, and I compared it with a Kafka text called *Before the Law*. It is a story that is both extraordinarily clear and as unclear as the question that is its crux: 'What is the law?' There is a peasant who was an honest man: he was the only one who could have gone to the other side and seen the law – seen, therefore, that it doesn't exist. Because the door could be opened only for him. He didn't go in there. How could he have gone 'there' since the law that doesn't exist was himself? All that was needed was a door and a doorkeeper: he was the one who constantly fabricated the law, and he never saw that the law did not exist.

C: Do you know what that story makes me think of? The mirror stage – the fact that the chimpanzee looks behind the mirror to see who is there, another chimpanzee itself, or nobody – whereas man identifies and constitutes himself with the mirror. It reflects his image to him, *fixes* it as a subject and subjects it to the law, to the symbolic order, to language, and does it in a way that is both inalienable and alienating. The law exists.

H: Except that the chimpanzee actually is the chimpanzee and we are the result of our relationship to the door. What is the discourse of mastery? There is one. It is what calls itself 'the law' but is presented as 'the open door' in precisely such a way that you never go to the other side of the door, that you never go to see 'what is mastery?' So you never will know that there is no law and no mastery. That there is no master. The paradox of mastery is that it is made up of a sort of complex ideological secretion produced by an infinite quantity of doorkeepers.

Mastery ensures the transmission of knowledge

C: I wouldn't say that in the same terms. It has to be said straight out: for me mastery is fundamental and necessary. I don't particularly think one can transmit certain knowledges – *the* knowledges – except through mastery. That involves everything having to do with democratic transmission. Paradoxically, information contained in a system of knowledge cannot be transmitted outside of mastery. It is dependent on the 'law' of the Symbolic, like the doorkeeper , like the honest man. Subjectivity can be taken in, deluded, by it, of course, but it can also find there an explicit coherence, a certain number of connections shared by all, so that when the statement is transmitted, the receiver has access to it either immediately or through mediation.

Transmitting

C: What is at stake is connection and consistency. I know perfectly well you are not about to tell me that truth sticks to what is consistent and that you are going to call into questions the existence of other consistencies. As for me, the discourse of mastery exists; of course, it is ambivalent and full of traps as far as subjectivity is concerned: subjectivity finds the positions of psychoanalyst and professor to be almost equally untenable. But despite that, it is through the discourse of mastery that knowledge of the analytic act is *transmitted*. I am not talking about the rest of it.

H: I can't go along with you there. Your position, which I understand, disposes of a problem that is fundamental and primary for me: how is one to think and struggle against what mastery inevitably entails as a form of repression? A mastery's contradiction, if it isn't thought differently, is that, far from transmitting knowledge, it makes it still more inaccessible, makes it sacred. That is Law's dirty trick. Only those people who already have a relationship of mastery, who already have dealings with culture, who are saturated with culture, have ever dared have access to the discourse that the master gives.

C: Now, in this social and cultural system. But certainly you can conceive of societies structured differently, in which the conditions of access to knowledge would be profoundly different.

H: That's why I believe one has to take a thousand precautions. At the present time, it is impossible for me to use the term 'mastery' as it is currently used because of the repression it implies. Does someone

---

Culture, which is superstructure, must not be considered as a thing, a good, the result of an evolution, a stock converted into intellectual luxury, but rather as a factor in evolution (which cannot be solely a factor of income) and especially as a process' (Brecht, *Writings on Politics and Society*).

One can say that general culture is what permits the individual to fully feel his solidarity with other men, in space and in time, with the men of his generation as well as with the generations which have preceded him and those yet to follow. To be cultivated, then, is to have received and constantly developed an initiation to different forms of human activity independently of those which correspond to a profession, so as to be able to enter into contact and communion with other men (PAUL LANGEVIN).

already allied with a certain knowledge want to communicate it to others? Why does one want to communicate it to others? It's the usual question – 'what's the use?' Does it serve any purpose? I would say yes, obviously, it has to serve – not serve itself and not serve a superior cause, et cetera. There is a drawback we all know as teachers, which is the almost insurmountable difficulty of occupying a position of mastery.

Giving

H: The one who is in the master's place, even if not the master of a knowledge, is in a position of power. The only way to bar that is to execute the master, kill him, eliminate him, so that what he has to say can get through, so that he himself is not the obstacle, so it will be *given*. Something on the order of a personal gift, a subjective one.

C: I don't like that term – personal gift, it tends toward oblation and sacrifice…

What one knows…
What one doesn't know.

H: Giving isn't sacrificing. The person who transmits has to be able to function on the level of knowledge without knowing. I'm not at all referring to Socrates now. Just that one should be in a state of weakness, as we all are, and that *it be evident*. That one have the guts to occupy the position one has no right to occupy and that one show precisely how and why one occupies it. I set my sights high: I demand that love struggle within the master against the will for power.

Mistress *woman or woman master*?

C: Just the same it will be mastery. When I hear *mastery*, I think of the present meaning of the word, which must come more or less from Hegel. Mastery, in Lacan, is inseparable from something fundamentally bound up with woman, with the hysteric, her referential figure. The hysteric puts the master and the academic, both power and knowledge, in check. What's more, this conjunction 'power-knowledge' and this division between the two seem to me to be on the border of myth, with its mythic power and arbitrary nature. Admitting these terms for what they are, would that mean that the hysteric and, hence, somehow, the woman does not have the right to move in the direction of mastery or academics or perhaps even toward the position of analyst? She has only one position, she 'puts in check'. That is inadmissible – grotesque. But the way you have defined a knowledge expounded with limits and holes is no longer, in effect, entirely mastery. It does correspond just the same to what I meant just now, that is to say, a discourse that – for its own subject, for what concerns knowledge – offers some connections, punctuations, scansions, demonstrations – through which the data of knowledge are transmitted. I see no way to conceive of a cultural system in which there would be no transmission of knowledge in the form of a coherent statement. Right now, for social and ideological reasons, this coincides with a position of mastery.

H: I don't know what you call 'right now'; it has always been like that in our western societies. In our own history, the one we are still reacting to, that is what has happened and keeps on happening.

C: That's not entirely true. There is a history of mastery, for us among others, that runs through the history of national education, via the major schools of teacher instruction, via Jules Ferry, via the struggles for a state school, et cetera. And I really think that, from women's point of view, there have been some rays of light in that history and some moments when women had mastery. Not that they have had economic mastery, of course, but it has come about that they had symbolic management of an intellectual activity. An example would be the time

---

'Common public instruction for all citizens is to be created and organized and to be free with regard to those fields of instruction which are indispensable to all men' (French Constitution of 1791).

'The institutions of instruction in their entirety were opened up to the people free of charge, and, at the same time they were cleared of any interference by the Church and the State. Thus, not only was instruction made accessible for everyone, but knowledge itself was set free of the chains which class prejudices and governmental power had laid on it' (Karl Marx, *On the Commune*).

of the trouvères and troubadours...at the same time, what's more, as a mythology of the 'inspiring woman' opposing this mastery.

I believe that *cultural* oppression of women coincides with economic evolution and is accentuated by the development of capitalism. Think of the 'précieuses', who are not at all well known or well liked. There have sometimes been women in possession of knowledge.

H: There has always been a split between those who are in possession of knowledge and culture and who occupy a position of mastery and the others. I don't rule out women's having been on that side, but even then they are not in the masters' position. I am not saying that knowledge is always associated with power, or that it must be: but that is its danger. And I am not saying women are never on the side of knowledge-power. But in the majority of cases in their history, one finds them aligned with no-knowledge or knowledge-without-power.

C: By *power* you don't mean political power, you mean that scrap, that reflection of political power that the teacher exercises metaphorically and imaginarily. What exactly is the teacher's 'power'?

H: Where is the division between 'powers? It's impossible to separate them. I believe teaching goes hand in hand with ideology.

C: I don't think so. If that was true, there would be no reason at all to struggle for a truly democratic transmission of knowledge – on the contrary! It is true that whole segments of knowledge are 'trapped' in

---

The peoples whose women must work much more than is proper according to our ideas often have much more real consideration for women than our European populations. Civilization's 'lady', who is surrounded by feigned respect and who has become a stranger to any real work, has a far lower social position than the woman who is a barbarian, who worked hard, who counted as a real lady (*dame, froxa, Frau: domina*) and who, moreover, was one because of her character...

We are confronted with this new form of family in all its severity among the Greeks. As Marx noted, the position of the goddesses in mythology represents an earlier period, when women still occupied a freer and more respected place, in the Heroic Age, we already find women degraded owing to the predominance of the man and the competition of female slaves...The modern conjugal family is based on...admitted or masked domestic slavery of woman, and modern society is a mass made up exclusively of conjugal families, like so many molecules. In this day and age, man in the great majority cases, must support and nourish the family, at least in the propertied classes; and this gives him a sovereign authority which does not need legal privilege to back it up. Within the family man is the bourgeois; woman plays the part of proletariat. But in the industrial sphere, the specific character of economic oppression that weighs on the proletariat is only manifested in all its severity after all the legal privileges of the capitalist class have been suppressed and complete legal equality of the two classes has been established; the democratic republic does not suppress the antagonism between the two classes, the contrary is true: that is what, first of all, provides the ground where the struggle is going to be resolved (F. Engels, *The Origin of the Family, Private Property and the State*).

the dominant ideology, but still they are conveyed. There are, for example, Marxist historians; they teach history in a 'history' program. It is not because they are in a position of mastery within the teaching structure as it is now that the *content* of their knowledge goes hand in hand with ideology. The division is more complex: it is between the subject's position in relation to knowledge and *the specific effects of the knowledge itself.* The transmission is effective in any kind of structure; even if it is attenuated by the instructional system, it is not *wiped out.*

H: It is almost wiped out. Thank god there is always a tremendous resistance – young people's flexibility, for instance. Take people when they get out of high school, private schools, no matter what school, and see what you get. Zero.

C: But they are receivers and under difficult conditions...

H: Receivers are what they have received. Certainly there are always tightly held lines, like a certain type of philosophical instruction. But that never has more than a limited and postponed effectiveness. Despite absolutely incredible setbacks, it does keep alive a certain kind of spirit of change . But that's not what has taken power. Power lies always in the same direction. It always has.

C: In the same direction because the bourgeoisie, the dominant class, is in power. But you can't say that on one side there is the dominant class with its power, its system of transmission and the content of that system – and that is ideology, and on the other side is everything else. I don't think that is an actual split.

H: That there could be a culture without a culture or a world, a society without education is something I never thought.

C: At the moment, it seems to me, you are making mastery absolutely coincide with knowledge, except in a few exceptional cases.

H: Sure. But rather than mastery coinciding with knowledge, I would say that, with few exceptions, knowledge is constantly caught up in, is entrapped by a will for power. I know which people conveying knowledge don't seem to be dealing with the exercise of power. There are very few. In reality, most of the people I know make use of knowledge, consciously or unconsciously, and use it for something else for themselves.

C: It is inevitable on a certain level that they make it serve themselves, nothing can ever be done about that. Satisfaction is essential to avoid falling into what I've called 'oblativity'. The desire to teach has to find some satisfaction!

The non-master must be imagined

H: It's a question of quantity. I'm saying that people for whom the process of return is a normal process of revenue are rare. They get a certain satisfaction, of course, that's normal, but that satisfaction can take any form. You can be gratified by the feeling of drawing others to your high level or, on the contrary, of going down to their level, et cetera. The most usual satisfaction is not generous. 'Masters', in general, try to really obtain an increase in value from mastery, a feeling of accrued superiority, an inflated narcissism...

C: Partly that's true. But all the more so when the knowledge has less support. It is particularly true, therefore, of the literary person – for example, where a personal gloss has considerable importance just now, where the discourse has progressed so slightly into theory that it is upheld only by a huge amount of inspiration, whose coherence is literally neurotic and which has no other way to defend itself. It is not knowledge that is being conveyed there but something on the order of the poetic. Perhaps the misunderstanding is about the idea of knowledge. When it is a question of knowledge, I am talking about a body of coherent statements that is not a neurotic coherence, hence one that isn't held together by the *singular* phantasmic specialty of the one who does the conveying.

Cultural prohibition

H: Mastery is at play in the Imaginary as well, where interpretation plays a part and is always cropping up. When one talks about mastery, it is a mastery that can very easily become permeated with something going beyond the object, something that is a mythical power, an Imaginary power that is held sacred and that adjoins a scene of a different sort from knowledge. Everything on the order of culture and cultural objects has a prohibition placed on it, which causes class positions in relation to culture. Likewise, woman is uneasy in relation to a certain sort of production – the production of signs...We don't go straight for it. We even wonder if we *can* go there. We say to ourselves: that possession is not for me. All that has been internalized for ever so long. What would this kind of power, belonging to the mastery of knowledge and, moreover, concealed, be in a field that doesn't pass through discourse? If, instead, it went through concrete practices, like manual work or even in the business world where there are mechanisms you can really dominate, where things probably don't escape you. Always for us, working in humanities and literature, there is a part that is uncontrollable. Mastery goes through real concrete power, in that case, political power, money, all the position forms of power that are the equivalents of the sacred power of the master's word.

C: What bothers me is this collusion between power/knowledge, invested with an effectiveness that I don't believe it has. The power to change – or to inhibit – knowledge comes through mediations that are too complex for us to judge what they might be. The power of power is first of all economic. What you describe is true on the level of a sort of huge, imaginary, mythical, ideological space. It is not true for things that are part of the real functioning of those structures.

What remains of me at the university, within the university?

H: For me ideology is a kind of vast membrane enveloping everything. We have to know that this skin exists even if it encloses us like a net or like closed eyelids. We have to know that, to change the world, we must constantly try to scratch and tear it. We can never rip the whole thing off, but we must never let it stick or stop being suspicious of it. It grows back and you start again.

C: Let's go back to the discourse of knowledge, the discourse of the university; as for myself I'm hanging on to it, I accept the dunce cap so readily put on the academic's head at the moment, but can I say that it is as a woman that I hold on to it, or not? I don't think the question is at all pertinent.

H: You're right that it has no pertinence in that instance. As a subject, I always suffered from being made inferior or was crushed by what comes through the surrounding knowledge, even if, to defend myself and out of curiosity, I said to myself: 'I'm going to go see what it is.' I didn't do as Kafka's peasant did; I went to see, but that comes from the fact that when I was in ignorance – which I was for a very long time – when I was 'theoretically naive', as they say, I felt myself constantly under attack, aggressed, because it is very hard for people with a knowledge at their disposal not to be aggressive sometimes, even the best of masters. I'm thinking of B…who is a very intelligent woman with extraordinary talent. Recently I saw she was deeply troubled; a few people whom she had just seen had told her, 'You know, women don't have to enter the Symbolic anyhow.' It's ridiculous. For her it didn't mean anything, and for good reason – how could one expect her to know what 'enter into the Symbolic' meant? The people she was talking to didn't even bother to say to themselves: she doesn't know what the Lacanian concept of the Symbolic is. It's not exactly your everyday word after all. From the moment one begins to *use* what can be called a concept, when it is mastered and enters your discourse and gets lost, it becomes an ordinary word; but that isn't true at all for everybody else. That is mastery's trap. Being so much a master that you forget you are one.

Give me the password

C: What you said was 'the best of masters', but then you described a mockery of a master. In other respects, however, I gladly invest a positive value in aggressivity, even that of the master, even that of the best of masters. Being aggressive is also allowing the other self-definition, it is *showing* oneself as a subject.

H: Being able to organize or give order to a discourse and being able to make progress are absolutely indispensable, but there are opposite, negative effects as well. For example – controlling and censoring imagination, free production, other forms, et cetera. As a writer, even though I don't know very much, I'm already saying to myself, 'That's enough. I know almost too much about it. Let's not slow down.'

C: With that, let's get back to writing, words, thought, feminine thought processes, whether there is coherence or not. You and I immediately agreed that when one made use of this discourse for transmitting, it didn't matter whether one was a man or a woman. Why did we agree so easily about that? Why is that so obvious?

H: Because precisely, I think it is a discourse that annihilates sexual difference – where there is no question of it.

C: So – in other discourses it could be a question?

H: It is a discourse agreeing more with masculinity than with femininity.

C: We don't have any way to know that.

H: Yes, I have ideas about it. There is something in woman's libidinal organization that doesn't enjoy this kind of discourse...

C: When you say that, you are moving in the direction of the women who say that feminine discourse can come only from splitting?

H: No. I was very exact. I said, 'Woman doesn't enjoy herself in it.' I never said she was incapable of it. And I am sure of it – femininity doesn't enjoy itself there. I keep coming back to this: we are all bisexual. The problem is, what have we done with our bisexuality? What is becoming of it?

The Untenable

Double history of seduction.
What woman is not Dora?
She who makes the others (desire).
The servant-girl's place. Does the hysteric change
the Real? Desire, the Imaginary, class struggle -
how do they relate? What are the yields?

H: I got into the sphere of hysteria because I was drawn – called. I knew
absolutely nothing about it. I had read 'The Dora Case', but didn't see
myself in it. Once into it, though, I made great headway.

First, still rather naïvely, I produced a text on it. Later, I had a sort of
'aftertaste', and I started working on the question. I arrived at a whole
series of positions; some of these positions, perhaps, are contestable. It
is impossible to have a single, rigid point of view about it. If it is only a
metaphor – and it's not clear that this is so, it functions well, it has its
use. I started with Dora; I read that text in a sort of dizziness, exploding
over the situation presented, where at heart I found myself siding
frenetically with the different characters. I immediately worked out a
reading that was probably not centered the way Freud had wanted it to
be. I had to bring center page obliterated characters, characters
repressed in notes, at the bottom of the page, and who were for me in
the absolute foreground, I read it like fiction. I didn't worry about an
analytic investment at that moment, and besides, I couldn't have.

She identifies herself

H: One never reads except by identification. But what kind? What is
'identification'? When I say 'identification', I do not say 'loss of self' I
become, I inhabit, I enter. Inhabiting someone, at that moment I can
feel myself traversed by that person's initiatives and actions.
(Actually, that has always disturbed me. When I was younger, I was
afraid because I realized I was capable of mimicry. Then I accused
myself of thieving flight.) I turned round and round. I found myself
caught up in those characters' same state, because they too were
identifying ... Almost all those involved in Dora's scene circulate
through the others, which results in a sort of hideous merry-go-
round, even more so because, through bourgeois pettiness, they
are ambivalent. All consciously play a double game, plus the
game of the unconscious. Each one acts out the little calculations
of classic bourgeois comedy – a comedy of clear conscience on

the one hand, a comedy of propriety on the other. First of all, 'you don't divorce', then you make a combination of structures with interchangeable elements to get the greatest possible pleasure from an adulterous situation. And that can hold only if there is a social pact that is observed. That pact is, 'no one will say what he knows'. Everybody knows, but everybody is silent, and everybody profits from it. Therefore, one is in a world that rests on a system of silent contracts, contracts of general hypocrisy. And it is a chain: '*I* won't tell what you are doing and *you* won't tell what I do'. As I was reading, I heard voices sighing in the text – voices of people who, in the chain, were finally those on whom weighed heaviest the great weight of silence, those who were crushed, who obtained no satisfaction in the roundabout. In the front line was Dora, who fascinated me, because here was an eighteen-year-old girl caught in a world where you say to yourself, she is going to break – a captive, but with such strength! I could not keep from laughing from one end to the other, because, despite her powerlessness and with (thanks to) that powerlessness, here is a kid who successfully jams all the little adulterous wheels that are turning around her and, one after the other, they break down. She manages to

---

'*Her or me*': if Dora felt for her father a more lively interest than that which one would have expected from a daughter, she felt and acted more like a jealous wife, as her mother would have been in the right to do, because it is the mother who has the right. But it is the *daughter* who has *the name*: if Dora said 'her or me' when she made scenes for him, when she had no right to do so, that bad little girl, it was because she was her father's daughter. He was a very active man, with unusual talent, an important manufacturer, enjoying a fine material position...when his daughter was born he felt fulfilled, having already had a son who would succeed him...He gave the baby the name Dora. All the other names in the story are without importance except for Dora's. During the first eight years of life, Dora was adored by her father. It was a love with no contract. From the age of eight, this little treasure suffered respiratory problems. She caused her father a great deal of worry. This kind man forced her to visit skillful doctors. What Mrs K was doing, couldn't Dora have done it?

not Mummy – DADDY –	put me to sleep – MUMMY –	some gold for Dora DORA	
Mr K MONSIEUR K –	MADAME K –	only for Mrs K – only for Daddy – not Mrs K - DADDY	MADAME K -
only for Dora – will have Daddy adore some gold for Daddy – golden case – won't get – DORA –		not my lady – DADDY –	MADAME K –
only for Mummy – MUMMY –	adore lie Daddy – not Dora – DADDY –	no gold to show – will have my treasure – DORA –	MY TREASURE –

say what she doesn't say, so intensely that the men drop like flies. We can very well see how – at what moment, in what scenes, by which meaning – she has cut through. Each time cutting through the marshmallow ribbon that the others are in the process of spieling. A hecatomb.

It is she who is the victim, but the others come out of it in shreds. The father, Mr K, Freud – everybody passes through. They all drop. Doubtless a symbolic carnage because the men always regroup. Then, afterward, comes a reflux and you have the party of men who came, reiterating the father, repeating the famous scene of Dora in bed, Dora lying down, Daddy standing and looking at Dora. In the end *she* makes *them* lie down; they fall; the most beautiful image is the one of Mr K's accident. Before Dora's eyes, he was run over by a cart. All of this was linked with a criticism of society which touches me because I belonged to that lower middle class when I was little: the criticism passing through a secondary figure. In the same way that the woman is the man's repressed in the conjugal couple, there is this little character who is in the process of disappearing from society and on whom rested the family structure: the servant-girl.

---

mummydaddy –		adore	
my goof	play Daddy –	not Dora –	will have –
MY PEARL –	MY GEM –	DADDY –	DORA –

get it? –		gold cage -	
my (chatter) box – play Mrs K – I gold –			Mrs F(reud)
MY GEMLET –	MADAME K –	JEOR –	MADAME F –

bick…

some gold for god –	my lady god –	will be –
DORA – GOD THE SECOND – MADAME GOD THE SECOND – MY BOX –		

show–		…er, bicker –	
my treasure –	but they have my marbles –		
MY TREASURE –	MY HOUSE –	MY MARBLES –	MY DAUGHTER –

get it ?

	(chatter) box		help!
notnot	play –		D's
DADDY –	MY GEMLET –	MY DICE –	

Madame K has rights
Mr K has rights
Daddy has rights
Mummy has rights
Only the gemlet has none
But she has the name

(HÉLÈNE CIXOUS, *PORTRAIT DU SOLEIL*).

Maid in the family

C: She is everywhere, in all Freud's analyses. The servant-girl is a
character who is just beginning to disappear from analyses. And she is
always on the side of eroticism.

H: The seductress. She is the hole in the social cell, 'it' goes through 'that',
it goes through her body. In 'Dora' what was terrifying was that these
archetypical servants were put by Freud himself in 'the maid's room' –
that is in the notes. There are two who are identical. Both are called 'the
servant-girl', 'the governess'. One succeeds the other in Dora's life,
with years in between but they have exactly the same role. They have
the same history: seduced by the boss and then eliminated for having
been seduced by the boss. Woman's situation carried to the paroxysm
of horror. So, the servant-girl is the repressed of the boss's wife.

C: The boss's wife is the lady: 'madame'. She spends her days in bed, or
she buys smoked salmon. She is a strange, absent face. But certainly
servant-girls are there only as fantasy objects, like animals. Grouscha,
in the analysis of *The Wolfman*, is both the maid and a pear – the child
says it straight out. He links it together loud: pear striped with yellow,
maid, butterfly, sex between a woman's legs. There are the servant-
girls, stuck in between fruits and bugs. Elsewhere Freud speaks of a
bottle of pineapple liqueur; it is spoiled, this liqueur; it smells bad. And
Martha Freud, the slut, makes the most of it by saying: 'It should be
given to the servants'.

And Freud says: 'No, because it's spoiled we can throw it away'.
Good soul...unless, because it concerns one of Freud's own dreams, he
made the most of it by blaming the sentence on his wife...

H: That situation – why doesn't it appear in the cases that Freud recounts?
Dora's case is archetypical, 'the servant-girl is the boss's wife's
repressed', but in Dora's case, Dora is in the place of the boss's wife: the
mother is set aside. She is dead, she is nothing, and everybody has
agreed to bury her. Including Freud. Not for a moment does he analyze
the reports given him about the mother.

She is 'in the hole'. Which is exactly what permits Dora's rising to the
fore and this sort of Oedipal idyll that is going to be played out
between her and daddy. What does that mean? It means that, for Freud,

---

In my opinion, it still had to be explained why Dora felt so offended by Mr K's
advances – the more so because I began to understand that, in this affair, for Mr
K, it was no frivolous attempt at seduction. I interpreted the fact that she
informed her parents of this incident as an act which was already influenced by a
morbid desire for revenge...

We are back at the scene by the lake...Mr K began rather seriously; but she did
not let him finish. As soon as she understood what it was about, she slapped his

the mother, once her role is fulfilled, is through. As the Germans say: 'Der Mohr hat sein Pflicht getan, er kann gehen.' The Moor has done his job, out with him. Now he can go. That is Othello in ' The Moor of Venice'. You can replace 'the Moor' with the mother. She is done making kids, so she is made secondary in the story.

C: There is another reason, which is Freud's blindspot, not only about the Oedipal but also about class attitudes – a banality we must not forget to mention.

H: That is why I say that it is not significant that there is no boss's wife. It is significant that it is Freud who sets the stage, who puts covers on those things that are not important to him, who isn't in the play, and who puts the most important people in the best seats. It is certain that that corresponds socially to something quite real: the servant-girl, the prostitute....

C: Eroticism happens through what is 'clandestine', not through what is 'official'. Remember the text on sensual love and affectionate love in which Freud opposes them as almost incompatible. But Engels, after all, doesn't say anything different. That is all very coherent, and at the same time, there are sharp contradictions. What is coherent is the opposition of the legal wife and the prostitute and their complementarity in the family. The contradictions would be Freud's silences – the things he couldn't see in his own ideological misunderstanding. The family does not exist in isolation, rather it truly supports and reflects the class struggle running through it. The servant-girl, the prostitute, the mother, the boss's wife, the woman: that is all an ideological scene.

H: Freud didn't give the servant-girl enough recognition. Never do you see her in the body of the text – she is always in the kitchen, in her station: she appears in the notes. When Freud speaks of Dora's sexual

---

face and ran off. I wanted to know what words he had said; she did not remember anything except this explanation: 'You know that my wife is nothing to me.'

...For she understood perfectly well what her father, who couldn't sleep without his cognac, needed...Her father did not sleep, because relations with the beloved woman were lacking....'My wife is nothing to me.'

'I do not doubt', says the father 'that this incident is the cause of Dora's temperamental change...She demands that I break off my relations with Mr K, and especially with Mrs K, whom she used to adore. But I cannot do that because first I think Dora's story about Mr K's dishonorable proposals is a fiction that has forced its way on her; besides, I am deeply attached to Mrs K by real friendship, and I would not like to hurt her. The poor woman is very unhappy with her husband...We are two wretched people who...console each other with friendly sympathy. You know that my wife is nothing to me'(Freud, *Le cas Dora. Cinq Psychanalyses – The Dora Case. Five Psychoanalyses*).

initiation, entirely acquired from books, it is automatically attributed to the normal sources of this sort of pernicious education – it is probably the maid's doing, and indeed it is the servant-girl whom we find in a note.

Also, we always say that Freud failed to make the analysis of transferal – that he didn't see what was happening. The truth (which he saw only once when he was really put down) is that, in the system of exchange, me in your place, you in my place...Freud in relation to Dora was in the maid's place. It is Freud who was the servant-girl, and that is what is intolerable for Freud in the Dora case – that he was treated as one treats maids, having been fired the way you fire a servant-girl. There is no failure worse than that. The knot, the crux of the Dora case, is that Dora was afraid of being the maid, and on the other hand, she was afraid of being nothing, like her mother. That 'nothing' is stressed in the words the married men are saying. They are the words of comedy. At the same time, they pass on dramatic metaphors: Mr K says to Dora, and to the servant-girl whom he tried to seduce, 'You know very well that my wife is nothing to me.'

Freud as servant-girl

H: No woman tolerates hearing (even if it is about the other woman), 'My wife, a woman who is my woman, can be nothing.' That is murder. So Dora, hearing it, knowing that the servant-girl had already heard it , sees woman, her mother, the maid die; she sees women massacred to make room for her. But she knows that she will have her turn at being massacred. Her terrific reaction is to slap Mr K. This girl has understood; all her actions in the story Freud tells, and is telling, blindly show how she has seen each time the ignominy and the enactment of woman's murder. And to that must be added that in Dora there is a very beautiful feminine homosexuality, a love for woman that is astounding.

Dora seemed to me to be the one who resists the system, the one who cannot stand that the family and society are founded on the body of women, on bodies despised, rejected, bodies that are humiliating once they have been used. And this girl – like all hysterics, deprived of the possibility of saying directly what she perceived, of speaking face-to-face or on the telephone as father B, or father K, or Freud, et cetera do – still had the strength to make it known. It is the nuclear example of women's power to protest. It happened in 1899; it happens today wherever women have not been able to speak differently from Dora, but have spoken so effectively that it bursts the family into pieces.

Yes, the hysteric, with her way of questioning others (because if she succeeds in bringing down the men who surround her, it is by questioning them, by ceaselessly reflecting to them the image that truly castrates them, to the extent that the power they have wished to impose is an illegitimate power of rape and violence). – The hysteric is, to my eyes, the typical woman in all her force. It is a force that was turned back against Dora, but, if the scene changes and if woman begins to speak in other ways, it

---

There had been at the house a person who, prematurely, had wished to open Dora's eyes about her father's relations with Mrs K...That was her last governess...The teacher and pupil got along rather well for a while, then Dora suddenly became hostile to her and demanded her dismissal. As long as the governess had influence, she used it to stir Dora and her mother up against Mrs. K. ... But her efforts were in vain. Dora remained devoted to Mrs K and wanted to know nothing of the reasons there might have been to think her father's relations with her shocking. Dora, on the other hand, understood very well the governess's motives...She saw that the governess was in love with her father. When he was present, the governess seemed an entirely different person; then she was amusing and obliging...But Dora even let that pass. She only became angry when she realized that the love which had been lavished on her was really meant for her father...Then Dora broke off with her completely.

The poor governess had made Dora understand in an undesirable light part of her own behavior. Dora had acted with Mr K's children...as...the governess had with her.

'Do you know, doctor, that today is the last time I shall be here?'...(Freud): 'You know that you are always free to stop the treatment? When did you decide this?'

'Two weeks ago, I think.'

'Those two weeks remind me of the notice a servant or governess gives of departure.'

'There was also a governess who did that in the K's household.'

She was acting strangely towards Mr K. She didn't greet him, didn't answer him, she treated him as if he did not exist...'She told me that Mr K .... when Mrs K was absent for a few weeks, had wooed her and begged her to refuse him nothing. He told her that his wife was nothing to him and so forth' (Freud, *Le cas Dora*).

would be a force capable of demolishing those structures. There is something else in Dora's case that is great – everything in the nature of desire. A desire that is also, often, love – for love. The source of Dora's strength is, in spite of everything, her desire. The hysteric is not just someone who has her words cut off, someone for whom the body speaks. It all starts with her anguish as it relates to desire and to the immensity of her desire – therefore, from her demanding quality. She doesn't let things get by. I see the hysteric saying: 'I want everything.' The world doesn't give her people who are 'everythings'; they are always very little pieces. In what she projects as a demand for totality, for strength, for certainty, she makes demands of the others in a manner that is intolerable to them and that prevents their functioning as they function (without their restricted little economy). She destroys their calculations . The reckoning, for example, that consists of saying, 'My wife is nothing, therefore, you can be everything' – because she knows that it isn't true, she knows what 'everything' is, she knows what this false-nothing is, et cetera. I also thought the famous scene of the Madonna was terrific. It is the capacity for an adoration that is not empty – it is the belief in the possibility of such a thing.

The ones on the margins and social upheaval

C: That is certainly why it is somehow also a containment. It is metaphoric, yes – a metaphor of the impossible, of the ideal and dreamed of totality, yes, but when you say 'that bursts the family into pieces', no. It mimics, it metaphorizes destruction, but the family reconstitutes itself around it. As when you throw a stone in the water, the water ripples but becomes smooth again. The analysis I make of hysteria comes through my reflection on the place of deviants who are not hysterics but clowns, charlatans, crazies, all sorts of odd people. They all occupy challenging positions foreseen by the social bodies, challenging functions within the scope of all cultures. That doesn't change the structures, however. On the contrary, it makes them comfortable.

She sat for *two hours* in contemplative and dreamy admiration before the *Sistine Madonna*. When I asked her what she liked in the picture, she replied in a confused way. Finally, she said: 'The Madonna' (Freud, *Le cas Dora*).

H: I am not sure that is where I would put hysterics.

C: But yes – it all comes together. Ethnologists, analysts, or anyone naïvely able to say this, at the same time recognize in them an exceptional capacity for language and an *exclusion correlative to it*. In that position, they are part of one of the deepest reenforcements of the superstructures, of the Symbolic. It keeps the net of the Imaginary in a tight grip, and the hysterics are inside it. If I am the network between witch and hysteric, passing one on through the other, through the same signifiers, it is certainly because the hysteric seems to me to inscribe herself within that line.

H: I think there are degrees. I imagine hysteria as distributing itself along a scale of the possible intensity of disturbance. Along with, beyond a certain threshold, something that makes a complete victim of the hysteric. She loses all effectiveness, then, because she herself is the place where everything is turned back against her; she is paralyzed by it, physically or otherwise, and thus loses her impact. There are structures characteristic of hysteria that are not neuroses, that work with very strong capacities of identification with the other, that are scouring, that make mirrors fly, that put disturbing images back into circulation; because only if you are not an Iago can you play your little game of hypocrisy, only if you don't say to yourself, 'I – am a filthy creature.' Because in general the system's functioning is based on blindness, on denial. There is also the fact that there is no place for the hysteric; she cannot be placed or take place. Hysteria is necessarily an element that disturbs arrangements; wherever it is, it shakes up all those who want to install themselves, who want to install something that is going to work, to repeat it. It is very difficult to block out this type of person who doesn't leave you in peace, who wages permanent war against you.

The idiot in the family

C: Yes, it introduces dissension, but it doesn't explode anything at all; it doesn't disperse the bourgeois family, which also exists only through its dissension, which holds together only in the possibility or the reality of its own disturbance, always reclosable, always reclosed. It is when there is a crossing over to the symbolic act that it doesn't shut up again. At the back of my mind, I was thinking of Flaubert while you were talking to me. Flaubert the hysteric, Flaubert in the family circle...second son of the family. The father a very traditionalist doctor, a specialist in dissection at the charity hospital, one whose work is death. But also of the mother: they make a first son who is the true son, the heir. From that moment on, Mme Flaubert wants and expects a girl. She has male children who die. Gustave is the third, he survives; but there you have it, in his mother's desire, he should be a girl. Therefore, insofar as he is a boy, he must die. He stays alive but as the 'family idiot', not knowing how to read, stupid, considered abnormal. He is in a situation of exclusion, putting him obligatorily in a feminine position, both because he should be a girl and because the others are dead. Flaubert has no other solution than to go into writing, very precociously, and that is what Sartre demonstrates in his astonishing book. The first tales he writes are fantastic tales in which he is in the subjective position of the monsters. One of his first texts tells the story, in the first person, of a creature born of the encounter of a woman and a monkey. Later, to get on to other texts, he has to pass through crises whose immediate result is that his father mothers him. It is an absolutely pure schema. Yes, hysteria does upset and disturb the Flaubert family but very little in relation to his writing, which is the passage to the act, the political act, the passage to inscription in the Symbolic. But otherwise it doesn't, and Dora doesn't. For me the fact of being passed on to posterity through Freud's account and even Freud's failure is not a symbolic act. That is already more true of Freud and Breuer's hysteric who became the first welfare worker and who made something of her hysteria. The distinction between them , between those who nicely fulfill their function of challenging with all possible violence (but who can enclose themselves afterward) and those who will arrive at symbolic inscription, no matter what act they use to get there, seems essential to me. Raising hell, throwing fits, disturbing family relations can be shut back up.

H: It is that force that works to dismantle structures. There are some who are not effective, and others who are; it is a question of circumstances, of degrees. Dora broke something.

C: I don't think so.

H: The houses that 'resided' on her, whose stability was ensured by her...

C: What she broke was strictly individual and limited.

H: Because at that time, it was impossible to go any further.

C: Listen, you love Dora, but to me she never seemed a revolutionary character.

H: I don't give a damn about Dora; I don't fetishize her. She is the name of a certain force, which makes the little circus not work anymore.

C: Let's take that metaphorically: that is true of hysteria, agreed, but why limit that to the hysteric and hence to the feminine? From a certain point of view, the obsessive person does an equally destructive job, in the sense of passing limits in the direction of law, constraint, and conformity, which he transforms into caricature. In adding more to the rigidity of structures, and in adding more to ritual, he works destructively.

H: I'm not sure. When Freud says that what is obsessive, on a cultural level, yields the religious and that what is hysterical yields art, it seems right to me. The religious is something that consolidates, that will re-enclose, that will seal and fasten everything that is rigid in the social realm. There is a difference between what makes things move and what stops them; it is what moves things that changes them.

C: Do you know the games like 'taquin'? They are games where you move a piece in a system in which you can move only a limited number of pieces to explore the possibilities of permutation without the 'taquin's' moving. One shifts an element within a perfectly rigid structure, which is all the better for it. Language only moves one square to the place of another – that's all; the real distribution of elements, the real change cannot happen on that level.

Can one put desire to sleep?

H: I don't think that the revolution is going to happen through language either. But there is no revolution without a conscious grasp – without there being people who get up and begin to yell. I think that is where I make a connection with Bataille's analyses, I think that what cannot be oppressed, even in the class struggle, is the libido – desire; it is in taking off from desire that you will revive the need for things to really change. Desire never dies, but it can be stifled for a long time. For example, in peoples who are denied speech and who are on their last gasp. One ceases to move the moment one no longer communicates.

C: Except in taking what you say poetically, I have to admit that these

---

This land is not mine, nor this land, nor this land nor this land nor this sex nor this sex. I revolve around the Revolution as if around the sun with an unmoving, eternal desire like hell around heaven…A race of exhausted men take my place, they die easily: they tumble down the slopes beneath my eyes, these diminished men are merry…I imagine their burial…They imagine my burial but they think better of it: this land is not mine. And this belly and this History and this Sex?

They take their tommyguns and fire. Now that History is over, it is the unknown *outside*, banished but *where*, expropriated, but by what right? Emptied, in my own bosom where I have no place, I am witness to the violent debates of race and sex. I, my substitute. They ask me about Femininity. I keep down but standing. Substituting, can I affirm myself as substitute? And what is Mr Freud's position?

They are keeping me in a harness: men, and the men's women, and the women-men, and the two of them (Hélène Cixous, *Portrait du Soleil*).

sentences have no reality for me. Take an example. What is a people that doesn't communicate?

H: One can very easily smother desire. Let's take France, in fact. From the moment that you no longer circulate discourse, when you circulate only a dead, stereotypical discourse....

C: But who is 'one'? Who circulates? Who are the subjects? Where are they?

H: A certain power. The class that holds power has exercised it for a long time, but it has gotten worse, it is getting worse and worse, it systematically crushes all the places where the imagination is inscribed: the mass media, publishing – everywhere the word and its inventive forms can get through. This deals a heavy blow to political consciousness.

C: Obviously what you are describing is censorship....

H: Yes, and when one censors, one lowers the rate of desire and it takes forever for it to revive. It doesn't communicate. It doesn't know where to go. It is tired; it is going to sleep. That's how it feels. It is not going to budge. That doesn't mean it is dead but that censorship and prohibition are really very effective historic brakes.

C: That is a level of description where I do not recognize anything of what I think in political terms. Not that it is 'false', certainly. But it is described in terms that seem to me on the order of myth, of poetry. It describes a sort of collective subject, fictitious, desiring – a huge entity by turns free and revolutionary or subjugated, by turns sleeping or awake.... In reality these aren't subjects. Let's even admit into the political register the term desire, which in my sense and for the moment isn't pertinent: if you are thinking at the same time 'desire' and 'class struggle' but (they are heterogenous levels of language), the smothering of what you call 'desire' is impossible; the putting into sleep, unthinkable; the class struggle never ceases to become harsher and harsher, more and more stirred up through its contradictions. What you are feeling as censorship and the putting to sleep of imagination precisely correspond to a period of struggle such as there has not been in France for a long time; it is a reality that power is trying to erase. The stifling of it (which isn't the stifling of 'desire') happens through abusive use of all means of information. Not astonishing that one can feel that but is it necessary to be taken in by it? The idea of putting to sleep, therefore, is incompatible with the very notion of struggle contained in class struggle. Class struggle does not stop. There is imagination, desire, creation, production of writing (you see I am trying to find different names for the same experiences), and then somewhere else, on another level of reality, there is class struggle, and within it, women's struggle. There are missing links in all that, which we should try to think in order to succeed in joining our two languages. Sometimes desire and artistic production anticipate class struggle in its unfolding but also, dialectically, they are fallout from it, a more or less unconscious effect, with all its mediations, unthought at the present time. A conflict so fundamental for intellectuals that it informs the totality of consciousnesses, wherever they are situated, caught in impossible contradictions, whether consciously or not, whether they lean more toward guilty conscience or toward blindness. One is always situated there, in the struggle, in a precise position.

H: Class struggle is this sort of huge machine whose system is described by Marx, and, therefore, is now functioning. But its rhythm is not always the same; it is a rhythm that is sometimes very attenuated.

C: It can *seem* very attenuated, especially if you are bludgeoned into thinking so. But there is a considerable shift between the reality of class struggle and the way in which it is lived mythically, especially by intellectuals who have difficulty being able to size up the reality of the struggles directly, because they are in a position where work on language and work on the Imaginary have fundamental importance and can put blinders on them.

H: Right now, I am pessimistic. There is, in a very generalized manner, a loss of voice in the world of writing, of literature, of creation. It is symptomatic and it will have effects; it isn't by chance that reading is on the retreat in almost all countries of the West. So that means that all the governments united, whether right or reformist, are saying: 'You, if you still have eyes, shut them, and intellectuals of all countries, your mouths, and don't start making analyses, and besides, it isn't worth the trouble.' One sees the development of an international intrigue that is leading toward capitalist imbecilization in its most inhuman, most automatic, most formidable form. The selling out of all the countries, their handing themselves over the way France has done with the United States, is also done on condition of a complicitous silence. And to achieve it, they will not only silence the bulk of the production of writing – of literature in general, whatever it may be – but they will also silence poetry, even though poetry isn't going to talk about international relations. But somehow, they fear it, and they gag it.

'When a political man exercises pressure for the art of his time to express a given cultural world, it consists of political activity, not of artistic criticism: if the cultural world for which one struggles is a living and necessary fact, its expansiveness will be irresistible, and it will find its artists' (Antonio Gramsci).

C: And yet, in the same period, in the same movement whose capitalist reverse side you are describing, imperialism is coming apart, is defeated: in Indochina – what an event! in Europe. And that is fundamental. Pessimism should be only a limited look, only one point of view, only one perspective. I believe that the need for *dialectic* (which is how I always see it in depth) is making itself very real and that we will not succeed in thinking the struggle for women's liberation without this means of analysis and of comprehension, which is not natural for us, which is difficult, but which is the only true method.

H: History is always in several places at once, there are always several histories underway; this is a high point in the history of women.

5 Kate Millett and Cora Kaplan

KATE MILLETT *Sexual Politics**

It is difficult to overestimate the impact of Kate Millett's *Sexual Politics* – as literary criticism, as polemic, as cultural sign, as media event. The huge and politically essential task that Millett sets herself is to prove that relations between the sexes are not solely matters of personal choice or social organization, but intrinsically political. At the centre of this political relationship is an inequality of power, the dominance of men over women in patriarchy. The importance Millett gives to literature and psychoanalysis is indicated in the extract included here. Millett condemns the sexual ideology of D. H. Lawrence, where men are active and women passive, where men show prowess and women devotion. She questions also Freud's analysis of the Oedipus complex, noting how man becomes the centre of an adoring female circle and how the emotional needs of women are effaced. The need to explore a text in terms of its gender ideology has, post-Millett, become indubitable. At the same time, Millett initiates a debate on reading as a gendered activity; the affront which women can experience while reading texts which are lauded as models of imaginative insight or rational exposition needs to be explained, not dismissed (see Introduction, pp. 1–2, 17–18).

I Devotional

'Let me see you!'

He dropped the shirt and stood still, looking towards her. The sun through the low windows sent a beam that lit up his thighs and slim belly, and the erect phallus rising darkish and hot-looking from the little cloud of vivid gold-red hair. She was startled and afraid.

*KATE MILLETT, *Sexual Politics* (London: Virago, 1977), pp. 237–57.

135

'How strange!' she said slowly. 'How strange he stands there! So big! and so dark and cocksure! Is he like that?'

The man looked down the front of his slender white body, and laughed. Between the slim breasts the hair was dark, almost black. But at the root of the belly, where the phallus rose thick and arching, it was gold-red, vivid in a little cloud.

'So proud!' she murmured, uneasy. 'And so lordly! Now I know why men are so overbearing. But he's lovely, *really*. Like another being! A bit terrifying! But lovely really! And he comes to *me!* – ' She caught her lower lip between her teeth, in fear and excitement.

The man looked down in silence at his tense phallus, that did not change. ...'Cunt, that's what tha'rt after. Tell lady Jane tha' wants cunt. John Thomas, an' th' cunt o' lady Jane! – '.

'Oh, don't tease him', said Connie, crawling on her knees on the bed towards him and putting her arms round his white slender loins, and drawing him to her so that her hanging swinging breasts touched the top of the stirring, erect phallus, and caught the drop of moisture. She held the man fast.

'Lie down!' he said, 'Lie down! Let me come!'

He was in a hurry now.[1]

Lady Chatterley's Lover is a quasi-religious tract recounting the salvation of one modern woman (the rest are irredeemably 'plastic' and 'celluloid') through the offices of the author's personal cult, 'the mystery of the phallus'.[2] This passage, a revelation of the sacrament itself, is properly the novel's very holy of holies – a transfiguration scene with atmospheric clouds and lighting, and a pentecostal sunbeam (the sun is phallic to Lawrence's apprehension) illuminating the ascension of the deity 'thick and arching' before the reverent eyes of the faithful.

Lawrence's working title for the book was 'Tenderness', and although Oliver Mellors, the final apotheosis of Lawrentian man is capable of some pretty drastic sexual animosities (he'd rather like to 'liquidate' all lesbians, and what Freudians would call 'clitoridal' women, en masse, together with his own former wife), one still finds in this novel little of the sexual violence and ruthless exploitation so obtrusive in Mailer and Miller, nor, for that matter, the honest recognition of sexual caste one encounters in Genet. With *Lady Chatterley*, Lawrence seems to be making his peace with the female, and in one last burst of passion proposing a reconciliation for the hostilities embarked upon with the composition of *Aaron's Rod* in 1918, nearly ten years before. Compared with the novels and stories which preceded it, this last work appears almost an act of atonement. And so Constance Chatterley is granted sight of the godhead,[3] which turns out to be a portrait of the creator himself, nude, and in his most impressive state. Whereas the mood of *Kangaroo*, *Aaron's Rod* and *The Plumed Serpent* is homoerotic, here it is narcissistic.

In *Lady Chatterley*, as throughout his final period, Lawrence uses the words 'sexual' and 'phallic' interchangeably, so that the celebration of sexual passion for which the book is so renowned is largely a celebration of the penis of Oliver Mellors, gamekeeper and social prophet. While insisting his mission is the noble and necessary task of freeing sexual behavior of perverse inhibition, purging the fiction which describes it of prurient or prudish euphemism, Lawrence is really the evangelist of quite another cause – 'phallic consciousness'. This is far less a matter of the 'resurrection of the body', 'natural love', or other slogans under which it has been advertised, than the transformation of masculine ascendency into a mystical religion, international, possibly institutionalized. This is sexual politics in its most overpowering form, but Lawrence is the most talented and fervid of sexual politicians. He is the most subtle as well, for it is through a feminine consciousness that his masculine message is conveyed. It is a woman, who, as she gazes, informs us that the erect phallus, rising phoenix-like from its aureole of golden pubic hair is indeed 'proud' and 'lordly' – and above all, 'lovely'. 'Dark and cocksure' it is also 'terrifying' and 'strange', liable to give rise in women to 'fear' as well as 'excitement' – even to uneasy murmurs. At the next erection, Connie and the author-narrator together inform us the penis is 'overweening', 'towering' and 'terrible'.[4] Most material of all, an erection provides the female with irrefutable evidence that male supremacy is founded upon the most real and uncontrovertible grounds. A diligent pupil, Connie supplies the catechist's dutiful response, 'Now I know why men are so overbearing.' With the ecstasy of the devout, a parody of a loving woman's rapture and delight, she finds the godhead both frightening and sublime. Lawrence's own rather sadistic insistence on her intimidation before biological event is presumably another proof of inherent female masochism. One cannot help admiring the technique: 'But he's lovely, *really*... A bit terrifying! But lovely really! And he comes to *me!*' – out of the mouth of the inamorata the most abject piety. It is no wonder Simone de Beauvoir shrewdly observed that Lawrence spent his life writing guidebooks for women.[5] Constance Chatterley is as good a personification of counter-revolutionary wisdom as Marie Bonaparte.

Even Mellors is impressed, pleased to refer to his penis in the third person, coyly addressing it in dialect: 'Ay ma lad! Tha'rt theer right enough. Yi, tha mun rear they head! Theer on thy own ey? an ta'es no count o' nob'dy... Dost want *her?* Dost want my lady Jane?... Say; Lift your heads... that the king of glory may come in.'[6] John Thomas, this active miracle, is hardly matched by lady Jane, mere passive 'cunt'. Praise for this commodity is Mellors' highest compliment to his mistress: 'Th'art good cunt, though, aren't ter? Best bit o' cunt left on earth...Cunt! It's thee down theer; an' what I get when I'm i'side thee... Cunt! Eh, that's the beauty o' thee, lass'.[7] The sexual mystery to which the novel is dedicated is scarcely a reciprocal or co-operative event – it is simply phallic. Mellors' penis, even when deflated, is still 'that which had been the power': Connie moaning with 'a sort of bliss' is its 'sacrifice' and a 'new-born thing'.[8] Although the male is displayed and admired so often, there is, apart from the word cunt, no reference to or description of the female genitals: they are hidden, shameful and subject.[9] Male genitals are not only the aesthetic standard, '…the balls between his legs! What a mystery! What a strange heavy weight of mystery…The roots, root of all that is lovely, the primeval root of all full beauty',[10] they become a species of moral standard as well: 'The root of all sanity is in the balls.'[11] Yet all that is disreputable, even whole classes of society, are anathematized by the words 'female' or 'feminine'.

The scenes of sexual intercourse in the novel are written according to the 'female is passive, male is active' directions laid down by Sigmund Freud. The phallus is all; Connie is 'cunt', the thing acted upon, gratefully accepting each manifestation of the will of her master. Mellors does not even condescend to indulge his lady in foreplay. She enjoys an orgasm when she can, while Mellors is managing his own. If she can't, then too bad. Passive as she is, Connie fares better than the heroine of *The Plumed Serpent*, from whom Lawrentian man, Don Cipriano, deliberately withdraws as she nears orgasm, in a calculated and sadistic denial of her pleasure:

> By a swift dark instinct, Cipriano drew away from this in her. When, in their love, it came back on her, the seething electric female ecstacy, which knows such spasms of delirium, he recoiled from her…. By a dark and powerful instinct he drew away from her as soon as this desire rose again in her, for the white ecstasy of frictional satisfaction, the throes of Aphrodite of the foam. She could see that to him, it was repulsive. He just removed himself, dark and unchangeable, away from her.[12]

Lawrentian sexuality seems to be guided by somewhat the same principle one finds expressed in Rainwater's study of the working class (also the doctrine of the nineteenth-century middle classes) – 'sex is for the man'.[13] Lawrence's knowledge of Freud was sketchy and secondhand, but he appears to be well acquainted with the theories of female passivity and male activity and doubtless found them very convenient. Ladies – even when they are 'cunt' – don't move. In both novels there are a number of severe reprimands delivered against subversive female 'friction'.

The sexual revolution had done a great deal to free female sexuality. An admirably astute politician, Lawrence saw in this two possibilities: it could grant women an autonomy and independence he feared and hated, or it could be manipulated to create a new order of dependence and subordination, another form of compliance to masculine direction and prerogative. The frigid woman of the Victorian period was withholding assent, the 'new woman' could, if correctly dominated, be mastered in bed as everywhere else. The Freudian school had promulgated a doctrine of 'feminine fulfillment', 'receptive' passivity, the imaginary 'adult' vaginal orgasm which some disciples even interpreted as forbidding any penile contact with the clitoris. Notions of this kind could become, in Lawrence's hands, superb instruments for the perfect subjection of women.

In thanksgiving for her lover's sexual prowess, Lady Chatterley goes out into the rain before their hut to dance what the reader recognizes to be a mime of King David's naked gyrations before the Lord. Watching her, Mellors understands her to be performing a 'kind of homage toward him', while 'repeating a wild obeisance'.[14] Such satisfaction as she is granted by the lordly gamekeeper has converted her to a 'wonderful cowering female' whose flashing haunches Mellors perceives in terms of prey. Accordingly, he stirs himself to the chase. Having pursued and caught her, 'he tipped her up and fell with her on the path, in the roaring silence of the rain, short and sharp, he took her, short and sharp finished, like an animal'.[15]

Lawrence is a passionate believer in the myth of nature which has ordained that female personality is congenital, even her shame not the product of conditioning, but innate. Only the 'sensual fire' of the 'phallic hunt' can rout this 'old, old physical fear which crouches in the bodily roots'. On the occasion, when Lady Chatterley submits to Mellors' anal penetration, we are told that 'She would have thought a woman would have died of shame. Instead of which the shame died... she had needed this phallic hunting out, she had secretly wanted it, and she had believed that she would never get it.' The 'phallus alone' is competent to explore the 'core of the physical jungle, the last and deepest recess of organic shame'.[16] Having reached the 'bedrock of her nature', the heroine breaks off momentarily to preach to the reader that the poets were 'liars': 'They made one think one wanted sentiment. When one supremely wanted this piercing, consuming, rather awful sensuality...The supreme pleasure of the mind! And what is that to a woman?'[17] Lawrence has killed three birds here, the bluestocking, the courtly pose, and, it would seem, his own sodomous urges.[18] Although Constance Chatterley is more credibly a woman than most Lawrentian heroines (there are even casual references to her breasts and she becomes pregnant with the hero's child), the erotic focus of the novel is constantly the magnificent Mellors, 'remote', 'wild animal', with some superior and 'fluid male knowledge', the very personification of phallic divinity, described in caressing phrases which indicate Lawrence himself not only wishes to possess and partake of this power, but be possessed by it as well.

Lady Chatterley's Lover is a program for social as well as sexual redemption, yet the two are inextricable. Early in the novel, Tommy Dukes, one of the author's humbler mouthpieces, has deplored the fact that there are no 'real' men and women left in the world, predicting the fall of civilization on this account. We are all doomed unless the one hope of redemption is understood immediately: 'It's going down the bottomless pit, down the chasm. And believe me, the only bridge across the chasm will be the phallus!'[19] The metaphor is an unhappy one; in respect of penile length, the future hardly seems promising. Yet the program the novel offers against the industrial horrors it describes with such verve and compassion, is a simple matter: men should adopt a costume of tight red trousers and short white jackets and the working class should cease to desire money. In a single elaboration, Mellors suggests they busy themselves with folk art and country dances. This would be cruel, if it were not ridiculous. While a sexual revolution, in terms of a change in attitudes, and even in psychic structure, is undoubtedly essential to any radical social change, this is very far from being what Lawrence has in mind. His recipe is a mixture of Morris and Freud, which would do away with machinery and return industrial England to something like the middle ages. Primarily the thing is to be accomplished by a reversion to older sexual roles. Modern man is ineffectual, modern woman a lost creature (cause and effect are interchangeable in these two tragedies), and the world will only be put right when the male reassumes his mastery over the female in that total psychological and sensual domination which alone can offer her the 'fulfillment' of her nature.

This is why the novel concentrates on rehabilitating Constance Chatterley through the phallic ministrations of the god Pan, incarnated in Mellors. In the novel's early chapters we are instructed that her only meaningful existence is sexual and has been distorted by education and the indecent liberties of the modern woman. Married to an impotent husband, Connie mopes through some hundred and thirty pages of unfulfilled femininity. Neither a wife nor a mother yearning for a child, her 'womb' contracting at certain stated intervals, she seeks her fleeting youth in unsatisfactory trips to the mirror, and endless visits to some hen pheasants, whose 'pondering female blood' rebukes 'the agony of her own female folornness'[20] while affording her some solace by being 'the only things in the world that warmed her heart'.[21] In the presence of these formidable creatures she 'feels herself on the brink of fainting all the time',[22] and the sight of a pheasant chick breaking its shell reduces her to hysterical weeping. In the best tradition of sentimental narrative we first see 'a tear fall on her wrist', followed by the information that 'she was crying blindly in all the anguish of her generation's forlornness…her heart was broken and nothing mattered any more'.[23] Thereupon Mellors intervenes out of pity ('compassion flames in his bowels for her') and he invites her into the hut for a bit of what she needs.

He is characteristically peremptory in administering it: 'You lie there', he orders. She accedes with a 'queer obedience'[24] – Lawrence never uses the word female in the novel without prefacing it with the adjectives 'weird' or 'queer': this is presumably done to persuade the reader that woman is a dim prehistoric creature operating out of primeval impulse. Mellors concedes one kiss on the navel and then gets to business:

> And he had to come into her at once, to enter the peace on earth of that soft, quiescent body. It was the moment of pure peace for him, the entry into the body of a woman. She lay still, in a kind of sleep, always in a kind of sleep. The activity, the orgasm was all his, all his; she could strive for herself no more.[25]

Of course Mellors is irreproachably competent and sexuality comes naturally to him. But the female , though she is pure nature to whom civilized thought or activity were a travesty, must somehow be taught. Constance has had the purpose of her existence ably demonstrated for her, but her conversion must take a bit longer:

> Her tormented modern-woman's brain still had no rest. Was it real? And she knew, if she gave herself to the man, it was real. But if she kept herself for herself, it was nothing. She was old; millions of years old, she felt. And at last, she could bear the burden of herself no more. She was to be had for the taking. To be had for the taking.[26]

What she is to relinquish is self, ego, will , individuality – things woman had but recently developed – to Lawrence's profoundly shocked distaste. He conceived his mission to be their eradication. Critics are often misled to fancy that he recommends both sexes cease to be hard struggling little wills and egoists. Such is by no means the case. Mellors and other Lawrentian heroes incessantly exert their wills over women and the lesser men it is their mission to rule. It is unthinkable to Lawrence that males should ever cease to be domineering individualists. Only women must desist to be selves. Constance Chatterley was her husband's typist and assistant: she only ceases to serve this unworthy master when she becomes Mellors' disciple and farm wife. At no point is she given the personal autonomy of an occupation, and Lawrence would probably find the suggestion obscene. Even in the guise of a servant, Mellors has infinite assurance and a solid identity; Lady Chatterley appears an embarrassed impostor beside him.

Under the conventions of the eighteenth- and nineteenth-century novel, gentlemen entered into exploitative sexual liaisons with serving maids. Lawrence appears to have reversed this class relation by coupling the lady with her manservant, and his book is said to display an eloquent democracy by asserting that the class system is an 'anachronism'. Yet Mellors, a natural gentleman, and therefore Lord Chatterley's superior, is just as great a snob as Connie, whose sermons mouth Lawrence's own disgust with the proletariat from whence he was saved by virtue of exceptional merit. Mellors also despises his own class. The lovers have not so much bridged class as transcended it into an aristocracy based presumably on sexual dynamism rather than on wealth or position. The very obnoxious Lord Chatterley represents the insufferable white male of the master caste, pretending to be worthy of the term 'ruling class'. Mellors and Lawrence are born outsiders to the privileged white man's general sway of empire, mine ownership, and the many other prerogatives of a male elite. But this has not persuaded them to overthrow so much as to envy, imitate and covet. Rather in the manner of a black who is so corroded with white values that his grandest aspiration is sexual acceptance by the white woman, Lawrence's dark outsiders, whether Mexican Indian, or Derbyshire collier, focus their ambition on the 'white man's woman' – the Lady. Women of his own class and kind are beneath his contempt; the cruellest caricatures in the novel are Bertha Coutts and Mrs Bolton, from whom Mellors withholds himself in rigid distaste – they are unbearably 'common'. Dissatisfaction with Clifford Chatterley's impersonation of the 'ruling class' has by no means cured Lawrence of his allegiance to such a notion; to a large extent, his wish is only to install himself in this position. His plan is to begin by suborning the lady-class female, a feat which should give him courage to subordinate other males. Then he may enter upon his inheritance as natural aristocrat. Immersed in the ancient fantasy that he had the wrong father, he has converted his own father into a god; for in addition to being Lawrence himself and a desirable homosexual lover, Mellors is also supposed to be the surly and unpleasant miner of *Sons and Lovers*, Lawrence senior, rehabilitated and transformed into Pan. As it is improbable Mellors can acquire the artistic prestige or political power of other Lawrentian heroes, who are famous writers or generals, he is to be exalted by purely religious means. And although he is a social prophet, even this form of bettering his position is given little emphasis. Instead, he bases his entire claim upon John Thomas. The possession of a penis is itself an accomplishment of such high order (with the unimportant exception of a Venetian laborer who appears on only one page, no other male in the book gives any evidence of potency) that Mellors' divine nature is revealed and established through this organ alone.

When he began to compose his last novel, Lawrence was suffering in the final stages of tuberculosis. After *The Plumed Serpent* he admitted to being weary of the 'leader cum follower' bit and had despaired of political success.[27] All other avenues of grandeur appeared to be closed. Public power was a delusion, only sexual power remained. If the last Lawrentian hero is to have but one apostle to glorify him, let it be a woman. Sexual politics is a surer thing than the public variety between males. For all the excursions into conventional political fascism that occupy the middle and late period of his work, it was the politics of sex which had always commanded Lawrence's attention most, both as the foundation and as a stairway to other types of self-aggrandizement. *Lady Chatterley's Lover* is as close as Lawrence could get to a love story. It is also something of a cry of defeat, perhaps even of remorse, in a man who had aspired rather higher, but had to settle for what he could get. As a handbook of sexual technique to accompany a mood of reaction in sexual politics, it was not altogether a failure.

II Oedipal

In a letter to Edward Garnett written in 1912, Lawrence provided his own description of *Sons and Lovers:*

> A woman of character and refinement goes into the lower class, and has no satisfactions in her own life. She has had a passion for her husband, so the children are born of passion, and have heaps of vitality. But as her sons grow up, she selects them as lovers – first the eldest, then the second. These sons are *urged* into life by their reciprocal love of their mother – urged on and on. But when they come to manhood, they can't love, because their mother is the strongest power in their lives, and holds them… As soon as the young men come into contact with women there is a split. William gives his sex to a fribble, and his mother holds his soul. But the split kills him, because he doesn't know where he is. The next son gets a woman who fights for his soul – fights his mother. The son loves the mother – all the sons hate and are jealous of the father. The battle goes on between the mother and the girl, with the son as object. The mother gradually proves the stronger, because of the tie of blood. The son decides to leave his soul in his mother's hands, and like his elder brother, go for passion. He gets passion. Then the split begins to tell again. But, almost unconsciously, the mother realizes what is the matter and begins to die. The son casts off his mistress, attends to his mother dying. He is left in the end naked of everything, with the drift toward death.[28]

In the same letter Lawrence assured Garnett this would be a great book. Both the précis and the boast have truth, but the latter has more of it. *Sons and Lovers* is a great novel because it has the ring of something written from deeply felt experience. The past remembered, it conveys more of Lawrence's own knowledge of life than anything else he wrote. His other novels appear somehow artificial beside it.

Paul Morel is of course Lawrence himself, treated with a self-regarding irony which is often adulation: 'He was solitary and strong and his eyes had a beautiful light';[29] 'She saw him, slender and firm, as if the setting sun had given him to her. A deep pain took hold of her, and she knew she must love him' – and so forth.[30] In the précis, Lawrence (and his critics after him) have placed all the emphasis in this tale of the artist as an ambitious young man, upon the spectral role his mother plays in rendering him incapable of complete relations with women his own age – his sexual or emotional frigidity. That the book is a great tribute to his mother and a moving record of the strongest and most formative love of the author's life, is, of course, indisputable. For all their potential morbidity, the idyllic scenes of the son and mother's walking in the fields, their excited purchases of a flower or a plate and their visit to Lincoln cathedral, are splendid and moving, as only *Sons and Lovers*, among the whole of Lawrence's work, has the power to move a reader. But critics have also come to see Mrs Morel as a devouring maternal vampire as well, smothering her son with affection past the years of his need of it, and Lawrence himself has encouraged this with the self-pitying defeatism of phrases such as 'naked of everything', 'with the drift toward death', and the final chapter heading 'Derelict'.[31]

The précis itself is so determinedly Freudian, after the fact as it were,[32] that it neglects the two other levels at which the novel operates – both the superb naturalism of its descriptive power,[33] which make it probably still the greatest novel of proletarian life in English, but also the vitalist level beneath the Freudian diagram. And at this level Paul is never in any danger whatsoever. He is the perfection of self-sustaining ego. The women in the book exist in Paul's orbit and to cater to his needs: Clara to awaken him sexually, Miriam to worship his talent in the role of disciple and Mrs Morel to provide always that enormous and expansive support, that dynamic motivation which can inspire the son of a coal miner to rise above the circumstances of his birth and become a great artist. The curious shift in sympathy where she is a woman tied by poverty to a man she despises, 'done out of her rights'[34] as a human being, compelled despite her education and earlier aspirations, to accept the tedium of poverty and childbearing in cohabitation with a man for whom she no longer feels any sympathy and whose alcoholic brutality repels and enslaves her, to the possessive matron guarding her beloved son from maturity – is but the shift of Paul's self-centered understanding. While a boy, Paul hates his father and identifies with his mother; both are emotionally crushed and physically afraid before the paternal tyrant. The identification is real enough. When Walter Morel locks his pregnant wife out of the house in a boozy rage, it is Paul with whom she is pregnant, and the scene derives its conviction from the outraged prose of the precious burden himself. When Morel beats her and draws blood, it is Paul's snowy baby clothes that are stained with the sacrifice. As Mrs Morel cowers, sheltering the infant, a bond is sealed that will last past other attachments.

The book even provides us with glimpses of the Oedipal situation at its most erotic: 'I've never had a husband – not really… His mother gave him a long fervent kiss.'[35] At this critical juncture Walter Morel walks in, justifiably annoyed, to mutter 'at your mischief again'. Thereupon the two rivals square off and nearly fight it out. But Walter is beaten anyway, and one foresees that Paul is a son who will have much to atone for: 'The elderly man began to unlace his boots. He stumbled off to bed. His last fight was fought in that home'.[36]

But the Oedipus complex is rather less a matter of the son's passion for the mother than his passion for attaining the level of power to which adult male status is supposed to entitle him. Sexual possession of an adult woman may be the first, but is hardly the most impressive manifestation of that rank. Mrs Morel (in only one short passage of the novel is she ever referred to by her own name – Gertrude Coppard) has had no independent existence and is utterly deprived of any avenue of achievement. Her method of continuing to seek some existence through a vicarious role in the success she urges on her sons is, however regrettable, fairly understandable. The son, because of his class and its poverty, has perceived that the means to the power he seeks is not in following his father down to the pits, but in following his mother's behest and going to school, then to an office, and finally into art. The way out of his dilemma lies then in becoming, at first, like his mother rather than his father.

We are frequently told that Lawrence made restitution to his father and the men of his father's condition in creating Mellors and others like him. Such, alas, is not the case. Mellors is as one critic observes, 'really a sort of gentleman in disguise',[37] and if the portrait of the broken drunkard in *Sons and Lovers* is cruel, and it is undeniably, it is less cruel than converting this victim of industrial brutality into a blasé sexual superman who is too much of a snob to belong to either the working or the middle classes. The late Lawrentian hero is clearly Lawrence's own fantasy of the father he might have preferred. In the same way, Lady Chatterley is a smartened-up version of his mother herself. Like his own wife Frieda von Richthofen, she is a real lady, not that disappointed little woman of the mining village with chapped red hands who fears her clothes are too shabby to be seen in Lincoln cathedral. Yet Mrs Morel is a brave, even a great woman though waitresses in teahouses snub her when she can only order custard, too poor to pay for a full meal. *Sons and Lovers* gives us Lawrence's parents without the glamour with which his snobbishness later invested them. All the romances of his later fiction are a reworking of his parents' marriage, and of his own too, modeled on theirs, but a notable advance in social mobility. For Lawrence saw his course, saw it with a Calvinistic sense of election, as a vocation to rise and surpass his origins.

When Paul's ambition inspires his escapes from identical circumstances it will be upon the necks of the women whom he has used, who have constituted his steppingstones up into the middle class. For Paul kills or discards the women who have been of use to him. Freud, another Oedipal son, and a specialist in such affairs, predicted that 'he who is a favorite of the mother becomes a "conqueror."'[38] Paul is to be just that. By adolescence, he has grown pompous enough under the influence of maternal encouragement to proclaim himself full of a 'divine discontent'[39] superior to any experience Mrs Morel might understand. And when his mother has ceased to be of service, he quietly murders her. When she takes an unseasonably long time to die of cancer, he dilutes the milk she has been prescribed to drink: '"I don't want her to eat... I wish she'd die"... And he would put some water with it so that it would not nourish her.'[40] By a nice irony the son is murdering her who gave him life, so that he may have a bit more for himself: he who once was fed upon her milk now waters what he gives her to be rid of her. Motherhood, of the all-absorbing variety, is a dangerous vocation. When his first plan doesn't work, he tries morphine poisoning: 'That evening he got all the morphia pills there were, and took them downstairs. Carefully, he crushed them to powder.'[41] This too goes into the milk, and when it doesn't take hold at once, he considers stifling with the bedclothes.

A young man who takes such liberties must be sustained by a powerful faith. Paul is upheld by several – the Nietzschean creed that the artist is beyond morality; another which he shares with his mother that he is an anointed child (at his birth she has the dream of Joseph and all the sheaves in the field bow to her paragon); and a faith in male supremacy which he has imbibed from his father and enlarged upon himself. Grown to man's estate, Paul is fervid in this piety, but Paul the child is very ambivalent. Despite the ritual observances of this cult which Paul witnessed on pay night[42] and in his father's feckless irresponsibility toward family obligations, he was as yet too young to see much in them beyond the injustices of those who hold rank over him as they did over his mother. Seeing that his father's drinking takes bread from his young mouth, he identifies with women and children and is at first unenthusiastic about masculine prerogative. When a crony comes to call for his father, Paul's vision makes us aware of the man's insolence: 'Jerry entered unasked, and stood by the kitchen doorway...stood there coolly asserting the rights of men and husbands.'[43]

Lawrence later became convinced that the miner's life and the curse of industrialism had reduced this sacred male authority to the oafishness of drinking and wife- and child-beating. Young Paul has been on the unpleasant end of this sort of power, and is acute enough to see that the real control lies in the bosses, the moneyed men at the top. Under industrialism, the male supremacy he yearns after is, in his eyes, vitiated by poverty and brutality, and it grants a noisy power over all too little. This is part of the unfortunately more ignoble side of Lawrence's lifelong hatred for industrialism. In his middle period he was to concentrate his envy upon the capitalist middle classes, and in his last years he championed primitive societies, where he was reassured male supremacy was not merely a social phenomenon all too often attenuated by class differences, but a religious and total way of life.

The place of the female in such schemes is fairly clear, but in Lawrence's own time it was already becoming a great deal less so. As in *The Rainbow*, this novel's real contrasts are between the older women like his mother, who know their place, and the newer breed, like his mistresses, who fail to discern it. Mrs Morel has her traditional vicarious joys: 'Now she had two sons in the world. She could think of two places, great centers of industry, and feel she had put a man into each of them, that these men would work out what she wanted; they were derived from her, they were of her, and their works would also be hers.'[44] When Paul wins a prize for a painting at Nottingham Castle, she crows, 'Hurrah, my boy! I knew we should do it!'[45] For the rest, she is an eager devotee: 'He was going to alter the face of the earth in some way which mattered. Wherever he went she felt her soul went with him. Whatever he felt her soul stood by him, ready, as it were, to hand him his tools.'[46] She irons his collars with the rapture of a saint: 'It was a joy to her to have him proud of his collars. There was no laundry. So she used to rub away at them with her little convex iron, to polish them till they shone from the sheer pressure of her arm.'[47] Miriam's mother, Mrs Leivers, also goes a way toward making a god of the young egoist: 'She did him that great kindness of treating him almost with reverence.'[48] Lawrence describes with aplomb how Miriam idolizes Paul; even stealing a thrush's nest, he is so superior that she catches her breath: 'He was concentrated on the act. Seeing him so, she loved him; he seemed so simple and sufficient to himself. And she could not get to him.'[49] Here we are treated not only to idealized self-portraiture but to a preview of the later godlike and indifferent Lawrentian male.

Paul is indeed enviable in his rocklike self-sufficiency, basking in the reverence of the bevy of women who surround him, all eager to serve and stroke – all disposable when their time comes. Meredith's *Egoist* is comic exposure; Lawrence's is heroic romance. When Paul first ventures forth into the larger male world, it is again the women who prepare the way for his victories. In a few days he is a favorite of all the 'girls' at Jordan's Surgical Appliances. 'The girls all liked to hear him talk. They often gathered in a little circle while he sat on a bench and held forth to them, laughing.'[50] We are told that 'they all liked him and he adored them'.[51] But as Paul makes his way at the factory the adoration is plainly all on their side. They give him inordinately expensive oil colors for his birthday and he comes more and more to represent the boss, ordering silence, insisting on speed and, although in the time-honored manner of sexual capitalism, he is sleeping with one of his underlings, he insists on a rigid

147

division between sex and business.[52]

The novel's center of conflict is said to lie in Paul's divided loyalty to mother and mistresses. In *Fantasia of the Unconscious*, one of two amateur essays in psychoanalysis in which Lawrence disputes with Freud, he is very explicit about the effect of doting motherhood:

> The son gets on swimmingly... He gleefully inherits his adolescence and the world at large, mother-supported, mother-loved. Everything comes to him in glamour, he feels he sees wondrous much, understands a whole heaven, mother-stimulated. Think of the power which a mature woman thus infuses into her boy. He flares up like a flame in oxygen.

'No wonder they say geniuses mostly have great mothers.'[53] 'They mostly have sad fates', he immediately adds with the same sort of self-pity one detects in the précis.[54] About its negative effects on sons, he is equally explicit, for there comes a time when the mother becomes an obstacle: 'when faced with the actual fact of sex-necessity', the young man meets with his first difficulty:

> What is he actually to do with his sensual, sexual self? Bury it? Or make an effort with a stranger? For he is taught, even by his mother, that his manhood must not forego sex. Yet he is linked up in ideal love already, the best he will ever know... You will not easily get a man to believe that his carnal love for the woman he has made his wife is as high a love as that he felt for his mother or sister.[55]

What such a sceptic will do instead is outlined fairly succinctly in Freud's, 'The Most Prevalent Form of Degradation in Erotic Life', he will make a rigid separation of sex from sensibility, body from soul; he will also develop a rationale to help him through this trying schizophrenic experience. The Victorians employed the lily-rose dichotomy; Lawrence appeared to have invented something new in blaming it on his mother. But the lily/rose division, which Lawrence is so harsh in excoriating in Hardy,[56] is also a prominent feature of *Sons and Lovers*. Miriam is Paul's spiritual mistress, Clara his sexual one – the whole arrangement is carefully planned so that neither is strong enough to offset his mother's ultimate control. Yet the mother too is finally dispensable, not so that Paul may be free to find a complete relationship with either young woman, but simply because he wishes to be rid of the whole pack of his female supporters so that he may venture forth and inherit the great masculine world which awaits him. Therefore the last words of the book are directed, not at the self-sorrowing of Paul's '*nuit blanche*', his 'dereliction' and 'drift towards death', but at the lights of the city, the brave new world which awaits the conqueror.

When Paul wonders incoherently aloud – 'I think there's something the matter with me that I can't...to give myself to them in marriage, I couldn't ...something in me shrinks from her like hell' – just as when Miriam reproaches him, 'It has always been you fighting me off', the reader is expected to follow the précis and the critics and understand that this is all part of the young man's unfortunate Oedipal plight. Lawrence himself attempts to provide a better clue to Paul's type of fixation:

> ...the nicest men he knew...were so sensitive to their women that they would go without them forever rather than do them a hurt. Being the sons of women whose husbands had blundered rather brutally through their feminine sanctities, they themselves were too diffident and shy. They could easier deny themselves than incur any reproach from a woman; for a woman was like their mother, and they were full of the sense of their mother...[57]

Yet all this well-intentioned puritanism dissolves before the reader's observation of the callowness with which Paul treats both Miriam and Clara. The first girl is, like Paul himself, a bright youngster restless within the narrow limitations of her class and anxious to escape it through the learning which has freed Paul. Less privileged than he, enjoying no support in a home where she is bullied by her brothers and taught the most lethal variety of Christian resignation by her mother, she retains some rebellious hope despite her far more discouraging circumstances. Having no one else to turn to, she asks Paul, whom she has worshipped as her senior and superior, to help her eke out an education. The scenes of his condescension are some of the most remarkable instances of sexual sadism disguised as masculine pedagogy which literature affords until Ionesco's memorable *Lesson*.

Paul has grandly offered to teach her French and mathematics. We are told that Miriam's 'eyes dilated. She mistrusted him as a teacher.'[58] Well she might, in view of what follows. Paul is explaining simple equations to her:

> 'Do you see?' she looked up at him, her eyes wide with the half-laugh that comes of fear. 'Don't you?' he cried... It made his blood boil to see her there, as it were, at his mercy, her mouth open, her eyes dilated with laughter that was afraid, apologetic, ashamed. Then Edgar came along with two buckets of milk.
> 'Hello!' he said. 'What are you doing?'
> 'Algebra,' replied Paul.
> 'Algebra!' repeated Edgar curiously. Then he passed on with a laugh.[59]

Paul is roused by the mixture of tears and beauty; Miriam is beautiful to him when she suffers and cringes; 'She was ruddy and beautiful. Yet her soul seemed to be intensely supplicating. The algebra book she closed, shrinking, knowing he was angered.'[60]

As she is self-conscious and without confidence (Miriam's sense of inferiority is the key to her character), she cannot learn well: 'Things came slowly to her. And she held herself in a grip, seemed so utterly humble before the lesson, it made his blood rouse.'[61] Blood rouse is, of course, the Lawrentian formula for sexual excitement and an erection; the algebra lesson is something of a symbol for the couple's entire relationship. The sight of Miriam suffering or humiliated (she later gives Paul her virginity in a delirium of both emotions) is the very essence of her attractiveness to him, but his response is never without an element of hostility and sadism. His reaction here is typical: 'In spite of himself, his blood began to boil with her. It was strange that no one else made him in such a fury. He flared against her. Once he threw the pencil in her face. There was a silence. She turned her face slightly aside.'[62] Of course, Miriam is not angry, for one does not get angry at God. 'When he saw her eager, silent, as it were, blind face, he felt he wanted to throw the pencil in it...and because of the intensity with which she roused him, he sought her.'[63] The reader is made uncomfortably aware that 'pencil' is etymologically, and perhaps even in the author's conscious mind as well, related to 'penis' and both are instruments which have here become equated with literacy and punishment.

Miriam's aspirations are not respected; her failures are understood to be due to inferiority of talent. There are also a great many explanations provided the reader that she is frigid, and everything in her situation would seem to confirm this. Her mother's literal Victorian repugnance toward sexuality is the most plausible explanation, even without our knowledge of Miriam's debilitating insecurity. When she thinks of giving herself to Paul, she foresees beforehand that 'he would be disappointed, he would find no satisfaction, and then he would go away'. The chapter where Paul finally brings her to bed is entitled, 'The Test on Miriam'. Needless to say, she does not measure up, cannot pass his demanding examination. So her prediction comes true and Paul throws her away and takes up Clara. Yet the situation is somehow not this simple; even within the muddled explanations of Lawrence's text, it is several times made clear that Paul withholds himself quite as much as does Miriam.[64] Her famous frigidity appears to be his excuse. In the classic dilemma of the lily/rose choice Paul has been provided with an alibi which passes responsibility on to his mother.

While the first half of *Sons and Lovers* is perfectly realized, the second part is deeply flawed by Lawrence's overparticipation in Paul's endless scheming to disentangle himself from the persons who have helped him most. Lawrence is so ambivalent here that he is far from being clear, or perhaps even honest, and he offers us two contrary reasons for Paul's rejection of Miriam. One is that she will 'put him in her pocket'. And the other, totally contradictory, is the puzzling excuse that in their last interview, she failed him by not seizing upon and claiming him as her mate and property.

It would seem that for reasons of his own, Lawrence has chosen to confuse the sensitive and intelligent young woman who was Jessie Chambers[65] with the tired old lily of another age's literary convention. The same discrepancy is noticeable in his portrait of Clara,[66] who is really two people, the rebellious feminist and political activist whom Paul accuses of penis envy and even man-hating, and who tempts him the more for being a harder conquest, and, at a later stage, the sensuous rose who by the end of the novel is changed once again – now beyond recognition – into a 'loose woman' whom Paul nonchalantly disposes of when he has exhausted her sexual utility. Returning her to her husband, Paul even finds it convenient to enter into one of Lawrence's *Blutbruderschaft* bonds with Baxter Dawes, arranging an assignation in the country where Clara, meek as a sheep, is delivered over to the man she hated and left years before. The text makes it clear that Dawes had beat and deceived his wife. Yet, with a consummate emotional manipulation, Paul manages to impose his own version of her marriage on Clara, finally bringing her to say that its failure was her fault. Paul, formerly her pupil in sexuality, now imagines he has relieved Clara of what he smugly described as the *femme incomprise* quality which had driven her to the errors of feminism. We are given to understand that through the sexual instruction of this novice, Clara was granted feminine 'fulfillment'. Paul is now pleased to make a gift of Clara to her former owner fancying, that as the latter has degenerated through illness and poverty (Paul has had Dawes fired) he ought to be glad of salvaging such a brotherly cast off.

Even before it provides Paul with sexual gratification, the affair offers considerable opportunities for the pleasure of bullying:

'Here, I say, you seem to forget I'm your boss. It just occurs to me.'
'And what does that mean?' she asked coolly.
'It means I've got a right to boss you.'
'Is there anything you want to complain about?'
'Oh, I say, you needn't be nasty,' he said angrily.
'I don't know what you want,' she said, continuing her task.
'I want you to treat me nicely and respectfully.'
'Call you, "sir", perhaps?' she asked quietly.
'Yes, call me "sir". I should love it.'[67]

The sexual therapy Clara affords to Paul is meant to be a balm to his virulent Oedipal syndrome, but is even more obviously a salve to his ego. Only in the fleeting moments of the orgasm can the egoist escape his egotism, but Lawrence's account fails to confirm this:

> She knew how stark and alone he was, and she felt it was great that he
> came to her, and she took him simply because his need was bigger than
> either her or him, and her soul was still within her. She did this for him
> in his need, even if he left her, for she loved him.[68]

This is a dazzling example of how men think women ought to think, but
the book is full of them. By relieving his 'needs' with a woman he rigidly
confines to a 'stranger in the dark' category, Paul has touched the great
Lawrentian sexual mystery and discovered 'the cry of the peewit' and the
'wheel of the stars'.[69]

Having achieved this transcendence through Clara's offices, he finds it
convenient to dismiss her. While watching her swim far out at sea during
a holiday they have taken together, Paul converts himself into a species of
god in the universe before whom Clara dwindles to the proportions of
microscopic life: 'Look how little she is!' he said to himself. 'She's lost like
a grain of sand in the beach – just a concentrated speck blown along, a tiny
white foam-bubble, almost nothing among the morning... She represents
something, like a bubble of foam represents the sea. But what is *she*. It's
not her I care for.'[70] This is an impressive demonstration of how subject
diminishes object and having, through his sexual magnetism, reduced this
once formidable, independent woman to the level of quivering passion,
Paul cannot help but find her a nuisance. What if their affair were
discovered at work? We are told that 'She invariably waited for him at
dinner-time for him to embrace her before she went.'[71] Paul reacts to such
attentions like the bumptious young clerk he has become:

> 'Surely there's a time for everything... I don't want anything to do with
> love when I'm at work. Work's work – '
> 'And what is love?' she asked. 'Has it to have special hours?'
> 'Yes, out of work hours.'...
> 'Is it only to exist in spare time?'
> 'That's all, and not always then.'[72]

It is Paul's habit to lecture his mistresses that, as women, they are
incapable of the sort of wholehearted attention to task or achievement that
is the province of the male and the cause of his superiority: 'I suppose
work can be everything to a man... But a woman only works with a part
of herself. The real and vital part is covered up.'[73] The idea seems to be
that the female's lower nature, here gently phrased as her 'true nature' is
incapable of objective activity and finds its only satisfactions in human
relationship where she may be of service to men and to children. Men in
later Lawrence novels, men such as Aaron, constantly ridicule trivial
female efforts at art or ideas.

Given such views, it is not very surprising that Paul should make such excellent use of women, Clara included, and when they have outlived their usefulness to him, discard them. As Clara is a creature of the double standard of morality, the woman as rose or sensuality, he invokes the double standard to get rid of her , declaring sententiously that 'after all, she was a married woman and she had no right even to what he gave her.'[74] He finally betakes himself to a fustian view of the indissolubility of marriage, decrees that she is completely Dawes's property, and with a sense of righteousness, returns her no worse, indeed, much the better, for wear.

Having rid himself of the two young women, time-consuming sex objects, who may have posed some other threat as well, possibly one of intellectual competition, Paul is free to make moan over his mother's corpse, give Miriam a final brush-off, and turn his face to the city. The elaborate descriptions of his suicidal state, however much they may spring from a deep, though much earlier, sorrow over the loss of his mother, appear rather tacked on in the book itself, as do certain of the Freudian explanations of his coldness as being due to his mother's baneful influence. Paul is actually in brilliant condition when the novel ends, having extracted every conceivable service from his women, now neatly disposed of, so that he may go on to grander adventures. Even here, the force of his mother, the endless spring of Lawrence's sacred font, will support him: 'She was the only thing that held him up, himself amid all this. And she was gone, intermingled herself.'[75] But Paul has managed to devour all of mother that he needs; the meal will last a lifetime. And the great adventure of his success will henceforward be his own. 'Turning sharply, he walked toward the city's gold phosphorescence. His fists were shut, his mouth set fast.'[76] Paul may now dismiss his mother's shade with confidence, all she had to offer is with him still.

Notes

1. D. H. LAWRENCE, *Lady Chatterley's Lover*, written 1928, (New York: Random House, 1957), pp. 237–8.

2. Ibid., p. 238.

3. It had been Lawrence's consistent practice to veil the sanctities of sex in vague phrases about cosmic flight, movement into space, and so forth, while the trademark adjectives droned its tedious 'deep, deep, deep' refrain at the reader. *Lady Chatterley* contains the only wholly explicit sexual descriptions in his work.

4. D. H. LAWRENCE, *Lady Chatterley's Lover*, p. 238.

5. SIMONE DE BEAUVOIR, *The Second Sex* (New York: Knopf, 1953), p. 209.

6. LAWRENCE, op. cit., p. 237.

7. Ibid., p. 201.

8. Ibid., p. 197.

9. This is true despite the great insight Lawrence displays about the nature of sexual inhibition and prurience, brutality and shame in A *Propos Lady Chatterley's Lover* and in his other critical essays on sex and censorship. Here, too, he is busy affirming that the phallus is not only the bridge to the future, but the very essence of marriage and life itself. His silence as regards to female genitals is most remarkable, and evidence, I believe, of considerable inhibition and very probably of strongly negative feelings. In Henry Miller one encounters the same phenomenon in a more severe form.

10. Ibid., p. 197.

11. Ibid., p. 246.

12. D . H. LAWRENCE, *The Plumed Serpent*, written 1923 (New York: Knopf, 1951), p. 463.

13. LEE RAINWATER, *And the Poor Get Children* (Chicago: Quadrangle, 1960).

14. LAWRENCE, *Lady Chatterley's Lover*, p. 250.

15. Ibid., pp. 250–1.

16. Ibid., pp. 280–1.

17. Ibid., p. 281.

18. One remembers that Mellors' first love was his colonel. With the exception of *Sons and Lovers* and *The Rainbow*, every Lawrence novel includes some symbolically surrogate scene of pederasty: the rubdowns in *The White Peacock* and *Aaron's Rod*, the consecration scene in *The Plumed Serpent*, the kiss denied in *Kangaroo* and the wrestling scene in *Women in Love*.

19. LAWRENCE, *Lady Chatterley's Lover*, p. 82.

20. Ibid., p. 127.

21. Ibid., p. 126.

22. Ibid., p. 127.

23. Ibid., p. 129.

24. Ibid., p. 130.

25. Ibid., p. 130.

26. Ibid., pp. 130–1.

27. D. H. LAWRENCE, *The Letters of D.H. Lawrence*, ed. Aldous Huxley (New York: Viking, 1932), p. 719. To Witter Bynner, 13 March, 1928:

> I sniffed the red herring in your last letter a long time: then at last decided it's a live sprat. I mean about *The Plumed Serpent* and 'the hero'. On the whole, I think you're right. The hero is obsolete, and the leader of men is a back number...the leader-cum-follower relationship is a bore. And the new relationship will be some sort of the tenderness, sensitive, between men and men and men and women, and not the one up, one down, lead on I follow, *ich dien* sort of business.... But still, in a way, one has to fight... I feel one still has to fight for the phallic reality...

28. LAWRENCE, *The Letters of D.H. Lawrence*, pp. 78–9.

29. LAWRENCE, *Sons and Lovers* (1913). (New York: Viking, 1958), p. 356.

30. Ibid., p. 166.

31. One of the most influential essays on *Sons and Lovers* is Van Ghent's article, which describes Paul as a victim of scheming and possessive women. Dorothy Van Ghent, *The English Novel: Form and Function* (New York: Rinehart and Company, 1953).

32. Lawrence rewrote the book at least twice. The final version, like the précis, was done after Frieda 'explained' Freudian theory to Lawrence.

33. The narrative of William's funeral, especially the moment when the coffin is brought into the house, the class honesty of the Christmas parties, and the daily life of Mrs Morel, are, in my opinion, the most convincing and poignant prose Lawrence ever wrote.

34. LAWRENCE, *Sons and Lovers*, p. 66.

35. Ibid., p. 213. 'I was born hating my father: as ever I can remember, I shivered with horror when he touched me… This has been a kind of bond between me and my mother. We have loved each other, almost with a husband and wife love… We knew each other by instinct.' From a letter to Rachel Annand Taylor, 3 Dec., 1910. From the *Collected Letters of D. H. Lawrence*, Vol I, ed. Harry T. Moore (New York: Viking, 1962) , pp. 69–70.

36. Ibid., p. 214.

37. GRAHAM HOUGH, *The Dark Sun, A Study of D. H. Lawrence* (New York: Capricorn, 1956), p. 31.

38. See Alfred Kazin, 'Sons, Lovers and Mothers', in the *Viking Critical Edition of Sons and Lovers*, ed. Julian Moynahan (New York: Viking, 1968), p. 599.

39. LAWRENCE, *Sons and Lovers*, p. 388.

40. Ibid., pp. 388, 393.

41. Ibid., p. 394.

42. The miners divide their money out of the presence of women, who are thereby prevented from interfering on the behalf of household and child-rearing expenses. See pp. 6, 17, 196, 200.

43. LAWRENCE, *Sons and Lovers*, p. 20.

44. Ibid., p. 101.

45. Ibid., p. 253.

46. Ibid., p. 222.

47. Ibid., p. 55. (*Portnoy's Complaint* is a healthy antidote to this sort of thing.)

48. Ibid., p. 223.

49. Ibid., p. 223.

50. Ibid., p. 110.

51. Ibid. In Lawrence's day, as in ours, it is customary in business to refer to all low-status female employees, e.g., the vast majority of women workers, as 'girls', whatever their age, and some of Paul's co-workers were twice or thrice his age. The custom bears a curious resemblance to that one whereby black men are addressed as 'boy' right through senility.

52. JULIAN MOYNAHAN, 'Sons and Lovers; the Search for Form', in the Viking critical edition of *Sons and Lovers*, p. 569. Like much else in the novel, Paul's phenomenal success with the factory women appears to be an instance of wish fulfillment. Lawrence quit a similar factory job 'after a few weeks because the factory girls jeered at him and one day removed his trousers in a dark corner of the storerooms'.

53. D. H. LAWRENCE, *Fantasia of the Unconscious* (1922). (New York: Viking, 1960), p. 159.

54. Ibid.

55. Ibid., pp. 169–70.

56. D. H. LAWRENCE, 'A Study of Thomas Hardy', reprinted in *Phoenix, the Posthumous Papers of D. H. Lawrence* (New York: Viking, 1936).

57. LAWRENCE, *Sons and Lovers*, p. 279.

58. Ibid., p. 155.

59. Ibid., p. 156.

60. Ibid.

61. Ibid.

62. Ibid., p. 157.

63. Ibid.

64. Ibid., p. 284.

65. See Jessie Chambers, *D. H. Lawrence, A Personal Record*, By 'E.T' 2nd revised ed. (New York: Barnes and Noble, 1965).

66. Actually, Clara is nobody at all. Tradition has it that Lawrence's initiatrix was a Mrs Dax who simply took pity on the lad: 'She took him upstairs one afternoon because she thought he needed it.' Julian Moynahan, *op. cit.*, p. 569.

67. LAWRENCE, *Sons and Lovers*, p. 266.

68. Ibid., p. 353.

69. Ibid.

70. Ibid., pp. 357–8.

71. Ibid., p. 355.

72. Ibid.

73. Ibid., p. 416.

74. Ibid., p. 352.

75. Ibid., p. 420.

76. Ibid.

Cora Kaplan 'RADICAL FEMINISM AND LITERATURE: RETHINKING MILLETT'S *SEXUAL POLITICS*'*

Cora Kaplan's essay, 'Radical Feminism and Literature: Rethinking Millett's *Sexual Politics*' (1979), lambasts Millett. Kaplan's exasperation at what she sees as the weaknesses of a radical-feminist reading of literature is held in check only by the keen intelligence of her argument. Though recognizing Millett's important role in undermining the 'liberal consensus about sexual representation', Kaplan complains that Millett's understanding of ideology, of the work of Freud, of the political nature of literary criticism, are all unsatisfactory. Kaplan believes that Millett's preoccupation with a patriarchal ideology and power which supersedes all other differences – class, or race, or culture – fails to account for the complex interrelation of determinants in the life of any woman. She finds Millett's reading of Freud partial and resolved to prove a consistent misogyny. Finally, Kaplan claims that in Millett's literary analysis the fictive nature of writing is ignored; anti-women comments in the text are interpreted as the author's firmly held opinion. Other critics have been somewhat kinder to Millett, concentrating on the historical and political significance of Millett's text rather than its theoretical weaknesses. But Kaplan's essay retains its status as a powerfully argued critique (see Introduction, pp. 17–18).

With the publication of Kate Millett's *Sexual Politics* (1970) radical feminist theory can be said to have 'come out', costumed, not surprisingly, in something old – refurbished bits and pieces of sixties New Left radicalism – as well as something new – 'a systematic overview of patriarchy as a political institution'.[1] Millett's reworking of 'patriarchy' is conceptually co-ordinated with the left-libertarian policies that underwrote the civil rights, anti-imperialist and counter-culture movements. From this tendency *Sexual Politics* retained a violent hostility to the 'functionalist' bias of the academy coupled with a mildly receptive if somewhat duff ear for Marx and Engels, the latter modified by a firm rejection of Stalinist old-left politics. Patriarchy was defined as 'a political institution' rather than an economic or social relation and political institutions were in their turn conceived as hierarchical power relations. Institutions were conceptualized as expressing oppression in homologous or analogous ways, so that the State, the Family, the University, the Mental

---

* CORA KAPLAN, 'Radical Feminism and Literature: Rethinking Millett's *Sexual Politics*', *Red Letters*, 9, 1979. Reprinted in Kaplan, *Sea Changes: Essays on Culture and Feminism* (London: Verso, 1986), pp. 15–30.

Hospital or the Army, instead of having differentiated structures and a complex articulation were, instead, metaphors for each other, emphasising through their similarities the dominance relations of the society as a whole, which were characterized by racism, sexism and capitalism. This type of analysis, which owed a great deal to the functionalism it refused, provided a theoretical justification for struggle on all possible sites in the sixties. The campus thus became as valid a place to fight as Mississippi. While it is unfair to ridicule or denigrate the resistance of the decade, it is crucial for us now to understand where this analysis, so simple and often so simply wrong, was instrumental in the creation of radical feminist theory.

Millett's influential book is especially useful if one asks why so disproportionate a number of declared feminists have chosen literature as the particular object of their analysis of female subordination. For even given the relatively large numbers of academic women who read arts subjects rather than economics, politics or labour relations, and taking into account the primacy that 'ideology' holds in feminist theories of all political complexions, the attention given to literature as a source of patriarchal ideology or feminist liberation is peculiar, and surely requires some explanation and political justification. *Sexual Politics*, one of the most readable and innovative texts of the modern women's movement, helps to make sense of this tendency. Almost half the book is devoted to the theoretical and historical development of patriarchy; the third section examines *The Literary Reflection* as revealed in the work of four male authors, D H Lawrence, Henry Miller, Norman Mailer and Jean Genet. In this final section Millett has made a lasting intervention in literary criticism. Since *Sexual Politics* it has been difficult for critics to ignore the wider social and political implications of the representation of sexual practice in fiction. In taking issue with Millett's interpretations, critics, myself included, have been forced on to her ground, made to admit that the depiction of sex in literature is an ideological issue for author, reader, and critic. Once you have read Millett, an 'innocent' enjoyment of the sexual in literature is almost sure to be lost. This breaking-up of an unthinking 'broadminded', liberal consensus about sexual representation has been a major achievement. *Sexual Politics* sets another excellent precedent, not generally acknowledged. Unlike most recent feminist books on literature, even including Ellen Moers' brilliant, eclectic study of *Literary Women*,[2] *Sexual Politics* sets literary analysis against a specific theory of women's subordination, in relation to ideologies of gender difference inscribed in other contemporary discourses and practices. The book provides the material for its own critique.

Rereading the first half of *Sexual Politics* is still rewarding. Millett had researched very widely; she touched most of the issues that feminists had developed in the seventies. The historical section marks off the period

1830–1930 as a time of 'Sexual Revolution' and the period of 1930–60 as
'The Counter-revolution'. Even this periodizaton, indicating a radical
putsch and inevitable backlash, harks back to a very sixties left description
of the ebb and flow of radical movements. In the course of her historical
exposition there are valuable discussions of Mill and Engels, and a more
central if wildly uneven account of the sinister patriarchal implications in
the development of psychoanalytic and social theory.

Millett's prose is often richer than her arguments, but even so the first
half of the book is so full of matter that it is sometimes difficult to keep
track of the logic of her analysis. She is centrally concerned to show how
patriarchal ideology has kept pace with profound changes in attitudes
towards sexuality, which in Millett's broad definition generally means
social, economic and political relations between men and women, but
occasionally means sexuality alone. It would require a much longer piece
to deal fully with Millett's concept of the workings of patriarchy; for the
purposes of this essay I want to concentrate on two theoretical issues
which have far-reaching implications for Millett's literary analysis: the
first is her understanding of 'ideology' within her larger definition of
patriarchy, and the second, related to the first but narrower in scope, is her
critique of Freud. Once Millett's position on these subjects has been
located it becomes much easier to see why she has tackled literature
through male writers almost exclusively, and why Lawrence, Miller,
Mailer and Genet have been chosen instead of an alternative group
composed say, of James, Fitzgerald, Updike and Baldwin, novelists
equally obsessed with the social and political implications of sexuality. We
can see why literature, such an important area of concern for radical
feminism, remains, even in the hands of a skilful and academically trained
critic like Millett, virtually untheorized.

Radical feminism and ideology

Under the sixties' slogan 'the personal is political' a space was made for
feminists to include the psychological effects of female socialization as one
of the principal oppressions suffered by women in male-dominated
societies. Franz Fanon and Kenneth Clark (the Black sociologist) had
offered prior analyses of the internalized effects of racism in colonial
countries and in the United States. It was easy to see that if racial
stereotyping could induce feelings of inferiority and difference, gender
distinctions, even more widely held by human societies, could be instilled
at a deep level. Successful struggle by Africans and American Blacks
against racism showed that its effects were damaging but not permanent.
At the same time as Fanon, Clark and others were exploring the

psychological implications of racist and imperialist ideologies, the radical right were heralding the end of ideology – by which they meant the political and social theories held by the left. In choosing a working definition of ideology, feminists did not hesitate to choose a loosely Marxist conception in which ideology was a world seen upside-down, alienated, mystified – a false representation that reflected the alienating conditions in which people lived. This definition is largely drawn from early Marxist texts that liberal academics in the sixties were pulling out of the dying fires to which they had been consigned by zealous book-burning McCarthyites a few years earlier. However, both the early and late Marx held that ideologies are formed by material conditions of existence related to historically specific modes of production. One may go quite far in insisting on the relative autonomy of ideology, and still call oneself a Marxist, but one can never see ideology escaping a necessary dialectical relation with a given mode of production. However much the American New Left in the sixties concentrated on the political at the expense of the economic, however much it confused consciousness with struggle, it never quite forgot about capitalism, nor did it generally abandon the Marxist concept of determination by the base, the economy, in the last instance, even if the last instance seemed as far off as the last trump. However, a sea change occurs with the development of radical feminist theory, which insists on the primacy of gender difference over all other determinations. In Marxist theory ideologies of the bourgeoisie and the proletariat were seen as class specific ideologies dictated by class divisions created by capitalism, with bourgeois ideology dominant. 'Ideology' in Marxist shorthand means bourgeois ideology. In radical feminist theory the notion of a dominant ideology, of a ruling group as distinct, say, from a 'national' ideology is retained, as is the concept of ideology as a false representation. However, now *only* patriarchal ideology ruled, an ideology that ignored and/or transcended class division. Radical feminism is by no means a theoretical unity, any more than Marxism, or Marxist-feminism. Within radical feminism the origin of women's subordination is variously described, yet it is always at pains to point out that the transhistorical, transcultural, transclass character of women's oppression proves that patriarchy is much more fundamental in the determination of women's condition of existence than the effects of any given mode of production. The original conditions under which men seized power over women, or maintained it at subsequent historical moments, hardly matters. What does matter is that power is maintained by men through ideologies of gender inequality. Just as Marx characterises capital as having as its *raison d'être* the extraction of surplus value (unpaid labour) from the worker, so patriarchy's reason-for-being in this unmediated definition is to ensure the domination of men over women. It is easy to see how patriarchy becomes, given this emphasis, primarily a power relation, and patriarchal ideology its energy source.

Millett on Freud has become so familiar a part of anti-patriarchal rhetoric that there is some danger when looking again at Millett's anti-Freud passages[3] of watching mesmerized as the knife blade makes a telling stroke here and there at Viennese phallocentrism and assuming the rest of the argument, as it has been taken up by Shulamith Firestone and others.[4] A more dutiful rereading is interesting. Millett's technique is to isolate elements of Freudian theory drawn from different periods and kinds of writing in order to emphasise the gross chauvinism of certain passages on women – as well as to ridicule the methodology together with the conclusions. She sees Freud's work on women as giving a pseudo-scientific imprimatur to biological determinism, and, further, to be motivated centrally by Freud's distaste for 'feminist insurgence'. Penis envy, Millett's particular *bête, noire* or *blanche*, was 'in fact a superbly timed accusation, enabling masculine sentiment to take the offensive again as it had not since the disappearance of overt misogyny when the pose of chivalry became fashionable'.[5] As Millett herself points out later, in a rather more acute and milder discussion of Erik Erickson on women, chivalry is simply a polite form of misogyny. In any case her dating of the disappearance of overt misogyny is fuzzy. Did it ever disappear? Or does it simply recede in Millett's account so that she can place Freud in the foreground as the arch-enemy of feminism? Here is an unhappily typical example of Millett's polemic, which itself commits the errors which she lays at Freud's door:

> Freud's circular method in formulating penis envy begins by reporting children's distorted impressions, gradually comes to accept them as the correct reaction, goes on to present its own irresponsible version of the socio-sexual context, and then, through a nearly imperceptible series of transitions, slides from description to a form of prescription which ensures the continuance of the patriarchal status quo, under the guise of health and normality. Apart from ridicule, the counter-revolutionary period never employed a more withering or destructive weapon against feminist insurgence than the Freudian accusation of penis envy.[6]

Note the ambiguous use of 'children's distorted impressions' and the substitution of 'irresponsible' for incorrect. Millett concentrates on Freud's ascription of penis envy, narcissism and masochism to women. She does not concern herself very much *here* with oedipalization and its consequences, or the concept of the unconscious, nor nearly enough with Freud's general point that our social identity is constructed through our taking on the position of one sex or another at an early age. Millett even feels that Freud's promisingly liberated theory that all humans are basically bisexual is vitiated because he still wishes to see healthy adults as normal at widely differentiated points in the spectrum of socialized gender difference. She insists that Freud's theories on women are an example of biological determinism, with women locked into their natural role of mothers. But even here she is convinced that Freud manages to denigrate women, denying them autonomy in this inferior role, by posing babies as penis substitutes. Freud's point is indirectly made but it seems pretty clearly to be about the unfair social overdetermination of the value of maleness in society. Millett opts for a deliberate misreading for the sake of a cheap flash: 'It somehow becomes the male prerogative even to give birth, as babies are but surrogate penises...were she to deliver an entire orphanage of progeny, they would only be so many dildoes.'[7]

Millett's comments on Freud's deeply contradictory writings on women are frequently illuminating, but the whole attack is conducted with so much blinding vitriol, and is so determined not to salvage even a castrated version of Freudian theory that she weakens her case. Freud did not, after all, invent patriarchy; his chauvinism is of a very old-fashioned kind. It is hard to believe that 'penis envy', crude as its application has been, has smashed more female ambitions than its older common sense cousin, which merely sneered that women who entered 'male' occupations were imitation men. Marxist-feminists, starting with Juliet Mitchell in *Psychoanalysis and Feminism*, feel that Freud and some modern members of his school have done more to enable understanding of gender construction in spite of the phallocentric bias of their work than other psychoanalytic theorists seemingly more sympathetic to women. These feminists are now concerned with revision and reinterpretation of Freud's work, and an exploration of its uses for materialist theories of ideology. Millett, however, had to reject the unconscious, the pivotal concept in Freud, and something common to human subjects of both sexes, because she is committed to a view that patriarchal ideology is a conscious conspiratorial set of attitudes operated by men against all empirical evidence of women's equal status, in order to support patriarchal power in office. It must be imposed on an essential, but already social, female subject who is not tainted with femininity, passivity, penis envy, narcissism, and so on. Freud's understanding of the internalization of femininity is indeed conservative, even pessimistic from certain feminist perspectives, and Millett is out to prove that, though the conspirators are formidable, the struggle is easier than we think. To this end she is not even afraid to misquote that most famous of Freud's pronouncements on women which comes at the end of his essay on 'Femininity' where he warns his readers that he has discussed women 'only insofar as their nature is determined by their sexual function'.[8] (This reservation, of course, governs most of his discussions of men, as well.) Millett naughtily clips this sentence so that 'Freud warns that "their nature is determined by their sexual function."'[9] Freud's destiny at Millett's hands is determined less by his anatomy than the 'cheap and chippy chopping' of his words.

Juliet Mitchell in *Psychoanalysis and Feminism*[10] refuses the simple homologies of Millett's analysis, and rehabilitates for English-speaking readers Freudian theory and its modern articulation, both as part of an analysis of femininity and as a way of introducing a more complex and comprehensible theory of ideology into Marxist-feminist thought. Her contribution is invaluable and has been widely influential in providing a powerful critique of Millett. But the integration of Marx and Freud, by Mitchell and others, has not proved easy. Mitchell, following Louis Althusser's use of Freud and Lacan, makes the unconscious central to the workings of ideology. She lays a heavy emphasis on the importance of oedipalization in the development of femininity. Ideology is endowed with a material existence and given a 'relative autonomy' from other determinations, thus avoiding a crudely economistic analysis of female subordination, but separating ideology from the mode of production so that their interrelation is hard to specify. For 'if the kinship system that defines matriarchy' (now redundant) is 'forced into the straightjacket of the nuclear family', the family in capitalism, how can it be forced out again?[11] The functionalist formulation of these problems may help to define the problem but it also tends towards the production of dualistic analyses of the economy and female socialization as they articulate women's subordination in modern industrial societies. Freudian theory, with its emphasis on repetition and reproduction of ideological positions, emphasises, perhaps too heavily, the unalterable distance between gender positions so that they remain rather like Marvell's 'Definition of Love' stuck at distant poles, 'begotten by Despair/Upon Impossibility'.

Moreover there is a peculiar congruence between Millett and Mitchell, which stems from their common preoccupation with 'ideology'. Millett's already constituted 'free' female subject, who has only to throw off her ideological bondage, boards in the same house where Mitchell's internally bound 'lady' lives her ideological imprisonment in material ideology. Neither of them really works for a living, or at least not in the sense in which women who are considered more fully in terms in class and gender work. For this establishment whether it goes under the name of Relative Autonomy or Idealism is marked by its transhistorical and transclass character, and houses only the oldest profession; its inmates are women who trade exclusively in their sexuality.

The tendency both of Mitchell's Marxist-feminist structuralism and Millett's radical feminist idealism is to displace the complex if mundane questions of women's subordination through the sexual division of labour under different modes of production. Mitchell poses the contradiction between patriarchy and capitalism as a loophole through which feminism can view the creation of the feminine unconscious, but like big Alice with her eye to the keyhole there's not much she can do about it. Patriarchy creates and recreates the psychic conditions for women's subordination which are not the thin voile of false consciousness, but rather the very flesh and blood of female subjectivity. It must be hoped, given this analysis, that struggle can take place where patriarchal ideology and capitalist ideology and interests clash. This is certainly an argument worth having and one which certain Marxist-feminists are taking up. Mitchell's own explorations of the problem run into difficulty where she continues to use a very formalist description of 'levels' in which women's work is the most remote and sketchy, and her psychic processes the most prominent and solid. In Millett, on the other hand, capitalism has disappeared except as an effect of patriarchy. Ideology is the universal penile club that men of all classes use to beat women. Women *do not* beat themselves. The unconscious, both its formulation and its effects, are denied and 'penis envy' has only to be exposed as the pathetic support to patriarchal power that it is for women, the real women hidden under male propaganda to be free in their individual consciousness if not yet *en masse*. As a consequence of this optimistic view very few women speak for themselves in the pages of *Sexual Politics*, maybe because a real woman is hard to find. Millett lets her male chauvinist social scientists and authors speak about them; even feminist fellow travellers like Mill and Engels are more prominent than nineteenth-century feminist voices. Gender renegades, such as Mill and Engels are allowed to espouse contradictions, but feminism itself must be positivistic, fully conscious, morally and politically correct. It must know what it wants, and since what many women wanted was full of contradictions and confusions, still entangled in what patriarchy wanted them to be or wanted for them, Millett does not let them reveal too much of their 'weakness'.

Ideology and Literature

In Millett's world weakness and masochism are male projections of women's character. She believes that Freud's theories and Lawrence's fictions are discourses of essentially the same order and type, except that one provides the scientific rationale for the other. Hardest to accept in Millett's literary analysis is the unproblematic identification of author, protagonist and point of view, and the unspoken assumption that literature is always a conscious rendering of an authorial ideology. Although this assumption slips now and then, it is always shoved back stage centre. For if the unconscious were allowed expression then the writer would be, like the dreamer, or the children with 'distorted' ideas about sexuality, off the hook. If he were, slyly, to disengage somewhat from his most monstrous creations then he would be like Freud lying in the name of objectivity. Millett loves Lawrence, Mailer, Miller and Genet because they seem to be so autobiographically centred in their work.

Consequently Millett has more respect for MCP novelists than for their brother psychoanalysts or social scientists, for although literature is, in her view, a 'reflection' of the reality of patriarchal ideology it at least admits to being an imaginary tale of male potency. It accepts, in part, its status as a fiction. Moreover it takes the place of the revelations of psychoanalysts in that it discloses the relationship between sexuality and sociality without reference to objective knowledge of their real relationship, that is without the intervention of social science 'proofs'. Lawrence, Miller and Mailer are analyst and patient rolled into one, the only begetters of male fantasies that they themselves interpret. And since, in Millett's words, literature affords large insights 'into the life it describes, or interprets, or even distorts',[12] the critic can make 'a radical investigation which can demonstrate why Lawrence's analysis of a situation is inadequate, or biased, or his influence pernicious, without ever needing to imply that he is less than a great and original artist, and in many respects a man of distinguished moral and intellectual integrity'.[13] One does not have to quarrel with this judgement of Lawrence to wonder why it cannot be applied equally to Freud, why in the midst of this radical reordering of values only great art, of all the patriarchal discourses, survives the dust heap or the pyre. It would be easy, too easy, to call Millett's preference for the true art of lying, bourgeois humanism, to see its conversion in the too uncritical praise of other feminist critics for women's art, cultural feminism, and to criticize both attitudes as 'elitist' or sentimental. There is another more disturbing element in Millett's stay of execution. Phallocratic novelists can survive in Millett's brave new world because they have performed exactly as patriarchal ideologists are supposed to. Caught in the missionary position, in the act of 'describing, interpreting and distorting life simultaneously', the male novelists can only plead guilty to creating women consciously to do his bidding and fulfil his desires. Literature emerges, in this view, as having a formal homology with the working of patriarchy, except in literature the male writer can, presumably, have it all his own way. Millett reads *Sons and Lovers, Tropic of Cancer* or 'The Time of Her Time' as models of patriarchal power in action, sadistic, depersonalized sexuality and the subordination of women in full swing. But since the writing is fiction the author can be represented as telling the truth about his desires and gross falsehoods about cultural reality. Millett's contempt for Freud is based on her belief that he is doing the same thing behind the mask of science. Writers are confessed criminals, or better still, criminal informers; they have integrity because they admit to their lack of it. Ironically, this is also why Millett prefers her phallocratic authors to be reliable narrators who identify wholly with their protagonists, although she recognizes uncomfortably that even these unregenerate chauvinists can occasionally act as double agents and project into their women characters. To fit her case they must be immersed, without contradiction, in their ideology of gender polarity and male dominance, so that their fictions become the ideal empirical verification of patriarchy's desired practice.

The consequence of this position is that Millett interrogates text and author simultaneously, using a popularized version of Freudian theory as it relates to male psychology as the major tool in her analysis. Discrete points are often sharp and revealing but since three different objects, author, text and social relations not to mention 'politics' have been collapsed into a single object the conclusions she draws from her readings are inevitably muddled. One can only look at a few examples of this process in action.

Millett has especial trouble in making *Lady Chatterley's Lover* fit her schema. She acknowledges that it is Lawrence's most sympathetic book about women, his 'attempt to make his peace with the female',[14] that it contains little of the sexual violence so prominent in Miller and Mailer, and even offers 'a program for social as well as sexual redemption'.[15] Generously, she reminds us that Lawrence's working title for the novel was 'Tenderness'.[16] Then she launches her attack on the book, using the crudest form of Freudian literary interpretation which reduces the author's work to his early familial relationships. As with penis envy, but with less justification, Millett assumes that the Oedipus complex is inevitably a pathological diagnosis instead of an essential process in human development which can under certain circumstances produce adult neurosis or pathology. She intimates somehow that Freud has invented it because he suffers from it, calling him 'another Oedipal son', like Lawrence.[17] As Millett deals with the relationship between author and character, the latter becomes transformed into a real historical figure.

We are frequently told that Lawrence made restitution to his father and the men of his father's condition in creating Mellors and others like him. Such, alas, is not the case. Mellors is as one critic observes 'really a sort of gentleman in disguise', and if the portrait of the broken drunkard in *Sons and Lovers* is cruel, and it is undeniably, it is less cruel than converting the victim of industrial brutality into a blasé sexual superman who is too much of a snob to belong to either the working or the middle-classes. The late Lawrentian hero is clearly Lawrence's own fantasy of the father he might have preferred. In the same way, Lady Chatterley is a smartened-up version of his mother herself. Like his own wife Frieda von Richthofen, she is a real lady, not that disappointed little woman of the mining village with chapped red hands who fears her clothes are too shabby to be seen in Lincoln cathedral. Yet Mrs Morel is a brave, even a great woman, though waitresses in teahouses snub her when she can only order custard, too poor to pay for a full meal. *Sons and Lovers* gives us Lawrence's parents without the glamour with which his snobbishness later invested them. All the romances of his later fiction are a reworking of his parents' marriage, and of his own too, modeled on theirs, but a notable advance in social mobility. For Lawrence saw his course, saw it with a Calvinistic sense of election, as a vocation to rise and surpass his origins.[18]

Millett doesn't expand upon what could or ought to constitute literary 'restitution' to one's father. *Pace* Graham Hough, the most superficial reading of *Lady Chatterley* will show that Mellors is not drawn as a 'gentleman in disguise', but as a type still extant in British life, an embittered, educated man of working-class origins, unwilling quite to become a class renegade, but cut off from class identity.[19] He is not drawn as a blasé sexual superman, but rather as someone whose sexual experience has been bad enough to make him temporarily continent. Connie may owe something to Frieda, but the only thing that she has in common with Mrs Morel is her gender, though Millett is free to prefer the latter character. They are quite distinct portraits of two different women with different class backgrounds, psychology and experience. Millett's claim that writing about the aristocracy if you are not yourself of it is an attempt at class mobility makes a snob of everyone from Shakespeare – no, wait a minute, Chaucer – on upwards. If you're black and write about whites, or female and write about men or Irish and write about the English...?

These are all minor cavils however. What is worst about this passage is not its *ad hominem* attack on Lawrence's supposed regressive, snobbish and false use of his personal history, but Millett's wish to eat her Freud and castrate him too. She does not seem to see that you can't demolish a psychic schema of development for one sex and accept its linked application to the other without a much more elaborate and careful critique than she has presented. Thus she accepts Freud's assessment of masculinity – aggressive, sadistic, Oedipally bound, terrified of castration, fetishistic, and so on, but rejects the sexual bipolarity implied by identifying real men (admitted homosexuals excepted) with these attributes.

The whole of *Sexual Politics* is permeated by a coercive sexual morality, meant to replace those mores inscribed in patriarchy. Typical of the early years of the modern women's movement, it borrows from the sexual libertarianism of the alternative ideologies of the 1960s, which in turn reacted against the macho poses of the post-war fifties. It is marked, among other things, by an extreme distaste for the recrudescent sado-masochistic elements of sexuality, however 'playfully' practiced. Surprisingly it has very rigid notions of sexual health. Thus in spite of Millett's sympathy towards overt homosexuality she is clinically severe towards authors who seem to identify with their heroines. Tennyson is a case in point and she puts this tendency in his work down to his 'problems of sexual identity', unconsciously lining herself up with the very normative views she ascribes to Freud, Lawrence, Miller, Mailer.[20] Now that it has become less fashionable to promote a 'correct' feminist sexuality, so that it is no longer so important to be clitoral and/or gay as opposed to vaginal and straight, most of this moralizing comes over as specious and naïve, especially in regard to literature. Millett comes close, but never close enough, to understanding that literature is the place where bisexuality is spoken even by the most consciously phallocratic authors.

A less positivistic but equally 'feminist' literary criticism would read not only *Lady Chatterley* but many of Millett's chosen texts quite differently. Mailer's 'The Time of Her Time', for instance, need not be read as a serious account of how Mailer-the-cocksman triumphs again, but rather as a Feiffer-like send up of the Greenwich Village macho scene, where Mailer's fake Irish bullfighter goads and gores his way through elaborate sexual games, in a parody of machismo and Hemingway. Mailer encourages such a reading by giving the girl the last word, allowing her to undermine with language the 'manhood' that had just been physically vindicated.[21] Mailer is hard to interpret because his writing about America identifies fascism and imperialism with male fantasies about power and sexuality. These are fantasies that Mailer shares: at certain points they seem to take over his work, as in *An American Dream*, a tendency that suggests the instability of the metaphor between sexuality and politics. Perhaps what these writers ought to have suggested to Millett is that the sociology of sex, particularly sexuality as expressed in literature, is not the key to or the symbol of power politics. (She does seem to lean towards this view somewhat in her treatment of Genet.) If there is a central conviction in Mailer it is his unshaken belief that the sexual is political and vice-versa. He keeps snapping away at the same view from every possible angle. In this belief Mailer and Millett are united and equally stubborn. *Flying*, Millett's feminist rewrite of Mailer, gets no closer to the relationship between sex, gender and politics than Mailer's work, though it contains as much coupling and campaigning.

Millett may take her authors seriously, but it is hard for her, given her rejection of formalist or structuralist methodologies of literary criticism, to stay with a single text long enough to let the contradictory elements in its ideological inscription play themselves out in her analysis. She tends to note them in passing as detours from the general coherence of her readings, but since these readings must support such literature as the vanguard of an ideological counter revolution with a well-planned, coherent, fully conscious attack on women it would be counterproductive of her to foreground conflict and sabotage, even fragging,[22] within the ranks. She looks for, and in most cases finds, a concrete reading, ties it to the text and heaves it over the side.

This method adds nothing to the development of a Marxist feminist literary criticism, which must look more carefully at the complex interrelation of class and gender ideologies in literature written by men and women, and must attempt to theorize imaginative writing as something more specific, strange and fragmented than a 'reflection' of either patriarchal ideology or real social relations. A socialist cultural criticism may wish to cut loose, finally, from feminism's overemphasis in the last decade on high culture as a leading influence, benign or vicious, on women's subordination or struggle. Millett's radical feminism is quite clear about culture's central place in the sexual revolution. Given the errors in her definition of patriarchy and the function of patriarchal ideology we should, as Marxists and feminists, be wary of placing all of our hopes and fears on the revision of culture. In her postscript, Millett concludes:

> The enormous social change involved in a sexual revolution is basically a matter of altered consciousness, the exposure and elimination of social and psychological realities underlining political and cultural structure. We are speaking then, of a cultural revolution, which while it must necessarily involve the political and economic reorganization traditionally implied by the term revolution, must go far beyond this as well. And here it would seem that the most profound changes implied are ones accomplished by human growth and true re-education, rather than those arrived at through the theatrics of armed struggle – even should the latter become inevitable.[23]

Much of this statement is politically impeccable, but its emphasis, written as it was in the midst of the Vietnam war, is a little worrying. The realities of armed struggle are made to seem more distant and fictional than those of altered consciousness and human growth.

Notes

1. KATE MILLETT, *Sexual Politics* (London: Virago Press, 1977), p. xi.

2. ELLEN MOERS, *Literary Women* (London: Women's Press, 1978).

3. MILLETT, pp. 176–203.

4. SHULAMITH FIRESTONE, *The Dialectic of Sex* (London: Women's Press, 1979).

5. MILLETT, p. 189.

6. Ibid.

7. MILLETT, p. 185.

8. SIGMUND FREUD, 'Femininity', in *New Introductory Lectures on Psychoanalysis*, James Strachey, ed. (London: Penguin, 1973), p. 169.

9. MILLETT, p. 202.

10. JULIET MITCHELL, *Psychoanalysis and Feminism* (London: Allen Lane, 1974).

11. MITCHELL, p. 412.

12. MILLETT, p. xii.

13. Ibid.

14. Ibid., p. 238.

15. Ibid., p. 242.

16. Ibid., p. 238.

17. Ibid., p. 248.

18. Ibid.

19. GRAHAM HOUGH, *The Dark Sun, a Study of D. H. Lawrence* (London: Duckworth, 1968), p. 31.

20. MILLETT, p. 76–7.

21. NORMAN MAILER, *Advertisements for Myself* (New York: Putnam, 1959).

22. 'Fragging', slang word coined in the Vietnam War for attacks on US officers by their own men.

23. MILLETT, pp. 362–3.

6   Mary Jacobus and Stephen Heath

MARY JACOBUS 'Is There a Woman in This Text?'*

In the Preface to her collection of essays, *Reading Woman: Essays in Feminist Criticism* (1986), Mary Jacobus explains her decision not to use any of her pre-1978 work. She sees the advent of French feminism, from the mid-1970s onwards, as having a decisive influence on her own thinking and generally on disputes within feminist criticism. Thus Jacobus situates her recent work in the context, firstly, of Freudian and Lacanian psychoanalysis and, secondly, in a dialogue with wider developments in critical theory. In both debates her aim is to work dialectically, moving between psychoanalysis and feminism, literary theory and feminist criticism. This aim is well realized in her essay, 'Is There a Woman in This Text?' which explores the unhappy part that both women and 'woman' can play in the construction of theory. Working through a series of compellingly different examples – an academic joke, Freud's interpretation of Jensen's *Gravida*, James Watson's account of the discovery of the structure of DNA, Mary Shelley's *Frankenstein* – Jacobus examines the function, meaning and place of the woman. Though psychoanalysis is the major critical partner in her feminist reading, Jacobus does not disregard Anglo-American approaches. Her account of the relationships between the male professors and the female student, or between James Watson and Rosalind Franklin are intelligible also as examples of sexual politics. Ultimately, however, when Jacobus sets side by side Anglo-American and French feminist responses to theory, her

---

* Mary Jacobus, 'Is There a Woman in This Text?' *New Literary History* (Autumn, 1982), 14 (1). Reprinted in Jacobus, *Reading Woman: Essays in Feminist Criticism* (London: Methuen 1986), pp. 83–109.

preference for textuality over sexuality, woman as writing-effect rather than source of meaning, representation rather than empiricism, becomes clear (see Introduction pp. 13–20).

Let me start with an anecdote. Readers of Stanley Fish's *Is There a Text in This Class? The Authority of Interpretive Communities* (1980) will recognize in my title an allusion to the anecdote which gives him his. It's also, appropriately enough, an interpreter's joke (though at whose expense is not immediately clear); and, since it involves the triangulation of two men and a woman, a joke that falls structurally into a category defined by Freud as at once seductive and aggressive. Seductive, because you'll recall that for Freud this is always the aim of the sexual joke directed at a woman; aggressive, because the presence of another man turns desire to hostility, enlisting the originally interfering third party as an ally. The function of this kind of joke is both to humiliate and to eliminate the woman, becoming a joke at the precise point when it is directed no longer at her but at the onlooker-turned-listener.[1] Here, then, is Fish's anec-joke, which involves two male professors of differing critical persuasions and a female student whose theoretical innocence has already been violated by one of them:

> On the first day of the new semester a colleague at Johns Hopkins University was approached by a student who, as it turned out, has just taken a course from me. She put to him what I think you would agree is a perfectly straightforward question: 'Is there a text in this class?' Responding with a confidence so perfect that he was unaware of it (although in telling the story, he refers to this moment as 'walking into the trap'), my colleague said, 'Yes; it's the *Norton Anthology of Literature*', whereupon the trap (set not by the student but by the infinite capacity of language for being appropriated) was sprung: 'No, no', she said, 'I mean in this class do we believe in poems and things, or is it just us?'[2]

Despite the ritual allusion to language's infinite capacity for appropriation, it's not hard to see that the student here, rather than language, is being appropriated as two professors vie for possession of the untutored female mind. But the woman student – described by the unnamed professor as one of Fish's victims – is not simply the victim of Fishy doctrine (parodically rendered as the instability of the text and the unavailability of determinate meanings); she's also the fall doll who sets Fish's theoretical discourse in motion – the idiot questioner disguised as dumb blonde. For one professor after another's ego, she voices a satisfyingly reductive version of Fish's critical position; but for Fish himself, she provides the opportunity to complicate it and finally cast it out in favor of a more finely tuned position (limited indeterminacy and a situational definition of meaning). By the end of the book the trap contains, not Fish's unwary colleague, still less the agile Fish, but the dumb blonde's misinterpretation.

If an anecdote tells us something the teller knows, a joke may reveal something he doesn't. Fish's anecdote tells us that he doesn't hold the absurd view ascribed to him by his opponents, that poems and things are 'just us'. But his joke tells us something else. Of the many constitutive meanings in this first-day-of-term encounter that Fish goes on to ponder, there is one he does not mention: the interpretive wrinkle introduced by the sexual triangle. Of course it could be argued that in most American universities, and especially at Johns Hopkins, such gender arrangements are the norm and so they are. But the overwhelming likelihood that in the interpretive community which concerns Fish – the English department of a major university – two professors at odds about critical theory will be male, and the student female, doesn't quite account for the effect. One has only to substitute a male 'victim' for laughter to turn to pedagogic exasperation (can't students get anything right?). Lurking behind Fish's bonhomous opening gambit is a tinge of gender harassment – not institutional but structural. There's no reason to think Fish himself anything but well disposed toward women students, or indeed feminist criticism, though one might justifiably take him to task for ignoring gender as a constitutive element in the interpretive community, especially in the light of current feminist concern with the woman reader. Rather, we glimpse here a paradigm commonly found when professors anxiously rebut their critics or covertly compete with one another. One might speculate that the function of the female 'victim' in scenarios of this kind is to provide the mute sacrifice on which theory itself may be founded; the woman is silenced so that the theorist can make the truth come out of her mouth. Freud himself, in similar circumstances, rebuts doubts thrown on his professional competence and on the rightness of his theories with his 'Dream of Irma's Injection', obliging a recalcitrant young patient to swallow the interpreter's 'solution' which she has resisted in real life. If (as the dream enabled him triumphantly to prove) *'when the work of interpretation has been completed, we perceive that a dream is the fulfilment of a wish'*, then Freud not only exonerates himself as physician and as analyst, but enacts a satisfying revenge on resistant patient and skeptical colleagues alike.[3] The sickly Irma has violence done to her body – in particular, to her remarkable oral cavity – in order that Freud's solution to the secret of dreams may be swallowed by his readers. One might say that the wish fulfilled by this dream is that dreams should be the fulfillment of wishes.

Like Fish's anec-joke, Freud's dream can be misread as an example of the role frequently played by a woman in a theoretical context. It's no part of my purpose to indict 'theory' as such – on the contrary; still less to imply, as some feminist critics have tended to do, that theory is of itself 'male', a dangerous abstraction which denies the specificity of female experience and serves chiefly to promote men in the academy. Instead, I want to offer some thoughts about the relation between women and theory – about the deflection of gender harassment (aggression against the class of women) or sexual harassment (aggression against the bodies of women) onto the 'body' of the text. The result might be called textual harassment, the specular appropriation of woman, or even her elimination altogether. It's not just that women figure conveniently as mirrors for acts of narcissistic self-contemplation on the part of some male theorists, or that the shutting up of a female victim can open theoretical discourse. It's also a matter of the adversarial relation between rival theorists which often seems to underline a triangle such as the one in Fish's anecdote. This triangle characteristically invokes its third (female) term only in the interests of the original rivalry and works finally to get rid of the woman, leaving theorist and theorist face to face. My first extended example of the textual relation between a woman and a theory will be *Delusions and Dreams in Jensen's Gradiva* (1907), Freud's reading of a *fin-de-siècle* novella. Painstaking yet wishful, Freud's practice is a reminder that the word *theory* comes from the Greek verb to look on, view, or contemplate, and that self-regard can never be far away in such a context. My second example will center on Mary Shelley's *Frankenstein* (1818), and especially on Frankenstein's uncreation of his female monster, while drawing on a theoretical debate which similarly has as its focus the elimination of the woman. Finally, I'll return briefly to another way of asking the question 'Is there a woman in this text?' in order to relocate it within current feminist critical theory – putting the question back where it belongs for feminist critics themselves.

Gradiva Rediviva

> Then thou our fancy of itself bereaving,
> Dost make us Marble with too much conceaving ...
>
> (MILTON, 'On Shakespear')

Recognizing the violence done by Freud to the literary text in the interests of analytical 'truth', Sarah Kofman writes in *Quatre romans analytiques* (1973) of the impossibility of analytic interpretation without countertransference; 'the unconscious of the analysis, like that of everyone, can never be eliminated'.[4] What form does this countertransference take in the case of Freud's analysis of Jensen's 'Pompeian phantasy', *Gradiva* (1903)? Freud himself was bound to read it in the light of his own theories, but did he also read his theories into it?[5] As it happens, he was himself alert to the possibility of having found in Jensen's 'phantasy' only what he wanted to find: 'Is it not rather we who have slipped into this charming poetic story a secret meaning very far from its author's intentions?' (SE, 9, p. 43).* If so, he is implicated in the same delusional structure as Jensen's archeologist hero – guilty of 'introducing into an innocent work of art purposes of which its creator has no notion', and demonstrating 'once more how easy it is to find what one is looking for' (SE, 9, p.91).[6] Constructing an elaborate theory on the basis of his delusion, the young archeologist not only finds what he's looking for, but – and this is his chief value for Freud – reveals the artist-neurotic within the scientific scholar. In this sense (like Gradiva's own therapeutic dealings with the deluded hero), Freud's treatment of the novella might be said to take up the same 'ground' as the delusion itself. For Kofman, in fact, the hero's 'cure' at the hands of Gradiva parallels Freud's cure of the text – a cure whereby literature is ultimately consigned to the status of delusion, becoming a mere device for 'catching the carp truth: that of the literary text which must confirm that of psychoanalysis'.[7] Against his own better practice, Kofman argues, Freud is forced to align himself with the metaphysics of logocentricity – with 'truth' as opposed to 'fiction'. But perhaps there is another way of looking at the analytical countertransference at work in *Delusions and Dreams*. Freud's reading of Jensen's 'phantasy' proceeds by means of a series of important but unstated parallels between the role of Gradiva herself and that of the literary text; between the relation of a marble image to a living woman or of 'fiction' to real life. Above all, the doubling of Gradiva and the text bears on another unstated parallel, between 'woman' and 'theory'.

One might start by asking what are the resemblances between Norbert Hanold, the young archeologist, and Freud himself. Jensen's hero is at once a 'scientist' and a fantasist; his archeological obsession provides the basis for a delusion at odds with rational judgement and empirical realities, so that the original instrument of repression (archeology, or 'science' itself) becomes the vehicle for the return of the repressed. Defending himself against Eros, or life, Hanold becomes preoccupied with an ancient bas-relief of a young girl whom he identifies as being of Hellenic origin and names 'Gradiva' or 'the girl who steps along' (after the war god *Mars Gradivus*, 'striding into battle'), an allusion to her distinctive lift of the foot.[8] Norbert Hanold, we're told, 'took no interest in living women; the science of which he was the servant had taken that interest away from him and displaced it on to women of marble or bronze' (SE, 9, pp. 45–46). His fixation on a buried past and his unconscious mourning for the lost erotic possibilities of the present are vividly symbolized by a dream of Gradiva's transformation from a living woman, stepping along with her characteristic gait, into a recumbent marble form buried by the ashes of Vesuvius. Freud's own relation to his 'science' has

---

* SIGMUND FREUD, *The Standard Edition of the Complete Psychological Works of Sigmund Freud*. 24 vols. Ed. James Strachey (London: Hogarth Press, 1953–1974).

something in common with Hanold's. 'The author of *The Interpretation of Dreams*', he writes, 'has ventured, in the face of the reproaches of strict science, to become a partisan of antiquity and superstition' (SE, 9, p. 7). Whereas 'strict science' explains dreaming as a purely physiological process, the imaginative writer sides with the ancients, with the superstitious public, and with Freud himself to recognize 'a whole host of things between heaven and earth of which our philosophy has not yet let us dream' (SE, 9, p. 8). The ghost of Hamlet's murdered father becomes evidence for the uncanny power of the repressed – the unconscious itself, with its challenge to a materialist outlook. For Freud too 'science' becomes at once the instrument of repression and the means by which it is overcome. What returns is 'life', or 'Zoë' – the Greek name given by Jensen to his flesh-and-blood Gradiva; for the sculpted girl has a living double. Like the young archeologist, who 'had surrendered his interest in life in exchange for an interest in the remains of classical antiquity and who was now brought back to real life by a roundabout path which was strange but perfectly logical' (SE, 9, p. 10), a physiologically based science is revivified by what might be called the buried life of the mind.

Hence Freud's identification with his hero's growing impatience at a science unable to carry him back into the buried past of Pompeii: 'What (science) taught was a lifeless, archeological way of looking at things, and what came from his mouth was a dead, philological language' (SE, 9, p. 16). Like the real life Zoë's father, Hanold has been something of an 'archaeopteryx' – a 'compromise idea', Freud suggests, by which Zoë wittily satirizes both her father and her oblivious lover, identifying them with 'the bird-like monstrosity which belongs to the archeology of zoology' (SE, 9, p. 33). Zoë's father, whom we see in hot pursuit of the lizard *faraglionensis* among the ruins of Pompeii, has preferred the taxonomy of zoology to life itself; both he and Hanold, until now, have been 'absorbed by science and held apart by it from life and from Zoë' (SE, 9, p. 33). In a comically deluded moment, Hanold addresses the unlooked-for noontide apparition of Gradiva in Greek and Latin, forgetting, as he has done all along, that she is a 'German girl of flesh and blood'(SE, 9, p. 18); what comes from the mouth of science is a dead philological language. Ostensibly, the incident shows that 'his science was now completely in the service of his imagination'(SE, 9,p. 18). But it also raises a problem which Freud too must address in appropriate words. No less than Zoë's father, he runs the risk of becoming a taxonomist of life or, like Norbert Hanold, a strict scientist locked into a deadening technical vocabulary. As he embarks on the second, analytic phase of his reading of Jensen's novella in the light of his theories of dreams, neurosis and therapy, we find Freud anxious to 'repeat 'or 'reproduce' it 'in correct psychological technical terms', 'with the technical terminology of our science' (SE, 9, pp. 47, 44). Yet he is dissatisfied with the taxonomy of mental illness available to him – 'erotomania', 'fetishism', *dégeneré*, and the like – because 'all such systems of nomenclature and classification of the different kinds of delusion…have something precarious and barren about them' (SE, 9, p. 45). The 'strict psychiatrist' who would investigate Hanold's delusion in terms of heredity and degeneracy must give way to the student of the imagination, allied to artist and neurotic, and ultimately to Zoë herself, since her wooing of the young archeologist from his delusion is the model for Freud's own wooing of science.

If the story of Norbert Hanold's awakening to life and love provides Freud with an analogy for the awakening of 'strict psychiatry' to the existence of the unconscious, *Delusions and Dreams* also reveals a submerged concern with what might be called questions of mimesis; that is, with the relation between art object and observed life, the fidelity of literature to psychic laws and processes, and the status of the imagination itself in relation to Freudian theory. The central *donnée* of Jensen's 'Pompeian phantasy' is the 'far-reaching resemblance between the sculpture and the live girl' (SE, 9, p. 42), the improbable 'premiss that Zoë was in every detail a duplicate of the relief '(SE, 9, p. 70), the coincidence of there existing in antiquity a bas-relief which perfectly represents the appearance, and especially the characteristic walk, of a young girl of *fin de siècle* Germany. Another *donnée*, equally unlikely, is that Zoë's family name, 'Bertgang', might readily suggest translation as 'Gradiva'; fantastically, Freud allows himself to speculate that Zoë's family may be of ancient descent, having earned their name from their womenfolk's distinctive way of walking (SE, 9, p. 42). The peculiarity here doesn't lie in the fact of Hanold's repressed erotic feelings for his forgotten childhood playmate (for that is what she turns out to be) having settled unknowingly on her marble likeness. Rather, it lies in the uncanny priority of the representation over what it represents. This peculiarity exactly parallels the priority of Freudian theory over the literary text. As Gradiva is to Zoë, so theory is to Jensen's novella. At first sight, Freud had seemed to be arguing for the priority of literary insight over that of 'science'; as he poses it initially, the question is not whether this 'imaginative representation of the genesis of a delusion can hold its own before the judgement of science', since instead 'it is science that cannot hold its own before the achievement of the author' (SE, 9, p. 53). But by an unexpected sleight of hand, Freud ceases to emphasize the secondary status of science, instead asserting that his own prior views support all that Jensen has written: 'Does our author stand alone, then, in the face of united science? No, that is not the case (if, that is, I may count my own works as part of science), since for a number of years…I myself have supported all the views that I have here exacted from Jensen's *Gradiva* and stated in technical terms' (SE, 9, p. 53). This is the payoff for Freud's cautious but stealthily appropriative reading of Jensen's novella. Just as the marble bas-relief can figure in Jensen's 'phantasy' without seeming fantastic – indeed seeming rather to authenticate it, since such a bas-relief actually existed – so Freudian theory, granted independent existence, authenticates Jensen's literary insight, becoming the model for both art and life.

The resemblance of a marble bas-relief to a living girl is the single unexplained and inexplicable 'premiss' on which Jensen's novella and Freud's interpretation both depend. The double (Gradiva/Zoë) is also crucial to the way in which *Delusions and Dreams* poses the relation between theory and literary text, and in particular the relation between desire and the uncanny. Like Hanold, who sees in the sculpted figure 'something "of today"…as though the artist had had a glimpse in the street and captured it "from the life"' (SE, 9, p. 11), Freud goes through the motions of testing Jensen's 'phantasy' against empirical observation. Hanold takes to studying the feet of women in the street as a 'scientific task', trying to discover whether Gradiva's gait has been rendered by the artist 'in a life-like manner'; desire masks itself as an ostensibly scientific problem which called for a solution (SE, 9, pp. 11–2). The increasingly bodily nature of his curiosity surfaces later when he encounters the supposed ghost of Gradiva (actually Zoë) among the ruins of Pompeii. He longs to know 'would one feel anything if one touched her hand?' (SE, 9, p. 23) and seizes an opportunity to slap it (a piece of erotic aggression not lost on Freud). The question asked by the young archeologist at this point doubles exactly with the reader's, who as yet has no means of knowing from Jensen's narrative that a flesh-and-blood Zoë exists. In the second part of his analysis Freud takes a similar tack. Is Jensen's story indeed only a 'phantasy' (like Hanold's delusion) which renounces the portrayal of reality? Can his account of the construction of a delusion be verified from other sources? Does it lie within the bounds of possibility, like the sculptor's depiction of Gradiva's foot? (SE, 9, pp. 41–80). Ostensibly, Freud's answer is to assert its mimetic accuracy – Jensen's novella is 'so faithfully copied from reality that we should not object if *Gradiva* were described not as a phantasy but as a psychiatric study' (SE, 9, p. 41). Yet it is important to remember the earlier moment in Freud's account when the apparition of Gradiva amidst the ruins of Pompeii produces an experience of confusion and uncertainty, not only for Hanold but for the reader, forcing the conclusion that she is either 'a hallucination or a midday ghost' (SE, 9, p. 17). The unexpected discovery that – whether *rediviva* or not – she is corporeally present introduces the element of the uncanny, literally marking the return of the repressed. In his retelling of the story, Freud halts us here. The pause is significant, for both Gradiva and the text are alike in being uncanny, not because they are dead but because they are alive – living embodiments of desire. In Jensen's and Freud's texts, then, the uncanny moment occurs when what is supposed dead (Gradiva or science) comes to life again as 'Zoë' or 'theory'.

While seeming to test Jensen's 'phantasy' against reality, Freud ends by suggesting what is uncanny about his science of the mind (as about the unconscious) is that it is something we have always known but have forgotten, just as Hanold has forgotten his childhood playmate. Ostensibly, theory turns out to be life itself. But in the context of Gradiva's apparition in the streets of Pompeii, Freud has earlier asked whether the author intends to leave us in a world 'governed by the laws of science' or to transport us into an imaginary one (SE, 9, p. 17). Though he asserts that Jensen's story obeys the laws of science, these laws have a curious provenance. Like the resemblance of Gradiva and Zoë, the coincidence of Hanold's meeting with Gradiva in Pompeii, the very place to which he has fled in his unconscious avoidance of Eros, is represented as an illustration of 'the fatal truth that has laid it down that flight is precisely an instrument that delivers one over to what one is fleeing from' (SE, 9, p. 42). As for the transporting of Zoë herself from Germany to Pompeii, this is merely an instance of the author guiding his characters 'towards a happy destiny, in spite of all the laws of necessity' (SE, 9, p. 69); part, as it were, of the dream – and we know that Freud has throughout derived his 'rules...for the solution of dreams' from his own *Interpretation of Dreams* (SE, 9, p. 57). Not only is there no such thing as chance, but 'the laws of science' or mental life turn out to be uniquely authorized. Freud's complicity in the authorial manipulations of Jensen's text bears on an otherwise unrelated moment when he intrudes his own experience into the narrative. Recalling the uncanny resemblance between a dead woman and her sister, whose unexpected appearance in his consulting room momentarily convinced him 'that the dead can come back to life' (SE, 9, p. 71), Freud not only implicates himself in the delusional structure; he reveals his own residual belief in the omnipotence of thought. Having considered himself responsible for the woman's death, he sees in her apparent restoration to life a restoration of his infallibility as a doctor. The *revenant* doubles as his own lost ideal. Commenting on Freud's account of the narcissistic 'essence of woman' who must fully correspond to male desire, Sarah Kofman writes that 'men's fascination with this eternal feminine is nothing but fascination with their own double, and the feeling of uncanniness, *Unheimlichkeit*, that men experience is the same as what one feels in the face of any double, any ghost, in the face of the abrupt reappearance of what one thought had been overcome or lost forever.'[9] If Freud's experience of the uncanny in his consulting room was nothing less than a pang of gratified narcissism, then the sighting of Gradiva by the deluded Hanold, by the confused reader, and by Freud himself becomes the magical moment when the fantasists of archeology, literature, and psychoanalysis confront themselves restored to wholeness.

It is surely in this moment that we can identify the countertransferential aspect of *Delusions and Dreams*. Like the doll Olympia in Hoffmann's 'The

Sandman', who replies only 'Ach, Ach' to all that Nathanael proposes, the sculptured Gradiva had been a love object posing none of the risks of forbidden or potentially castrating sexuality.[10] But is the live Zoë finally very different? For all his emphasis on the accuracy of the copy – whether Gradiva's of Zoë or Jensen's of life – Freud implies that mimetic representation inevitably involves distortion or lack. Substituting Zoë for Gradiva, Hanold replaces his delusion 'by the thing of which it could only have been a distorted and inadequate copy' (SE, 9; p. 37). Similarly, 'dream images have to be regarded as something distorted', a mere copy of the dream thoughts they (mis) 'represent' (SE, 9, p. 59). The work of interpretation, then, seems to involve correcting the distortion and restoring dream thoughts to an imaginary wholeness. Despite his reductive statement that interpreting a dream (or, by analogy, a literary text) involves translating 'manifest content' into 'latent dream-thoughts' (SE, 9, p. 59), Freud seems actually to be proposing something more like the effect of the *revenant's* apparition in his consulting room. Both delusion and theory become a desired supplement to the empirically observed world of the 'strict psychiatrist'. That Zoë herself, no less than Gradiva, is made in the image of Hanold's, Jensen's, and Freud's own desire emerges most clearly from the charming concluding scene of the 'Pompeian phantasy'. In a moment which Freud takes evident pleasure in rehearsing, Norbert Hanold asks Zoë Bertgang to step back once more into his dream of Gradiva and reenact for him the distinctive lift of the foot on which his delusion has centered:

> The delusion had now been conquered by a beautiful reality: but before the two lovers left Pompeii it was still to be honoured once again. When they reached the Herculenean Gate, where, at the entrance to the Via Consolare, the street is crossed by some ancient stepping-stones, Norbert Hanold paused and asked the girl to go ahead of him. She understood him, 'and pulling up her dress a little with her left hand, Zoë Bertgang, Gradiva *rediviva*, walked past, held in his eyes, which seemed to gaze as though in a dream; so with her quietly tripping gait, she stepped through the sunlight over the stepping-stones to the other side of the street.'
>
> (SE, 9, pp. 39–40)

'With the triumph of love', Freud concludes, 'what was beautiful and precious in the delusion found recognition as well' (SE, 9, p.40). This, unmistakably, is the Pygmalion story, in which the coming to life of the ideal beloved, modeled on the lover's desire, figures the artist's narcissistic relation to his Galatea-like creation. Nathanael's Olympia is simply the demonic version of the same myth. In the passage Freud quotes so affectingly, we witness not only the triumph of love but the triumph of specular appropriation ('held in his eyes, which seemed to gaze as though in a dream'). Freud's proof that theory is only the life we have forgotten turns on a moment when the living Zoë gets reappropriated as an uncanny representation: Gradiva *rediviva*.

The Bride of Frankenstein

> Many and long were the conversations between Lord Byron and Shelley, to which I was a devout but nearly silent listener. During one of these, various philosophical doctrines were discussed, and among others the nature of the principle of life, and whether there was any probability of its ever being discovered and communicated.
>
> (MARY SHELLEY, 'Introduction' to *Frankenstein*)

Lacan ventriloquizes the meaning of Freud's 'Dream of Irma's Injection' as a plea for forgiveness for having transgressed a limit previously uncrossed, that of curing the sick whom before no one had wished or dared to cure; 'for to transgress a limit hitherto imposed on human activity is always culpable'.[11] The magical word of Freud's dream solution ('Trimethylamin'), linked by Freud himself to the chemistry of sexual processes, suggests that Freud's morbid fascination with Irma's deep throat figures the broken taboo – that of looking too closely at the 'immensely powerful factor of sexuality' which he believed to be the origin of the nervous disorders he aimed to cure (SE, 4, pp. 116–17). In his *Autobiographical Study* (1925), recalling that as a boy he was moved 'by a sort of curiosity' about human concerns, Freud speaks of the influence on him both of an older boy and of the theories of Darwin, which 'held out hopes of an extraordinary advance in our understanding of the world' (SE, 20, p. 8). The two impulses behind his decision to become a medical student were male bonding and curiosity about the origins of life; later, his work in physiology was to focus on the central nervous system. His remark apropos of Norbert Hanold's researches into women's feet, that 'the scientific motivation might be said to serve as a pretext for the unconscious erotic one' (SE, 9, p. 52), could stand as the epigraph not only to his own researches but to all scientific quests for the origins of life, whether organic or mental. Before moving on to *Frankenstein Or the Modern Prometheus*, whose own origins – according to Mary Shelley herself – lie in conversations between Byron and Shelley about 'the nature of the principle of life',[12] I want to look briefly at another scientific autobiography, James Watson's *The Double Helix: A Personal Account of the Discovery of the Structure of DNA* (1986). Watson's and Crick's pursuit of 'the Rosetta Stone for unravelling the true secret of life',[13] the very basis of genetic reproduction, unexpectedly repeats the paradigm of the scientific triangle which Mary Shelley had anticipated in her gothic novel, bringing together motifs of curiosity, ambition and scientific inquiry in the context of an undercurrent of male bonding which has as its necessary victim a woman.

One might speculate that the unconscious motive of Watson's pursuit of the structures of DNA was twofold: that of engaging in intense oedipal rivalry with a distinguished older scientist, Linus Pauling, while attaching himself closely to another (younger) man, Francis Crick; or perhaps, as one scientific observer has suggested, Pauling and Crick were really interchangeable – 'The love and the competition are one and the same'.[14] In any event, both kinds of oedipal relation – rivalry or love – are profoundly misogynistic, demanding as they do the sacrifice of a living woman. As is well known, the 'race' for the secret of DNA involved not only Watson and Crick in Cambridge versus Pauling at California Institute of Technology, but a London-based team consisting of Maurice Wilkins, who later received the Nobel prize along with the Cambridge pair, and a young woman named Rosalind Franklin. The competition derived some of its excitement from contrasting temperaments and styles, but above all from the radically different approaches involved. While Watson and Crick adopted the inspirational, hit-or-miss methods of theoretical model building, the London-based team used as its principal research tool the findings of X-ray diffraction – painstakingly empirical techniques of measuring molecular cell structures. This is the context in which a misogynistic element enters, and for a while dominates, Watson's 'personal account'. Wilkins' co-researcher, whom Watson refers to throughout as 'Rosy', as if she were a kind of scientific charlady, had been brought in because of her expertise in X-ray diffraction technique; presumably Wilkins hoped that she would speed up his research. But 'Rosy' refused to regard herself as Wilkins' assistant (which she was not) and – worse still – persisted in thinking that DNA was as much her problem as his. In Watson's eyes, this made her a furious feminist who ultimately posed a threat not simply to men but to science itself: 'Clearly', he writes, 'Rosy had to go or be put in her place. The former was obviously preferable because, given her belligerent moods, it would be very difficult for Maurice (Wilkins) to maintain a dominant position that would allow him to think unhindered about DNA' (p. 20). And go she finally did, but not before she had unknowingly provided the empirical data on which Watson and Crick based their final model of the double helix.

For Norbert Hanold, science becomes a discarded, unlovely mistress, or 'an old, dried up, tedious aunt, the dullest and most unwanted creature in the world' (SE, 9, p. 65). Something similar happens to 'Rosy' in *The Double Helix*; at once virago and dowd, she is represented as the sour spinster science by which theory knows itself young and virile. Not content with stressing her lack of feminine desirability – the absence of lipstick or attractive clothes – Watson speculates that she is 'the product of an unsatisfied mother who unduly stressed the desirability of professional careers that could save bright girls from marriages to dull men' (p.20); how unlike Zoë. Later, giving an important talk on DNA (whose implications Watson was at that point in no position to understand), she is represented as the product of 'careful, unemotional crystallographic training', and hence as hostile to the idea of using 'tinker-toy like structures' for solving theoretical problems in biology. As she calls for more refined crystallographic analysis, Watson labels her the schoolmarm 'labwork': 'Certainly', he recalls, 'a bad way to go out into the foulness of a heavy, foggy November night was to be told by a woman to refrain from venturing an opinion about a subject for which you were not trained. It was a sure way of bringing back unpleasant memories of lower school' (p. 52). In her sympathetic biography of Rosalind Franklin, Anne Sayre was struck by one detail in Watson's recollection of this talk, his reference to 'Rosy's' glasses ('momentarily I wondered how she would look if she took off her glasses'). Ms Franklin did not wear glasses.[15] For her biographer, this was the giveaway that Watson had substituted fiction for fact – just as he failed to give 'Rosy' credit for providing him with crucial data. For us, perhaps, it throws light on other, seemingly unrelated aspects of Watson's account: his allusions to what he calls 'popsies'; the preoccupation with the sexual life of Cambridge au pair girls which (according to Watson) constituted Crick's main topic of conversation apart from DNA; and his habit of referring to plausible theoretical solutions as 'pretty'. In his recent book, *Life Itself* (1981), Crick playfully calls RNA and DNA 'the dumb blondes of the biomolecular world'.[16] Like Gradiva, the model of the double helix is narcissistically invested with desire; unlike 'Rosy' – Nathanael's Klara to the Olympian DNA – the double helix replies only 'Ach, Ach' when spoken to.

Brash and unconsciously misogynistic as it is, *The Double Helix* offers a clear-cut view of the Girardian triangle at work. The 'pretty' object of desire (whether the solution to DNA or a Nobel prize) is pursued less for itself than for being desired by another scientist. The function of the object of desire is thus to mediate relations between men; female desire is impossible except as a mimetic reflection of male desire.[17] The same paradigm shapes Mary Shelley's *Frankenstein* – at once a drama of Promethean scientific enquiry and of oedipal rivalry, a myth of creation that encompasses both a quest for the origins of life and the bond of love and hate between creator and creation; 'Did I request thee, Maker, from my clay/To mould Me man?' (*Paradise Lost*, X, 743–4) demands the novel's Miltonic epigraph, in Adam's words to God. Significantly, what Mary Shelley recalls at the inception of her novel are conversations between Byron and Shelley in which she took almost no part. Perhaps we should see *Frankenstein* not simply as a reworking of Milton's creation myth in the light of Romantic ideology but as an implicit critique of that ideology for its exclusive emphasis on oedipal politics.[18] *Frankenstein* would thus become the novel that most accurately represents the condition of both men and women under the predominantly oedipal forms of Byronic and Shelleyan Romanticism. Read in this light, the monster's tragedy is his confinement to the destructive intensities of a one-to-one relationship with his maker, and his exclusion from other relations – whether familial or with a female counterpart. The most striking absence in *Frankenstein,* after all, is Eve's. Refusing to create a female monster, Frankenstein pays the price of losing his own bride. When the primary bond of paternity unites scientist and his creation so exclusively, women who get in the way must fall victim to the struggle. Indeed, if we look in this text for a female author, we find only a dismembered corpse whose successful animation would threaten the entire structure of the myth. It was more appropriate than he knew for James Whale to cast the same actress, Elsa Lanchester, as both the angelic Mary Shelley and the demonic female monster in his 1935 film sequel to the novel, *The Bride of Frankenstein.*[19]

In Mary Shelley's own version (see note 12), Frankenstein's creation of the monster is immediately followed by the vivid nightmare and yet more appalling awakening which had been her own waking dream and the starting point of her novel. Frankenstein's postpartum nightmare strikingly conflates the body of his long neglected fiancée and childhood sweetheart, Elizabeth, with that of his dead mother:

> I thought I saw Elizabeth, in the bloom of health, walking in the streets of Ingolstadt. Delighted and surprised, I embraced her; but as I imprinted the first kiss on her lips, they became livid with the hue of death; her features appeared to change, and I thought that I held the corpse of my dead mother in my arms; a shroud enveloped her form, and I saw the grave worms crawling in the folds of the flannel. I started from my sleep with horror; a cold dew covered my forehead, my teeth chattered, and every limb became convulsed; when, by the dim and yellow light of the moon, as it forced its way through the window shutters, I beheld the wretch – the miserable monster whom I had created.
>
> (p.58)

The composite image, mingling eroticism and the horror of corruption, transforms Frankenstein's latently incestuous brother-sister relationship with Elizabeth into the forbidden relationship with the mother.

The grave as well as the source of life, brings birth, sex, and death together in one appalling place; the incestuously embraced mother figures Frankenstein's unnatural pursuit of nature's secrets in his charnel house labors. Like Irma's throat, the mother's shrouded form is unwrapped to reveal decay and deformity in the flesh itself.[20] It's not just that the exclusion of woman from creation symbolically 'kills' the mother, but that

Frankenstein's forbidden researches give to the 'facts of life' the aspect of mortality. Elizabeth in turn comes to represent not the object of desire but its death. In a bizarre pun, the monster – 'the demonical corpse to which I had so miserably given life' – is compared to 'a mummy again endued with animation' (p. 58). Exchanging a woman for a monster, Frankenstein has perhaps preferred monstrosity to this vision of corrupt female flesh. From this moment on, the narrative must move inexorably toward the elimination of both female monster and Elizabeth herself on her wedding night. Only when the two females who double one another in the novel – the hideous travesty of a woman and her anodyne ideal – have cancelled each other out is the way clear for the scene of passionate mourning in which the monster hangs, loverlike, over Frankenstein's deathbed at the conclusion of Walton's narrative.

In Mary Shelley's novel, intense identification with an oedipal conflict exists at the expense of identification with women. At best, women are the bearers of a traditional ideology of love, nurturance, and domesticity; at worst, they are passive victims. And yet, for the monster himself, women become a major problem (one that Frankenstein largely avoids by immersing himself in his scientific studies). A curious thread in the plot focuses not on the image of the hostile father (Frankenstein/God) but on that of the dead mother who comes to symbolize to the monster his loveless state. Literally unmothered, he fantasizes acceptance by a series of women but founders in imagined rebuffs and ends in violence. Though it is a little boy (Frankenstein's younger brother) who provokes the monster's first murder by his rejection, the child bears the fatal image of the mother – the same whose shroud had crawled with grave worms in Frankenstein's nightmare:

> As I fixed my eyes on the child, I saw something glittering on his breast: I took it; it was a portrait of a most lovely woman. In spite of my malignity, it softened and attracted me. For a few moments I gazed with delight on her dark eyes, fringed by deep lashes, and her lovely lips; but presently my rage returned: I remembered that I was for ever deprived of the delights that such beautiful creatures could bestow; and that she whose resemblance I contemplated would, in regarding me, have changed that air of divine benignity to one expressive of disgust and affright.
> Can you wonder that such thoughts transported me with rage?
> (p.143)

Immediately after the monster has his vision of this lovely but inaccessible woman, shifting in imagination from looks of benignity to disgust, he finds Frankenstein's servant girl Justine asleep in a nearby barn: 'She was young: not indeed so beautiful as her whose portrait I held; but of an agreeable aspect, and blooming in the loveliness of youth and health. Here, I thought, is one of those whose joy-imparting smiles are bestowed on all but me. And then I bent over her, and whispered, "Awake, fairest, thy lover is near – he who would give his life but to obtain one look of affection from thine eyes: my beloved awake!"' (p. 143). But in this travesty of the lovers *aubade*, the beloved's awakening will shatter the dream, so she must sleep forever. On Justine's person the monster wreaks his revenge on all women, planting among her clothes the incriminating evidence of the mother's portrait as the supposed motive for her murder of the little boy. She is duly tried and executed, even confessing to the crime – for in the monstrous logic of the text, she is as guilty as the monster claims: 'The crime had its source in her: be hers the punishment!' (p.144).

In this bizarre parody of the Fall, Eve is to blame for having been desired. By the same monstrous logic, if woman is the cause of the monster's crimes, then the only cure is a mate, 'one as horrible and deformed as myself' (p.144). The monster's demand for a mate provides the basis for James Whale's sequel. In *The Bride of Frankenstein*, Frankenstein and his crazed collaborator Dr Praetorius undertake what neither Mary Shelley nor her hero could quite bring themselves to do – embody woman as fully monstrous. Shelley's Frankenstein gives several different reasons for dismembering the female corpse which he is on the point of animating: that she might prove even more malignant than her mate; that between them they might breed a race of monsters to prey on mankind; and that 'they might even hate each other' – he loathing her for a deformity worse than his because it 'came before his eyes in the female form', while 'she also might turn in disgust from him to the superior beauty of man' (p.165). This last fear, taken up by James Whale's horror movie, is a demonic parody of the moment in Milton's creation myth when Eve prefers her own image to that of Adam – 'less fair,/Less winning soft, less amiably mild,/Than that smooth watery image' (*Paradise Lost*, IV:478–80). As in Renaissance representations of the Fall, where the serpent's face is hers, Eve appears in the guise of the narcissistic woman – that self-sufficient (the more desirable because self-sufficient) adorer of her own image.[21] God tells her firmly that Adam is 'he/Whose image thou art' (*Paradise Lost*, IV:471–2), but she knows better. If it is the function of *Paradise Lost* to cast out female self-love, it is the function of *The Bride of Frankenstein* to destroy its own monstrous version of Eve's rejection of Adam. Behind this fantasy lies yet another, that of the female monster who might desire men instead of monsters. The threat to male sexuality lies not only in her hideous deformity, refusing to accommodate the image of his desire, but in the dangerous autonomy of her refusal to mate in the image in which she was made. It is as if Irma's throat had suddenly found its voice.

At this juncture it seems appropriate to return to the Girardian triangle and to Sarah Kofman's reading of Freud – in particular, to the Girard-Kofman argument over the narcissistic woman. Since the narcissistic woman has enjoyed some vogue as the point of resistance both to specular appropriation by male desire and to the phallocentic system whereby the term *woman* is reduced to *man-minus*, denying sexual difference, the argument is worth recapitulating.[22] Perhaps, too, the stakes are not quite what they seem. The theory of narcissism itself – an almost tautologous concern, given the reflexivity of looking at oneself as a love object finds an apt emblem in this self-involved figure, who comes to represent for Girard the illusion at the center of Freud's theory, and for Freud himself, the barely repressed possibility that all love might turn out, at bottom, to be narcissistic. In 'On Narcissism: An Introduction' (1914), Freud allows himself to speculate about a female type which he calls 'the purest and truest one', (SE, 14, p. 88), a type who achieves the 'self-sufficiency' of loving only herself. According to Freud, such women exercise a special attraction because – like children, cats, large beasts of prey, criminals and 'humorists' – they seem to have kept intact an original, primary narcissism which the adult male has lost. Her fascination is that of representing a lost paradise of narcissistic completeness, while leaving the lover forever unsatisfied. For once, Freud defines *woman* not in terms of lack but in terms of something she has; primary narcissism replaces the missing phallus. In Kofman's reading, the narcissistic woman is important because she refutes Freud's tendency elsewhere to reduce the 'enigma' of woman to categories of penis envy, castration and veiling. But she writes, what is frightening about such a woman is 'woman's indifference to man's desire, her self-sufficiency…it is what makes woman enigmatic, inaccessible, impenetrable'.[23] And so Freud must finally redeem her, by way of pregnancy and motherhood, for the ethical superiority of object love. For Girard, however, the narcissistic woman had never been anything but a phantasmatic projection on Freud's part. Her self-sufficiency is an illusion, the strategy of a coquette aware that desire attracts desire, merely 'the metaphysical transformation of the rival-model'.[24] Failing to recognize the mimetic essence of desire, Freud has allowed himself to be entrapped by a woman.

In Kofman's eyes, Girard is responding to the intolerable idea of female self-sufficiency (as Freud himself does elsewhere) by denigrating it. But there is more at stake. Girard contends not simply that Freud is entrapped by a fantasy but that his entire theory of narcissism is a chimera. Freud's status as the theorist of desire is undermined in order to reduce narcissism to a merely mythical disguise for Girardian strife between doubles; eliminating the narcissistic woman, Girard also eliminates sexual difference, since in his scheme there is only male desire which the woman mimics. If the narcissistic woman stands, Eve-like, at the center of Freud's theory of desire, Girard's is the James Whale-like scenario of her destruction. What is left without her is the collaboration of Frankenstein and Dr Praetorius – or if you like, a struggle for primacy between Freud and Girard in which Girard employs Proust as his front man, using the metaphors of *À la recherche du temps perdu* to prove that Proust not only understood desire better than Freud but that he demystifies the concepts which buttress the theory of narcissism. The artist knows better than the scientist, for all his technical terms. There is a familiar ring to this. Freud's own arguments – about Jensen's *Gradiva,* for instance – are marshalled by Girard to prove the superiority of literary over scientific insight; Proust, moreover, doesn't really stand alone, since in this Freud himself supports him. But if all Girard wants to do is assert the primacy of the literary text as a source of theory, why this onslaught on the narcissistic woman? To start with, she is easier to unveil than Freudian theory; her coquettish self-sufficiency can stand in for its formidable appearance of wholeness. In addition, her elimination allows the literary text (Proust's) or the critical text (Girard's) to enjoy unmediated dialogue with the psychoanalytic text. Girard's final contention is not that Freud needs the narcissistic woman but that Freud and Proust (or rather, Girard) need one another: 'a dialogue between the two, a dialogue of equals that has never occurred so far'. But just as the monster comes finally to dominate Frankenstein, Girard has in mind something other than equality; 'After countless Freudian readings of Proust, we can propose, for a change, a Proustian reading of Freud.'[25] Next we will have the spectacle of the monster lamenting the destruction of his maker; for to destroy the loved and hated rival is to destroy what is, for Girard himself, the very essence of desire.

In Freud's reading of *Gradiva,* theory steals a march on the literary text which it invokes as proof of its rightness. In Girard's reading of Freud, the literary text usurps on theory – to reveal theory once more. The play of desire proves to be a power play; but either way, the name of the game is theoretical priority. Freud's tendency to suggest, despite himself, not that theory is life but rather that life is always theory, has some bearing on the narcissism debate. The threat posed by the narcissistic woman is that she may reveal the primacy of narcissism, undercutting object love and mimetic desire alike. Perhaps the ultimate function of both 'life' (Zoë) and the narcissistic woman is to defend against formlessness; indeed, one might speculate that this is the chief function of woman as such in theoretical discourse.

Just as the threat of castration may localize an anxiety less unmanageable than that glimpsed in the abyss of Irma's throat – the formless depths of female sexuality – so representing theory as a woman may defend against the indeterminacy and impenetrability of theory itself. It is better to be threatened by even a female monster than to be possessed by a theory whose combined insubstantiality and self-sufficiency are those of delusion. The so-called theorist's dilemma may be one source of the difficulty: if a theory serves its purpose, it should establish relationships among observable phenomena, yet if these relationship are so established, theory can be dispensed with. The dispensability of a good theory has as its obverse Hegel's contention that the innovation of theory is to transform an ungraspable reality into something representable.[26] On the one hand, the unprovability of theory is what constitutes its theoretical status; on the other hand, theory makes it possible to represent what would otherwise elude understanding. If we turn from Freud and Girard to feminist critical theory, it may be possible to see that feminists are caught in the dilemma of theory itself, particularly in their current concern not simply with sexual difference but with the issue of 'the woman in the text' or gendered writing. If 'theory' involves recourse either to the order of empirical observation (things as they are) or to delusion (things as they are not) or, on the contrary, a return to the field of representation (like patriarchal discourse, the traditional arena of women's oppression), would we do better to renounce it altogether?

And yet the question 'Is there a woman in the text?' remains a central one – perhaps *the* central one – for feminist critics, and it is impossible to answer it without theory of some kind. The respective answers given by Anglo-American and French criticism are defined, in part at least, by the inherent paradox of 'theory'. In America the flight toward empiricism takes the form of an insistence on 'woman's experience' as the ground of difference in writing. 'Women's writing', 'the woman reader', 'female culture' occupy an almost unchallenged position of authority in feminist critical discourse of this kind. The assumption is of an unbroken continuity between 'life' and 'text' – a mimetic relation whereby women's writing, reading, or culture, instead of being produced, reflect a knowable reality.[27] Just as one can identify a woman biologically (the unstated argument would run), so one can with a little extra labor identify a woman's text, a woman reader, the essence of female culture. Of course the category of 'women's writing' remains as strategically and politically important in classroom, curriculum, or interpretive community as the specificity of women's oppression is to the women's movement. And yet to leave the question there, with an easy recourse to the female signature or to female being, is either to beg it or to biologize it. To insist, for instance, that *Frankenstein* reflects Mary Shelley's experience of the trauma of parturition and postpartum depression may tell us about women's lives, but it reduces the text itself to a monstrous symptom. Equally, to see it as the product of 'bibliogenesis' – a feminist rereading of *Paradise Lost* that, in exposing its misogynist politics, makes the monster's fall an image of woman's fall into the hell of sexuality – rewrites the novel in the image not of books but of female experience.[28] Feminist interpretations such as these have no option but to posit the woman author as origin and her life as the primary locus of meaning.

By contrast, the French insistence on *écriture féminine* – on woman as a writing-effect instead of an origin – asserts not the sexuality of the text but the textuality of sex. Gender difference, produced, not innate, becomes a matter of the structuring of a genderless libido in and through patriarchal discourse. Language itself would at once repress multiplicity and heterogeneity – true difference – by the tyranny of hierarchical oppositions (man/woman) and simultaneously work to overthrow that tyranny by interrogating the limits of meaning. The 'feminine, in this scheme, is to be located in the gaps, the absences, the unsayable or unrepresentable of discourse and representation.[29] The feminine text becomes the elusive, phantasmal inhabitant of phallocentric discourse, as Gradiva *rediviva* haunts Freud's *Delusions and Dreams,* or, for the skeptical Girard, the narcissistic woman exercises her illusory power over the theory of narcissism. And yet, in its claim that women must write the body, that only the eruption of female *jouissance* can revolutionize discourse and challenge the Law of the Father, *écriture féminine* seems – however metaphorically – to be reaching not so much for essentialism (as it is often accused of doing) as for the conditions of representability. The theoretical abstraction of a 'marked' writing that can't be observed at the level of the sentence but only glimpsed as an alternative libidinal economy almost invariably gives rise to gender-specific images of voice, touch, anatomy; to biologistic images of milk or *jouissance*. How else, after all, could the not-yet-written forms of *écriture féminine* represent themselves to our understanding? Not essentialism but representationalism is the French equivalent of Anglo-American empiricism – an alternative response to the indeterminacy and impenetrability of theory. If the woman in the text is 'there', she is also 'not there' – certainly not its object, not necessarily even its author. That may be why the heroine of feminist critical theory is not the silenced Irma, victim of Freudian theory, but the hysterical Dora whose body is her text and whose refusal to be the object of Freudian discourse makes her the subject of her own. Perhaps the question that feminist critics should ask themselves is not 'Is there a woman in this text?' but rather: '*Is there a text in this woman?*'

Notes

1. See *Jokes and Their Relation to the Unconscious* (1905), SE, 8, pp. 97-101; and see also Jeffrey Mehlman.' How to Read Freud on Jokes: The Critic as Schadchen', *New Literary History* (Winter 1975), 6(2) pp. 439-61, for the suggestion that the interfering third party is the oedipal father.

2. STANLEY FISH, *Is There a Text in This Class? The Authority of Interpretive*

Communities (Cambridge, Mass: Harvard University Press, 1980) p. 305.

3. See *The Interpretation of Dreams* (1900), SE, 4, pp. 106-21. This was the dream apropos of which Freud wrote to Fliess in 1900, fantasizing that the house, where he had dreamed it might one day bear a marble tablet with the words : 'In this house, on July 24th, 1895, the Secret of Dreams was Revealed to Dr. Sigm. Freud'. See Jeffrey Mehlman. 'Thimethylamin: Notes on Freud's Specimen Dream', *Diacritics* (Spring 1976), 6(1) pp. 42-45: 'Freud...make(s) her cough up (his) truth.'

4. KOFMAN, *Quatre romans analytiques,* p. 133: 'L'inconscient de l'analyse, comme celui de tout homme, est inéliminable.'

5. As the editor of the *Standard Edition* notes, *Delusions and Dreams* contains 'not only a summary of Freud's explanation of dreams but also what is perhaps the first of his semi-popular accounts of his theory of the neuroses and of the therapeutic action of psycho-analysis' (SE, 9,p 5).

6. Compare Freud's own remark, in 'Construction in Analysis', that 'the delusions of patients appear to me to be the equivalents of the constructions which we build up in the course of analytic treatment ' (SE, 23, p. 268).

7. KOFMAN, *Quatre romans analytiques,* p. 16: 'Un appât pour mieux attraper la carpe vérité: celle du texte littéraire qui doit confirmer celle de la psychanalyse.'

8. A copy of the bas-relief – which Freud saw in the Vatican in 1907 as 'a dear familiar face' – hung in his consulting room; see Ernst L. Freud (ed.), *Letters of Sigmund Freud* (New York: Basic Books, 1960), p. 267.

9. SARAH KOFMAN, 'Narcissistic Woman', *The Enigma of Woman*, Catherine Porter, trans. (Ithaca: Cornell University Press, 1985), p. 56. See 'On Narcissism: An Introduction' SE, 14, pp. 73-102, especially pp. 88-9.

10. As Kofman suggests in *Quatre romans analytiques*, p. 124, stone is at once a symbol of castration and a defense against castration; Hanold's foot fetishism might be related to the obsessive question, Does Gradiva, or does she not, have a penis?

11. JACQUES LACAN, 'Le rêve de l'injection d'Irma', *Le Séminaire, Livre ll: Le moi dans la théorie de Freud et dans la technique de la psychanalyse* – 1954–55 (Paris: Seuil, 1978), p. 203: 'Car c'est toujours être coupable que de transgresser une limite jusque-là imposée à l'activité humaine.'

12. See Mary Shelley's 1831 'Introduction' to her *Frankenstein or the Modern Prometheus*, ed. M. K. Joseph, (London and New York: Oxford University Press, 1969), p. 8. Subsequent page references in the text are to this edition.

13. JAMES WATSON, *The Double Helix: A Personal Account of the Discovery of the Structure of DNA* (New York: Atheneum, 1968), p. 18. Subsequent page references in the text are to this edition.

14. Quoted by Horace Judson, *The Eighth Day of Creation: Makers of the Revolution in Biology* (New York: Simon and Schuster, 1979), p. 194. Judson's is perhaps the most balanced account of the relations between Watson, Crick, Wilkins, Franklin and especially of the work of the latter.

15. See Anne Sayre, *Rosalind Franklin and DNA* (New York: Norton, 1975), p. 21.

16. FRANCIS CRICK, *Life Itself: Its Origin and Nature* (New York: Simon and Schuster, 1981), p. 72. Crick has interesting things to say about theory apropos of his own

theory of 'Directed Panspermia' as the origin of life on earth, which his wife objects to as 'not a real theory but merely science fiction' (p. 148).

17. See Toril Moi, 'The Missing Mother: The Oedipal Rivalries of René Girard', *Diacritics* (Summer 1982), 12(2), pp. 21-31, for an excellent critique of Girard.

18. See also Mary Poovey, 'My Hideous Progeny: The Lady and The Monster', *The Proper Lady and the Woman Writer* (Chicago and London: University of Chicago Press, 1984), pp. 114-42, for a reading of Frankenstein in the light of its relation to Romantic egotism.

19. The film versions of Frankenstein, including Whale's, are discussed by Albert J. Lavalley, 'The Stage and Film Children of Frankenstein: A Survey', in George Levine and U. C. Knoepflmacher (eds.), *The Endurance of Frankenstein: Essays on Mary Shelley's Novel*, pp. 243-89, especially p. 273 (Berkeley: University of California Press, 1979); see also Donald F. Glut, *The Frankenstein Legend: A Tribute to Mary Shelley and Boris Karloff* (Metuchen, NJ: Scarecrow Press, 1973).

20. See Lacan's 'Le rêve de l'injection d'Irma', p. 186: 'Tout se mêle et associe dans cette image, de la bouche à l'organe sexuel féminin....Il y a là une horrible découverte, celle de la chair qu'on ne voit jamais, le fond des choses, l'envers de la face, du visage, les sécretats par excellence, la chair dont tout sort, au plus profond même du mystère, la chair en tant qu'elle est souffrante, qu'elle est informe, que sa forme par soi-même est quelque chose qui provoque l'angoisse.'

21. See, for instance, the paintings by Masolino, Pseudo Met de Bles, and Raphaël reproduced in Roland M. Frye, *Milton's Imagery and the Visual Arts: Iconographic Tradition in the Epic Poems* (Princeton: Princeton University Press, 1978).

22. KOFMAN's 'Narcissistic Woman', in *The Enigma of Woman*, pp. 50-65 debates René Girard's 'Le Narcissisme: le désir de Freud' in *Des choses cachées depuis la fondation du monde*, pp. 391–414 (Paris: B. Grasset, 1978), recast as 'Narcissism: The Freudian Myth Demythified by Proust' in Alan Roland (ed.), *Psychoanalysis. Creativity, and Literature*, pp. 293-311 (New York: Columbia University Press, 1978). For a related discussion of the narcissistic woman and her role in Kofman's writing, see Elizabeth Berg, 'The Third Woman', *Diacritics* (Summer 1982), 12(2) pp. 11–20.

23. KOFMAN, 'Narcissistic Woman', pp. 61–2.

24. GIRARD, 'Le Narcissisme: le désir de Freud', pp. 393–4: 'Ce qu'il appelle l'auto-suffisance de la coquette, c'est en réalité la transfiguration métaphysique du modèle-rival.'

25. GIRARD, 'Narcissism: The Freudian Myth', pp. 308, 309.

26. See Raimo Tuomela, *Theoretical Concepts* (New York: Springer-Verlag, 1973), pp. 3-4 and Nathan Rotenstreich, *Theory and Practice: An Essay in Human Intentionalities* (The Hague: Martinus Nijhoff, 1977) pp. 58–9; see also Clark Glymour, *Theory and Evidence* (Princeton: Princeton University Press, 1980).

27. See Jonathan Culler's discussion of the concept of 'the woman reader' in *On Deconstruction*, pp. 44–64.

28. See the respective readings of Frankenstein by Ellen Moers, 'Female Gothic' in Levine and Knoepflmacher, *The Endurance of Frankenstein*, pp. 77-78, and by Gilbert and Gubar, 'Horror's Twin: Mary Shelley's Monstrous Eve', *The Madwoman in the Attic*, pp. 313–47.

29. See, for instance, Hélène Cixous. 'The Laugh of the Medusa', in Marks and de

Courtivron, *New French Feminisms*, pp. 24–64 and 'Castration or Decapitation', trans., Annette Kuhn, *Signs* (Autumn 1981), 7(1), pp. 41–55; Luce Irigaray, 'When Our Lips Speak Together' and 'The Power of Discourse and the Subordination of the Feminine', in *This Sex Which Is Not One*, trans. Catherine Porter, (Ithaca: Cornell University Press, 1985), pp. 205–18, 68–85. For a recent critique of *l'écriture féminine*, see also Ann Rosalind Jones, 'Writing the Body: Toward an Understanding of *L'Écriture Féminine*', *Feminist Studies* (Summer 1981), 7(2): pp. 247–63, reprinted in Elaine Showalter, (ed.), *The New Feminist Criticism: Essays on Women, Literature, and Theory* (New York: Pantheon Books, 1985), pp. 361–77.

STEPHEN HEATH 'Male Feminism'*

Mary Jacobus's discussion in this book of the relationship between men, women and theory is given a sharper focus by Stephen Heath in his consideration of the specific relationship of men to feminism. In many ways the two essays intersect. For instance, both critics are preoccupied with issue of sexuality and textuality; both ponder the links between social experience and political allegiance; both explore the dangers and possibilities of marginality. But Heath's emphasis on men's role in feminism introduces some distinctive questions. Is men's interaction with feminism always 'impossible'? Can men be feminists, or can they at best merely hope to be anti-sexist or pro-feminist? For men, does feminism function partly as an object around which they can regroup? Heath exposes our present dilemma: men should take feminism seriously, but they should not appropriate it; women may welcome men to feminism but they need to remain cautious both about motives and possible consequences. Heath's essay is the first in a volume entitled *Men in Feminism* and many of the contributors respond to his thesis. The volume is resonant with anger and anxiety, claim and counter-claim. But an impressive intellectual energy also pervades and in this respect Heath's essay is a distinguished example (see Introduction pp. 13, 19–20).

Men's relation to feminism is an impossible one. This is not said sadly nor angrily (though sadness and anger are both known and common

---

*STEPHEN HEATH's 'Male Feminism' originally appeared in a longer format in *The Dalhousie Review*. Reprinted in Alice Jardine and Paul Smith (eds), *Men in Feminism* (New York and London: Methuen, 1987), pp.1–32.

reactions) but politically. Men have a necessary relation to feminism – the point after all is that it should change them too, that it involves learning new ways of being women *and men* against and as an end to the reality of women's oppression – and that relation is also necessarily one of a certain exclusion – the point after all is that this is a matter *for women,* that it is their voices and actions that must determine the change and redefinition. Their voices and actions, not ours: no matter how 'sincere', 'sympathetic' or whatever, we are always also in a male position which brings with it all the implications of domination and appropriation, everything precisely that is being challenged, that has to be altered. Women are the subjects of feminism, its initiators, its makers, its force; the move and the join from being a woman to being a feminist is the grasp of that subjecthood. Men are the objects, part of the analysis, agents of the structure to be transformed, representatives in, carriers of the patriarchal mode; and my desire to be a subject there too in feminism – to be a feminist – is then only also the last feint in the long history of *their* colonization. Which does not mean, of course not, that I can do nothing in my life, that no actions are open to me, that I cannot respond to and change for feminism (that would be a variant on the usual justification for the status quo, men are men and that's that); it just means that I have to realize nevertheless – and this is an effort not a platitude – that I am not where they are and that I cannot pretend to be (though men do, colonizing, as they always have done), which is the impossibility of my, men's relation.

Nothing in the above is intended to suggest a kind of criterion of immediacy. Women are not feminists by virture of the act alone of being women: feminism is a social-political reality, a struggle, a commitment, women *become* feminists. Simply, the negotiation between lived experience and feminism is for them direct, feminism includes that experience as its material and its energy, producing a knowledge of it for action, for change. The contradictions that may exist between, say, a woman's experience in her family in the defined roles of wife and housewife and mother which may be felt by her as the authentic terms of her being, where she is really 'herself', and the perspectives feminism will give on that experience, those defined roles, on her position as a woman, are what feminism is about, what it looks at, works from, involves, allowing the move and join from woman to feminist. For a man the negotiation is blocked, doubly contradictory: his experience is her oppression, and at the end of whatever negotiation he might make he can only always also confront the fact that feminism starts from there. To refuse the confrontation, to ignore, repress, forget, slide over, project onto 'other men' that fact, is for a man to refuse feminism, not to listen to what it says to him as a man, imagining to his satisfaction a possible relation instead of the difficult, contradictory, self-critical, painful, impossible one that men must, for now, really live.

'I am tired of men arguing amongst themselves as to who is the most feminist, frustrated by an object feminism becoming the stakes in a displaced rivalry between men because of a refusal by men to examine the structure of the relations between themselves,' Claire Pajaczkowska.[1] There we have an expression of anger from a feminist, tiredness and frustration. And I accept that. But how? At a distance? Of course I think that *I* never have argued about being 'the most feminist', others, not me. Yet I can hardly stay at that distance, self-assured, as if I do then, exactly, feminism *is* an object, something I *can* simply position myself in relation to, like some academic study. But then again, if I take it up into me, into my life, calling into question the assumptions of the position of myself (as opposed to just 'taking it up' like Sanskrit or Deconstruction), how do I develop a reflection on it, how do I think and talk and write about – *with* - feminism without falling back into the male argument, without producing another version of the object feminism up for grabs, 'the stakes'?

Pajaczkowska suggests an answer, by examining the structure of the relations between men, me in those relations. She says this, in fact, in an article on pornography, a response to two pieces by men on that topic; which reminds me of a remark by another feminist, B Ruby Rich, again in an article on pornography, to the effect that if 'the legions of feminist men' wanted to do something useful, 'a proper subject', they could 'undertake the analysis that can tell us why men like porn (not, piously, why this or that exceptional man does *not*).'[2]

Pornography and the relations between men and liking pornography... That pornography *is* a relation between men, nothing to do with a relation to women except by a process of phallic conversion that sets them as the terms of male exchange, is now an established part of radical critical awareness; the analysis has been made many times. Which still leaves theoretical-political *issues*: even if a typical reality of pornography can be recognized, is pornography only that, are there distinctions to be made, different kinds? Is all pornography violent and offensive? Are there connections between pornography and sexual liberation that are important, progressive? Are men's and women's pleasures in sexual imagery bound up with or separate – separable – from pornographic representations and how? Are pornographic images for male arousal necessarily the reproduction of domination? What should be done about pornography and how? Is it in itself a central target for action or does it deflect from the needed critique of a challenge to the violent sexual objectification of women running through the whole range of cultural forms that are socially accepted as non-pornographic? All these and more are issues that have been, are being debated by women, by feminists (for an argued account, from which I have borrowed here, I refer to the relevant chapter of Elizabeth Wilson's *What Is To Be Done About Violence Against Women?*[3])

My immediate concern though is male feminism. I once wrote, quoting a phrase coined by Robin Morgan and used in women-against-pornography movements: '"Pornography is the theory and rape the practice" – learning to understand the truth of that statement – and to understand it personally, with respect to one's own life – is a political-ethical necessity.'[4] I believe that, for men: if men do not grasp that in themselves, then I think the social structure of sexual oppression is still abstract for them and that feminism is beyond them, out there, just an object again. This is not, obviously, to say that feminism is merely about pornography, only that pornography in our societies, the capitalized circulation of images of sexual-commodity women, is one good crystallization of that social structure, that oppression (there are many others), whether or not those images are ostensibly violent or ostensibly not. 'Pornography is the theory and rape the practice' (says it exactly); and if, a reproach that is made, this is a crude position, and reading the feminist debate round the issues mentioned above does make the question complex, difficult, it must still be said that starting from it is necessary for men – do we want to be *subtle* about it, more prevarication, more defensiveness?

One way of grasping the structure of the relations between men is, indeed, with respect to pornography in these terms: what complicity of masculinity does pornography involve me in? Whether or not I have anything to do with it is in this context irrelevant (no need for personal piousness); it has to do with me, inescapably, not just because I live in its society but because too, which is what that means, pornography is this society's running commentary on the sexual for me, the final image I can have (how do I dissociate myself from that image and don't I in the very fact of dissociation recognize its involvement of me, in me?). And it runs into theory as well. For Freud after all, in the last years of his long life's work of the elaboration of psychoanalysis, 'the repudiation of femininity must surely be a biological fact, part of the great riddle of sex'.[5] Edged through by 'femininity' object and limit, explanation and enigma, psychoanalysis turns round and round again to its difficulties, all its insights and its blindness coming down into Freud's ultimate weariness, the gloom of understanding, 'the repudiation of femininity'. Pornography in its typical contemporary reality knows nothing but that: it gives a 'female sexuality' that fits and reassures the repudiation, the representation of her confirmed and confirming – woman as phallic, the same in a masculine sexual economy, and woman as passive, feminine, the exact and separate other half, the opposite sex, that that economy requires, allaying the fear of the non-identity of maleness, that men might really be feminine and passive too ('masculine' and 'feminine', those concepts that Freud rejects as 'of no use' in psychology but that he continues to use, filling them with 'active' and 'passive', and that he finds with the psychical 'bedrock' of every male or female individual: men fear passivity, women envy the penis, femininity repudiated). Pornography is developed to be about 'men together', in every sense of the term: all the figures in its system are male, masculinity from start to finish; its consumption defines a community of men; its aim is my identity as defined maleness, *me* together, untouched by real relations of sexual difference that include me in the fact of difference, in a sexuality that is heterogeneous, problematic, unstable, the process of my individual history, not just one sex, one's sex, the given heterosexual.

What can then be asked, I think, coming back to theory, coming back to male feminism, is whether that sexual system, that togetherness, is not always in danger of being replayed: contemporary theory as the rebonding of men round 'the feminine' (what exactly is happening when Derrida proclaims his wish to write 'as (a) woman' and all those deconstructing academics excel themselves for the time of a book or an article in woman's non-place, knowing as *'she* knows' that 'there is no truth'?[6]), male feminism as getting hold again – for the last time? – of the question of 'the woman' (are we sure that we are *so* far from the general cultural fascination with woman and 'liberation' and the sexual, from all its modes of recuperation?). Pajaczkowska's tiredness and frustration can go alongside and as a counterbalance to Freud's weariness: the repudiation of femininity and an object feminism, feminism as an expression of women that becomes an object for me, another way of retrieving her, very nicely, as mine, another view of the old enigma, woman again. Is it possible to wonder whether there is not in male feminism, men's relation to feminism, always . potentially a pornographic effect?

Which is said in difficulty, in recognition of something of the contradictions that there must be in this social reality for men who try to be with feminism. Society, Freud insisted, was rooted in male homosexual love, it was this which was compatible with group ties; women laid the foundations of civilization by the claims of their love which are then also its disturbance, an opposition of women little capable of instinctual sublimation, a sexual threat; so that society stands on the bond of men, repressed homosexuality, maintained in its patriarchal forms on the absolute distinction of the sexes, men as men, one and then the other, she as the difference, the projected 'dark continent', man's unknown. Recently, Rosalind Coward has stressed that it is in reality 'men's bodies, men's sexuality which is the true "dark continent" of this society.'[7] The risk of men's relation to feminism is that it stay a male affair, an argument round women that masks again its male stakes, that refuses again as women are projected back into the safeguard of our identity the real problem, the real point at which change must come, exactly ourselves, the end of 'masculinity' – which, of course, is the end of 'woman' too.

'What do men know about women's martyrdoms?' wrote Thackeray in 1848 in his novel *Vanity Fair*:

We should go mad had we to endure the hundredth part of those daily pains which are meekly borne by many women. Ceaseless slavery meeting with no reward; constant gentleness and kindness met by cruelty as constant; love, labour, patience, watchfulness, without even so much as the acknowledgement of a good word; all this, how many of them have to bear in quiet, and appear abroad with cheerful faces as if they felt nothing. Tender slaves that they are, they must needs be hypocrites and weak.[8]

Thackeray is sympathetic *and* patronizing *and* caught up in all the attitudes that help to make the situation of women he describes. Women are exploited but that exploitation is also their nature, they *are* tender slaves that is what makes them women. All the terms that Thackeray uses – gentleness, kindness, love, labour, patience, watchfulness – are women's qualities, the fact of their true womanhood, and the situation described is the context in which those qualities are brought out; so that what is at stake is not change but recognition – the acknowledgement of a good word, the due reward for the ceaseless slavery. Sincerely, Thackeray is locked into his perception of 'women's martyrdoms': women's lot is cruel and he is alongside them to express the cruelty; martydom is the very condition of saints and he is there to celebrate saintliness, reconfirming that lot.

We can see this easily now, looking back at the past, men as well as women. But how much of male feminism today may not also be analysable as a similar gesture of sympathy-reconfirmation? Can men see that? Suspicion of sympathy: *why, how* am I sympathetic?

Barthes one day in conversation: 'you study what you desire or what you fear.' In any formal sense I haven't studied feminism or feminist issues (is formal study anyway the point?) but I have read and thought about and written in relation to it and them, written on matters that are matters with which feminism is concerned – sexual difference, the contemporary construction of sexuality, the imaging and representation of men and women. Desire? Fear? Both? The questions are difficult to avoid. Writing after all is always an imaging and representation of myself, the passage of a certain desire: it takes a stance and asks for me to be seen in this or that way, even if I cannot control – master – its effects, how you will read me. Of course, there are conventions and genres of the elimination of desire, my writing as the voice of truth, reason, science, which is then the imaging and representation of an institutionalized mastery, my desire for that, that as my 'fitness'. To respond to feminism is to forgo mastery: 'the personal is political' tells me also that I cannot refuse to analyze my desire, that the impersonal safety of authority can no longer be mine. Is that then where the fear enters and connects? Feminism makes things unsafe for men, unsettles assumed positions, undoes given identities. Hence so often the violence of the reactions, that is clear. But hence too perhaps, less clear, elements in the relations men make with feminism, their sympathy. If I can move close to feminism, it may be that I can regain something of a male/female security, get back something of an identity. Do I write from desire-fear, to say simply in the last analysis 'love me', accept me at least as 'modestly, ingloriously marginal'? Which was indeed Barthes's definition of *the lover* today.

Desire and fear at any rate could serve as something of a genealogical probe for male feminism, somewhere from which to think about this or that manifestation and its implications. To think about, which does not mean to reduce to but merely to remember *as well* the sexual strategies of discourse, the subjectivity of the production of knowledge. One could, for example, think about Lacan and his work in this way, giving a different perspective to those of the accounts by followers and propagators. From the initial encounter with the woman, the enigma of her (in the 1930s, curiously coincidental with the beginnings of Freud's 'return' to 'feminity', the 'dark continent', Lacan confronts female paranoia, the Papin sisters and Aimée, the subject of his thesis) through to the Encore seminar and beyond (Lacan in the 1970s devoting himself explicitly to 'what Freud expressly left aside, the *Was will das Weib?*, the *What does woman want?*'[9]) we have what? The question, the woman, her non-existence, her not-allness, a pleasure – *jouissance* – proper to her, supplementary, beyond the phallus, related to God…and an address and a self-address in and out of all this which is at once provocative, Lacan putting feminists right, ah the phallus, and identificationary, Lacan a better woman and in love with him and herself, talking about love itself a *jouissance* and psychoanalysis nothing else but that anyway… 'When it comes down to it', announced Lacan on one occasion to his seminar audience, 'I am a perfect hysteric, that is to say, without symptoms, except from time to time mistakes in gender', having given an example of taking 'Miss' – *Mademoiselle* – for masculine.[10] The male analyst understands the woman and speaks in her place, is the perfection of the hysteric, no symptoms, save only the mistakes in gender, the misidentifications indeed, running in and out of her from *his* position, miss-taken but perfect – fear, desire, the love letter as regrounding of authority.

(And where does that leave the woman Lacanian analyst? In his place too? Exactly?)

When the Lacanian analyst sees young people on nude-bathing beaches, what does she know? 'They (the young people) want to go all the way to the end, but there is no end, other than castration and death.'[11] Naively, I understand death as an end, a final reality, but *castration*? The fact of sexual reproduction is also the fact of death, the continuation of the species at the cost of the individual who is transient, mortal. To say which, however, is not to say castration, castration as end, another final reality. There are lots of things one might grasp on nude beaches, and depending on their location: for instance, the beaches in the South of France which this analyst most likely has in mind raise questions to do with the treatment and place of the old (why 'young people'?), with racial inequality (how many of France's 'immigrant' population are to be seen?), with the whole economic definition of the body, the sexual. But *castration*?

'It's extraordinary', commented Juliet Mitchell in an interview recently, 'what happens when you get rid of the centrality of the concept of the phallus. I mean, you get rid of the unconscious, get rid of sexuality, get rid of the original psychoanalytic point.'[12] Just as on the beach we confront castration, so we cannot think without the centrality of the concept of the phallus – to do so would to be 'get rid of' the unconscious and sexuality. These latter are bound up with difference and division and language in the individual, the excess of the individual over the simple sexual function of species reproduction, the movement of desire that that excess constitutes in our particular histories as speaking beings. For psychoanalysis, which indeed opens for understanding this scene of the unconscious and sexuality, the phallus, the penis sublime as symbol, is *the* mark of division and difference, the ur-signifier, the ultimate and initial point of meaning, closing the unconscious and sexuality round it. And from there the scenario is everywhere played out, down to the young people on the beach, no other end, it's extraordinary....

What can I say to that? Apart from, in the crudest psychoanalytic response, *nothing*, since to say anything to it is merely an indication of my resistance, defence, denial, since the phallus and castration give the very structure from where I can speak at all. I can say and try to show that what is being described by psychoanalysis with the phallus and castration and all the other accompanying terms fits a specific social-historical definition and production of men, women, sexuality. I can say and try to show that the fact of division, the unconscious and the sexual is not by definition dependent on the primacy of the phallus, locked immutably in the same old fixed scenario (joining the whole debate on psychoanalysis and historical understanding to which Juliet Michell herself has contributed so much). The theoretical work is valuable and perhaps I can help in it. But what can I say from day to day, teaching, talking, just generally around? I find myself in fact continually defending and criticizing Freud and Lacan, psychoanalysis in their terms, rejecting and needing its descriptions, those terms. Which is where it is true that castration is the end, the final reality of this peculiar split, the original point to which it all comes down and from which, getting rid of the centrality of the concept of the phallus, it all has to be rethought, relived.

But then these are pious words and perhaps this is another way of saying the impossibility of men's relation to feminism. It is as though psychoanalysis is there as a kind of necessary impasse today, full of truth about the construction of our subjectivity, about the realization of the sexual identity of men and women, and full of an historical and social censorship, the foregone conclusion of the centrality of the concept of the phallus. The use of the truth against the censorship by women is one thing, but men after all *are* that truth, they can hardly simply use it against the censorship they today define and represent. I think of another analyst, close to and distant from Lacan, saying once: 'Imagine that it were a woman who had invented the unconscious...certainly she would not have invented that unconscious. Impossible, absolutely impossible.'[13] Yes and no? No doubt she would not have, but the unconscious that Freud invented he also found, found these particular structures and the phallus with them. Freud gets Dora right and she him, which is where the protest, the use, the critique, the reinvention begin, as they only can, from *her*.

Feminism is a subject for women who are, precisely, its subjects, the people who make it, it is their affair. Feminism is also a subject for men, what it is about obviously concerns them; they have to learn to make it their affair, to carry it through into our lives. Feminism speaks to me, not principally nor equally but *too*, to me too: the definitions and images and stories and laws and institutions oppressive of women that it challenges, ends, involve me since not only will I find myself playing some part in their reproduction but I too am caught up in them, given as 'man' in their reflection, confined in that place which is then presented as 'mine'. I have written about this, written about matters of feminism, for example in the book *The Sexual Fix* quoted above about the current construction of sexuality for men and women or in an essay entitled 'Difference' about psychoanalysis and sexual difference.[14] But I do not at all think, even less claim, that these are feminist writings; it is just that they depend on learning from feminism. This is, I believe, the most any man can do today: to learn and so to try to write or talk or act in response to feminism and so to try not in any way to be anti-feminist, supportive of the old oppressive structures. Any more, any notion of writing a feminist book or being a feminist, is a myth, a male imaginary with the reality of appropriation and domination right behind. But who am I to say this? But still, can't I say that this seems to me how we should see it, part of the ethics of sexual difference today?

Then I think of a counter-example, a bit of *evidence*. Isn't John Stuart Mill's *The Subjection of Women* evidently a feminist book? No doubt. Here is a book written by a man that was clearly progressive and important for feminism, part of its history; Mill's intervention into the debate over the equality of the sexes widely recognized by women in the late nineteenth-century and subsequently as 'an enormous advantage to the whole women's movement.'[15] No doubt. But *historically*. Today the history has changed, feminism has grown and advanced, there is no place in that way for a Mill.

And anyway Mill did not set out to write a feminist book, 'just' a book about the situation and rights of women. And anyway recognition of his book's very positive and effective contribution need not avoid the possibility of a negative aspect, Mill's work depending on his male authority and perhaps hiding the work of the women around him on whose actions and analyses he depended at the same time that his book would encourage them. And anyway, the point of this here, the *preoccupation* with acting, speaking, writing 'feminist', as opposed to the *fact* for women of being feminist, is male contemporary, observable now in certain groups of men (intellectuals, radicals): something to do with being right, correct, finding the authority of identity (and vice versa).

It happens often enough in meetings and discussions in which issues concerning feminism are involved and at which women are largely present that one hears a man preface what he wants to say with 'I live with a radical feminist' or 'I have talked about this with a lot of radical women' or some other, similar statement. What follows is then usually some objection, the expression of some effectively reactionary, very male-sexist position. This is a version, of course, of the some-of-my-best-friends-are ploy, as such not specific to debates about women and feminism, found also in, say, those about race, about racism.

What interests me, though, is that some of us have learnt not to say such things, have learnt that we cannot guarantee our position in that way, that *just because* the personal is political it cannot be used to shore up some purity of being – some rightness – for me. The personal as political means that I cannot simply refer to the personal as *my* identity, that I have to think that identity through in the social terms it carries at its center, as an *identity*: however many feminist women I know, it is not going to remove me from the structures of sexism, absolve me from the facts of male positioning, domination and so on. The oppression of women is not personal, it is social and I am involved in it as a person in this society; there is no personal guarantee against that. Though this is not to say that I am powerless to renegotiate my identity against those structures, that positioning – that after all has been the work of women in feminism, opposing the given terms for them, renegotiating *their* identity.

Where then am I when I hear 'I live with etc.?' Somewhere else. *I* know better. Do I? And really somewhere else? The problem is still one of guarantees: to believe I am somewhere else and know better is still to appeal to a personal distinction and to suggest an authorization. But what could this latter be? It is not, another version of the personal guarantee, that women's discourse is secured as feminist by the fact of their being women (there are reactionary and anti-feminist women) but that the relation between discourse and experience is *politically* negotiable by women in respect of the reality of their position as objects of oppression, inequality, sexism. Unable to make that negotiation, I am caught in the double bind of a position and a discourse that will always be today a reflection of domination, social maleness. Whenever I know, precisely I don't, and I have to accept a certain insecurity, the end of authority and authorization, to live a difficult and contradictory process of renegotiation in which *I* can never be assured (no matter what reassurance – the guarantees – I might try to claim). I have to beware too of turning this into some kind of existential tragedy (the tough-time-men-now-have on which popular magazines are always running stories); it's just a political fact, no more, no less.

One can also add to the 'I live with etc.' gesture the frequently observed ambition of men to be more radical, the most radical in feminism. Once again the more, the most, guarantees, proves correctness. Except, of course, that it doesn't; the extreme simply wipes out the experience it purports to represent (as men have always ordinarily done). So that 'radical' in what preceded ought to have been in inverted commas, since this 'radical' is literally reaction, male reaction, against the new reality of women and feminism that exactly it refuses in the very moment it speaks for it, for them.

In a lecture given a few years ago to the – shortlived – Cambridge Alternative English Faculty (the lecture subsequently became part of a chapter of his *Walter Benjamin or Towards a Revolutionary Criticism*), Terry Eagleton, after having reviewed some of the issues for a Marxist aesthetics and listed 'the major Marxist Aestheticians of the century to date' from Lukacs to himself, turned to 'feminist criticism' as 'a paradigm' for 'a "revolutionary literary criticism"', entering as he did so the following 'reservation': 'Feminist criticism is still notably underdeveloped, and much of it so far has been empiricist, unsubtle and theoretically thin.'[16] I think there was a little *frisson* in the audience, something rather daring had been said, and also some unexpressed rage.

'Reservation' is an interesting word in this context: the stance of the securely judging voice, commending and caveating; the indication of the containing place assigned, feminist criticism sent back to its reservation; and then, coming round to the voice again, the confirmation of the stance, this voice reserving its rights as it enters the reservation, seeing feminist criticism within the limits of its place. And in fact, 'feminist literary theory' as sighted by Eagleton is exactly a theoretical problem from the outside, the onlooker's worry about specificity and autonomy, about whether the people on the reservation have anything very much to say for themselves theoretically, depending as they do on other 'general theories' ('most notably, Marxism, semiotics and psychoanalysis'): 'There is, then, a theoretical problem about the meaning of an autonomous "feminist literary theory" of any developed kind.' Not that there isn't also a political problem, that of the '"radical-feminist" problematic', the 'jealous defence of feminist "autonomy" – *separatism*, in fact' which is 'a scandal that any revolutionary, man or woman, must surely denounce'. Feminism is found lacking in autonomy in theory, which is its failing (note the doubting quote marks, '"feminist literary theory"'), but when you get autonomy in practice it is another kind of failing, a real scandal (and the quote marks shift their position and attack, 'feminist "autonomy"').

Might not all this be completely irrelevant? Suppose we abandoned the judgement of autonomy, specificity and so on, stopped worrying about feminist theory in those terms, recognized it as strongly unreserved, not much bothered about where it might fit in some overall theoretical spectacle. Theory, we know, has its etymological roots in spectacle, the Greek *theoria* with its indications of sight and contemplation, and women have long been the point of its spectacular exclusion at best a voice-off (as with the 'woman from Mantinea, called Diotima' to whom Socrates appeals in *The Symposium* for his major speech on love).[17] Perhaps theory, not the theoretical but *theory* with all its reservations, is today a male move, an argument from men, their self-preserve, the dominant reservation (Irigaray has been saying and showing this in her work, to be greeted again and again with cries of 'irrationalism', another scandal).[18] And then what are men doing when they shift their gaze from theory to practice, a less controllable spectacle, and inveigh in their theory-books against '"radical feminism"' (more quote marks), against that 'feminist "autonomy"' which any revolutionary woman, he says, must surely denounce? Isn't feminism now exactly about women's autonomy and isn't the definition of the terms of that autonomy exactly an issue for women? Is it helpful, appropriate, feminist for men to stand in judgement of feminism and its theorical work and its political debates, brandishing an assumed standard of autonomy in the one hand and its foregone dismissal in the other?

None of this is written to be cleverer than or superior to Terry Eagleton (to whom, as my teacher, I anyway owe so much), even if in the reflection of writing I cannot – do not know how to – avoid that male image, the image of bettering, of asserting superiority. Given theory and reservations, Eagleton's 'theoretically thin' is probably right; he thinks it is. I think the contrary, that if we step outside the bounds of theory and reservations, stop waiting to see "what a 'feminist literary theory' as such might mean" (why are we waiting to see and should women wait too?) we shall find a range of work by feminists (Irigaray and Spivak and Bovenschen and Coward and…though the point is not to produce an imitation of Eagleton's list of 'major Marxist aestheticians') which can only make the judgement of 'theoretically thin' appear as a gesture of reaction and resistance (who cares if this work doesn't fit some decided image of what should be 'a "feminist literary theory" as such'?). Eagleton knows all this better than I do, but then he takes his position and I take mine; and in that movement I feel once again the difficulties, the conflict, the impossibilities of men's relation to feminism.

I experience embarrassment – a kind of critical unease – at writings by men on female sexuality: how can they, how can he still presume...? But then think of the reverse, women writing on male sexuality: Kate Millett in *Sexual Politics*, for example, or all the work on pornography by Andrea Dworkin, Angela Carter, Susan Griffin and so many others. That they know, that *she* knows something essential about male sexuality seems to me evident; I learn from them. So, reversing again, men can write on female sexuality and women can learn too.

   I hesitate, the embarrassment. All this reversing would be fine were it not that the two sides are neither equal nor symmetrical, are simply *not* the same. And this can be seen in the very idea of female sexuality, its construction as an object, something to write about. Take Freud: an essay entitled 'Female Sexuality' but not one entitled 'Male Sexuality', a chapter in the *New Introductory Lectures* on 'Femininity' but not on 'Masculinity'. Of course, Freud everywhere writes about men and sexuality, about the male sexual, but that is the norm, the point of departure, and as such at least unproblematic, not in question, not *the* question. When women around Freud write on female sexuality (Andreas-Salomé, Bonaparte, Deutsch, Horney...), often challengingly, they too are caught up in that question, his, and so contained nevertheless, as still by Lacan, still waiting contemptuously for women to come out with something of interest: 'since the time we've been begging them, begging them on our knees – I mentioned previously women analysts – to try to tell us, well, not a word! never been able to get anything out of them.'[19] He's right, they can't say anything interesting. How could they when the point is this *question,* which is always beyond whatever they might be able to say as the very fact of their being: they *are* the question. Female sexuality here is male sexuality, the male position and problem: woman as *my* other, she as the defining limit – the *jouissance au-delà*, as Lacanians put it – of my horizon as man.

   In the overall system of sexuality that is tightened to perfection in the nineteenth century and that still today determines so powerfully in so many ways the facts of our lives, male sexuality is repetition, female sexuality is query (darkness, riddle, enigma, problem, etc.). Of the former one can say nothing in as much as there is nothing to say beyond a few technical descriptions and a couple of moral injunctions or routine celebrations; men are men, there is no metaphysical agitation. Of the latter one can say nothing either in as much as women as women are the difference in the system so that there is everything to say; she is too much, a whole difficulty of knowing which is where female sexuality becomes the object, the topic, the title of the paper or the chapter or the book. We are in a long history from the nineteenth century through to today in which the self-evidence of sex (man, woman, the sexual act, reproduction) begins to weaken, in which 'sexuality' is the term of the recognition of everything that 'sex', 'one's sex', the 'two sexes' do not say, those notions unable to tell us much about sexual identity, about masculinity and femininity, about being a man, being a woman. Hence the tightening of the system, the definitions and redefinitions, the worried construction of 'female sexuality', all that writing; hence the constant return of sexuality to sex, to a phallic identity of man and woman, the sexual fix.

In a way, then, female sexuality is a bad question from a rotten history *and* a necessary one, for women against that history, disturbing its monolithic fiction (I pick up a feminist anthology, *Desire*: *The Politics of Sexuality*, not a single piece is called 'Female Sexuality' or 'Femininity' as though here the exploration of sexuality for women has already gone elsewhere to that construction).[20] While 'male sexuality' is a good question from a rotten history that could not pose it; an inevitable question for women, for Millett, for the writers on pornography, for those on rape, domestic violence, all the other matters of oppression. Instead of begging on our knees for women to go on silently proving their phallic otherness, we can listen to what they are effectively saying about *us*, about male sexuality, about the male operation of the sexual in our societies.

This is not to suggest that men might not have, ought not to have, something significant and real and unoppressive to say about women and sexuality: men's experience after all is part of many women's sexuality and men can know things in different ways, just as women can of men's sexuality. For the present though, in our societies, in our sexual history, I doubt in fact that men, that we, can. There is no equality, no symmetry, and so there can be no reversing: it is for women now to reclaim and redefine the terrain of sexuality, for us to learn from them. Which explains the unease, my opening embarrassment.

At a meeting of the Lacan School a woman analyst says this: 'The nature of femininity is to be cause of man's desire and, as corollary, not to be able to be recognized other than by a man is the nature of femininity. I know that the MLF (Women's Liberation Movement) will be "super-angry" but I'll carry on....'[21]

Whether or not feminists will be 'super-angry' (my rendering of the here trivializing *furax*, a kid's slang version of *furieux*, 'furious') will presumably depend on the stress given 'femininity'. If it is a matter of femininity as the constructed image of women, the image in which they are recognized and held as women, then what is being said is a truism: man's desire is set in relation to that construction of femininity which women are made to match and which thus exists precisely by virtue of its recognition by men. In that sense indeed, it really does take a man to know a woman, since she in this femininity is his knowledge, his image, the height of his imagination, – 'a real woman'. If it is a matter of something else, of femininity in connection with the reality and experience of women, being a woman, then what is being said might well give rise to anger, to political critique, to feminism.

Perhaps it is almost that 'feminine' and 'femininity' should be scrapped, their use abandoned; they come too loaded with the image, the construction, the monolithic male definition of the 'qualities' of women-woman. But not 'masculine' and 'masculinity', which *can* be used each time to name the elements of a system that assures male domination. The 'feminine' produced within that system is a male malady, fully masculine: *he* is sick from women, hence his endless attempts to confirm *her* as illness (the whole nineteenth-century coupling of women and sickness, 'for her own good'). 'Femininity': the woman you want, the woman you fear; 'masculinity': exactly the same.

Sometimes the sexologists ask us to consider and remember the terms of ownership in sexual exchange: 'Did you know that while it is true that anatomically a penis belongs to the man, his erection belongs to a woman?'[22]

Just about everything could be taken apart in that self-assured – Did you know? – sentence, from its hesitant grammatical logic (so that we might read the erection as belonging *anatomically* to a woman) to its instant heterosexuality (why can't the erection belong to him or to another man or, come to that, to no one at all in particular?). But my interest here is in the notion of belonging. Since I take it that it isn't a question of belonging anatomically for a woman, in what sense *does* his erection 'belong'? The flourished big deal for women in these ownership stakes, his erection belongs to her, is, of course, the reverse, is the reality of the same old story, *she* belongs to the erection: if there is an erection, then there must be 'a woman', she is its natural consequence, she's going to have to be around belonging – what, after all, does woman want? Somewhere at the far end of the sexologist's happy sentence is the philosophy of rape: his erection *belongs* to a woman, so she *must* want it and *ought* to get it, etc.

Perhaps there are different ways of thinking about belonging. Thus Michèle Montrelay: 'In the sexual act, the penis plunges into a "feminine" *jouissance* of which one no longer knows to whom it belongs.'[23] I am not sure about the 'one' there used to cover both men and women (is the experience of no longer knowing the same for a woman as for a man?) and the 'sexual act' is again heterosexual (how does the question of belonging carry over – should it? – to relations between men, between women?), but, that said, I can recognize what she describes as true, *possibly* true (this is a *version* of the sexual act). Montrelay also writes of a man as 'son of his mother, and as such participating in her femininity'. And I can recognize again what she is saying, despite the difficulties with 'femininity', can grasp it as experience, her way of talking about the instability, the breakdown of the phallic identities on which the discourse of belonging depends (note how the sexologists make everything turn in on penis and erection).

Belonging is a male problem in our existing system of man and woman, 'masculinity' and 'femininity'; it is the obsession of my identity as a man, getting things straight, knowing where I am and what I have and where she is and what she hasn't. Look at D H Lawrence, pioneer–philosopher and preacher–professor of the system: all that mulling over the sexual act, maleness and femaleness, keeping man and woman pure, bringing one into the singularity of one's male self through that act and the necessary passivity of the belonging woman claiming his erection as her object. Of course, we've made progress, look at any book or film, *Rich and Famous* for example, a film that acknowledges Lawrence as a 'sexual test pilot waiting to dive': Chris (Hart Bochner) a young male *Rolling Stone* journalist, 'I don't like girls of my age, they're always looking out for their orgasm'; Liz (Jacqueline Bisset), an older woman novelist, 'So?'; Chris, 'They should be looking out for ours.' Another big deal, belonging again, she *with me*. Of course, some of us have made more progress, look at…At what exactly? Have we? What is the relation between men and feminism and the sexual and belonging yet again? To what extent do men use feminism for the assurance of an identity, now asking to belong as a way of at least ensuring their rightness, a position that gets her with me once more?.

I can recognize what Montrelay describes, what she is saying, but she starts from the other side to the sexologists who themselves start from my side, the male assumption. She is utopian, about the confusion and disappearance of sides, no more belonging; they are realistic, within the reality of a system they repeat and thus support, a system of belonging. Male femininism is between the two, the impossibleness yet again: itself a long way off and itself very near to the reality of today which feminism precisely opposes for change.

'What does woman want?' said Freud, hardly jesting, and stayed too readily with the old answers – to be a man (penis envy), to be a woman (vaginal orgasm, a baby to make up for the penis she lacks) – and the old discomfiture -'the riddle of the nature of femininity' against which throughout history 'people have knocked their heads'. Freud wasn't alone with that question, he just happens to have given it its most famous and powerful formulation (and part of the power depends on the very real advance that psychoanalysis makes nevertheless in the exploration and understanding of sexuality, the complex individual history of sex and gender and identity). The problem of 'woman' was the great nineteenth-century thing, exactly in proportion as women became a problem, as they challenged, that is, their established institution and oppression as 'woman', 'womanhood', the sweetly serving Queens that Ruskin defensively celebrates in *Sesame and Lilies* (defensively because of the challenge. 'We hear of the mission and of the rights of Woman…'). Baudelaire knew how to answer the question: 'Woman is in heat and she wants to be fucked'; Freud knew from psychoanalysis that he didn't really know, hence the return to the enigma, the worry of the question. Which worry is anyway there in the very fact of the question, Baudelaire is as defensive as Ruskin, and the contempt and hatred increase in time of women's ideas of and demands for emancipation, self-definition, reaching a height in the early years of the twentieth century – they can be read, for instance, in T. S. Eliot's early poetry or in Otto Weininger's *Sex and Character* (Freud interrupts – he says ' I cannot interrupt' – his discussion of Little Hans to comment on the castration complex as both 'the deepest unconscious root of anti-Semitism', a Jew having 'something cut off his penis', and the strong 'unconscious root for the sense of superiority over woman', Weininger's book being then cited as an instance of this connection, this dual hostility; perhaps he might later have cited Eliot's poetry too, whose anti-Semitic elements have often been noted).

We now know another question, have learnt to move from 'What does woman want?' to 'What do women want?' And we know, in theory at least, that it is not for us to answer but to listen. Yet the new question is not so distant from the old one, from an 'a' to an 'e' is a long way and not so far. We know that there is no essence-woman (but should we know that, is that a refusal of something, of real difference to which we are then comfortably blind?) and we know that the plural is important, living women in the plural, not fitting our images and decrees of 'femininity' and 'masculinity' (but should we know that, shouldn't we know too that the plural is a singular force, the women's *movement?*). We know so much…But in all this women are still the thing, what we have and hold in the question; maybe for as long as *we* ask the question, think like that, it's too easy, too easy to *know*, maybe we're missing the point that the question has been taken away from us, maybe if we really listened that's what we'd hear, the end of *our* question, of our *question*.

Here's a better question for us, its particular reference is to 'male critics' and 'feminist criticism' but those terms could be appropriately extended to 'males' and 'feminism': 'Why is it that male critics in search of a cause find in feminist criticism their last hope?' Because…women have been men's problem, the question; and the historical reality of literature and theory over the last hundred and fifty years has been crucially bound up with that, a problematic of sexuality and sexual identity in which the pressure of women's struggles against the given definitions and representations has produced men's concern with that question and provided men today with a terrain which they can progressively and reappropriatingly occupy, a cause and a last hope. Because…the effects of feminism in academic institutions with the development of women's studies and an awareness generally of the need to consider women and their representation have led to a situation where 'things to do with women' are tolerated (up to a point, and with differences, of course, from particular institution to particular institution and then from department to department), if not accepted, as an area of interest, of possible study, with men thus able to make radical gestures at little cost, quite within the limits that the academy has already extended and reset. In that sense (I stress in that sense), feminism (but feminism has now come down to an 'interest', an 'area') is easy for white males in our Western universities, can readily be part of their profession; issues of class and race are much more difficult and much more absent (absent here meaning simply not recognized within the academic limits, remaining unspeakable and unspoken). As far as male critics are concerned, indeed, the meshing in the academy of some feminist criticism with French theory, deconstruction et al. has greatly helped, especially in the United States: I can do post-structuralism, Derrideanism, Lacanianism, and feminism in a guaranteed 'radical' cocktail, theory till the cows come home, or don't. Not that that flip way of putting it should let *me* out of criticism: after all, I participate in some of this too, am close to it; and however apart from it I may feel and believe myself to be, I cannot afford not also always to recognize the complicities that carry through against the apartness I try to maintain. Because…men have a social–sexual stake in feminism, in involving themselves with it . I don't want to imply that their relation to feminism is reducible merely and inevitably to a social–sexual strategy, an 'interest' of that kind, but we might as well admit that in the existing circumstances that relation cannot be magically free of the given terms of male/female positioning, of the general relations of men to women. Because … But all this is just my own paraphrase and realization of the answer suggested already by Gayatri Spivak when she asked the intial question: 'Perhaps because, unlike the race and class situation, where academic people are not likely to get much of a hearing, the women's struggle is one they can support "from the inside". Feminism in its academic inceptions is accessible and subject to correction by authoritative men.'[24]

Barthes: 'What is difficult is not to liberate sexuality according to some more or less liberatarian project, it is to disengage it from meaning, including from the transgression of meaning'; *Tillie Olsen*: let's ask 'the question of the place, proportion, *actual* importance of sexuality in our (now) longer-lived, more various, woman lives' (and I think we could add men into that question too, woman and man lives, even if it is then also asked differently) (and I think we can recognize in both Barthes and Olsen the Western and class elements – *whose* lives are longer-lived and more various, *who* can afford to talk of sexuality in this way?).[25]

There is a strange spiral of effects and retro-effects round 'sexuality' in relation to which we live (a limited 'we'). The development of a conception and understanding of sexuality, its extension of the sexual away from a mere perception of 'the sexual act' (the perception that is Marx's, for example, even as his daughter Eleanor is translating a major document in the history of the pressure of that extension, Flaubert's *Madame Bovary*), *is* liberating, our lives have changed; at the same time that (and here Marx's terms are right) sexuality has become a commodity definition, the fetish of sexual exchange, with a hyper-objectification of women in a circuit of 'pleasure' maintained by everything from sexology to advertising, what was and is liberating closed down into the ideological orders of 'liberation'. Sexuality, we now understand, is bound up with language and representation, the history of an individual's construction of identity in meaning, is a complex matter and movement of desire; and then again, our societies have produced sexuality as *the* meaning, including the meaning of feminism (thus equivalent to and contained within 'sexual liberation') as a kind of natural-essence bedrock, what it's all about, where we really are; which brings us back to a new version of 'the sexual act', equal opportunities, orgasm rewards, men and women, rich and famous...Sexual politics? Simple. *We know what it means.* Hence Barthes, the need to disengage sexuality from its meaning; hence Olsen, the need to question its place.

It is to psychoanalysis that we largely owe the conception and understanding of sexuality (psychoanalysis that began with Freud at a crucial moment of sexual concern, of challenge to the terms of the existing relations between men and women, women's protest against them; a moment that also saw the beginnings of sexology in the work of such as Krafft-Ebing and Havelock Ellis). 'The great enigma of the biological fact of the duality of the sexes', yes, but Freud hears, finds, learns an articulation of the sexual as sexuality in the process of the construction of the human subject, a difficult and precarious psychical reality. The key point of this articulation is, of course, the unconscious: 'the reality of the unconscious is sexual', says Lacan, but that sexual is not anchored in the body as its simple reflection or expression; the unconscious is 'discordant', it takes over and marks out the body, defines my sexuality which is thus not a pre-given content but, precisely, a process, a history.

Finally, however, it is not quite that easy. If the psychoanalyst's sexuality is not that of sexology and 'the sexual act' ('This is not its terrain' as Lacan insists),[26] it cannot be simply disconnected from the sexual, the duality of the sexes, Freud's enigma, male and female. Anatomy isn't destiny but neither is it just irrelevant, as Freud kept trying to say and wondering at and stumbling over, as Lacan with his determining phallus and castration somewhere knows, no matter how symbolically sublimated those references are supposed to be. Psychoanalysis indeed, part of its intense value, is exactly bound up with all the problems of the relationships, overlaps and breaks between the sexual as male and female for sexual reproduction and the individual's history as a speaking human being, given a definition as a man or a woman, produced in a particular patterning of 'masculinity', 'femininity', unconscious desire. The *Three Essays on the Theory of Sexuality* are a problematic story about the developing match and mismatch of the sexual and sexuality from infancy to adulthood; the case histories, Dora and the Rat Man, the Wolf Man and Schreber (Little Hans is too programmed to fit the norm, the child was painfully too little to have demonstrated how much more was at stake than the decreed scenario), are stories – novels – of the multiple, complex, heterogeneous mix-up of sexuality, sexual identity.

One of the most interesting things in Freud is that he recognizes sexual difference, and to start with between men and women. Pre Freud (I simplify, one can find exceptions, premonitions, bits and pieces of awareness), women were women, different to men, of course, potentially troubling, needing control, but women, woman, you *knew* that. With Freud, the recognition, they really aren't the same, they've gone out of the image of their mere identity as difference (she reflects my identity by the difference I know her to be as woman, my woman, my picture) and the disturbance is substantial, extensive (I too am disturbed, no longer identical with myself, assuredly man). The unconscious ruins everything and the sexuality then understood liberates women from the sexual: they are precisely not just the woman, organs, reproduction, biology. Freud begins again on those ruins the question of difference, the sexual-sexuality, men's and women's histories, noting, for example, that we must give up 'any expectation of a parallelism between male and female sexual development', recording his impression that 'a man's love and a woman's are a phase apart psychologically.'[27] Freud ends complementarity, the one for the other, the Adam and Eve syndrome, she made for him, 'two halves purely', as John Updike puts it in a novel entitled...*Marry Me*.

In Lacan this becomes the continual emphasis that there is no sexual relation, this indeed being the bedrock reality of analysis: 'the real, the only one to motivate the outcome of analytic discourse, the real that there is no sexual relation'.[28] Who would relate to who? The individual human subject caught up in meanings, representations, the movement of his or her desire is not to be brought down to *one* in an act of relation to some other one: the division, the excess, the unconscious runs through and across him or her; that I am one, finished, fixed, here and now simply present, one of a couple, is myth, imaginary. 'The only person with whom one wants to sleep is one's mother.'[29] I think the formulation is typically reductive (as so often in psychoanalysis it cannot allow for change, specific differentiations: to want to sleep with anyone is really to want to sleep with one's mother, the only person) but what it gets at is that relation is problematic, that one is never only 'one', belonging shot through by longing, the reality of one's construction from division.

There is no *sexual* relation because there are never two sexes but one and the other on both sides of the 'relation' (whether man and woman, woman and woman, man and man). One is always in my or yourself one and the other, or rather, in Lacan's writing, one and the Other, the symbolic as cause of the subject's identity-in-division, the chain of signifiers in which I take place. Relation, the idea of relation, depends on an imaginary other who will complement me as one, make up for the fact of division, stop the loss of identity. Women have been powerfully represented and held as 'woman' to be this other and then, the pressure of the reality of woman, feared and hated and attacked as the imaginary other of 'women' fails and his identity is questioned – at which point she finds herself carried over into the realm of the Other, projected as an enigmatic radical alienness, the back of beyond, and then made up all over again, with talk of her mystery, her ineffable *jouissance*, her closeness to the position of God and so on.

Two things interest me in all this: first that the division in which everyone, men and women, is inscribed as 'one' and the process of desire thus initiated do not express 'man' or 'woman' (part of what Freud says gropingly and conventionally when he makes libido 'masculine', not sex-expressive, and what the Lacanians follow when they insist that desire cannot be sexualized); second, that the division of everyone is also the difference, the out-of-phaseness, of male and female, man and woman. Psychoanalysis has a classic way of tying these two things together: the phallus, castration, different positions of male and female children in the Oedipus Complex, etc. Which may have its specific historical plausibility, its function as specific historical explanation given a particular social organization of the relations between men and women. But feminists have for long understood that the universalized primacy of the phallus in psychoanalysis, the phallus as aboriginal signifier, can only be maintained by fiat (it just *is*, there is nothing else to say), that, on psychoanalysis's own terms, exactly because the man's fright of castration at the sight of the female genital claimed by Freud is constructed from the paternal threat of castration recognized in the Oedipal moment, posing the problem of having or not-having, then the phallus cannot sustain the whole of sexual difference and sexuality, that the crucial matter of the relation to the maternal body, her sameness and difference and the articulations of that for the boy and the girl, is crucial, outside of any notion of the *pre*-Oedipal which just runs everything back from the phallus and relics off – Freud's buried civilization – the maternal as *before* and can then only see interest in it as regressive, exactly where you would expect women to be and where men shouldn't.

213

What has all this got to do with male feminism? Perhaps that men need to work out this not-simply Oedipal complex of division, difference, that they need to think through politically – sexual politics – sameness and difference and otherness (there's something extremely conventional about just assuming that women are defining their difference, that that's the way in which we are going to acknowledge their presence, again) that we should take seriously at last the 'hetero' in heterosexuality, which means the heterogeneity in us, on us, through us, and also take seriously the 'sexuality', which means, I think, giving up, precisely, heterosexuality, that oppressive representation of the sexual as act, complementarity, two sexes, coupling.

Difference as social and ideological limitation, the term of patriarchy: her difference gives the identity of the male position, she different is his reality, man and woman, 'the opposite sex', everything in place.

Difference as political opportunity she asserts, gains, realizes her difference, breaks the 'his' and 'her' identity, its imposition, women away from men, out of their place.

Difference as desire: no difference, only differences, no one and other, no his–her, man–woman, nor hetero–homo (another difference definition drawn up from the man–woman norm), a new sociality, deferring places, in that sense a utopia.

But *whose* desire?

There is a lot about psychoanalysis in these notes. I think, as so often, of Barthes: 'The monument of psychoanalysis must be traversed – not bypassed – like the fine thoroughfares of a very large city, across which we can play, dream etc.: a fiction.' And of Laura Mulvey: 'Psychoanalytic theory is…appropriated here as a political weapon.' And of Juliet Mitchell introducing in 1984 a piece written ten years earlier with 'then I was still hoping it would prove possible to use psychoanalysis as an incipient science of the ideology of patriachy – of how we come to live ourselves as feminine or masculine within patriarchal societies.'[30]

A fiction to be gone through, a political weapon to be appropriated as such, an analysis of patriarchal positioning in our lives as masculine or feminine (*perhaps*, 'then I was still hoping…'). I can use these three gestures to define psychoanalysis here, its use.The critique of the phallocentrism of psychoanalysis (Freudian, Lacanian) is now easy in many ways (which does not mean unnecessary) but the understanding that psychoanalysis produces remains nevertheless; the questions of subjectivity, of 'masculinity' and 'femininity', of sexual difference and identity in the individual's history remain to be worked through all the same: from within patriarchy the terms of patriarchy are analyzed *and* reproduced *and* then more than that, the remaining understanding and questions. Which doesn't make for a simple, cut and dry relation to psychoanalysis (hence, I think, the difficulties and shifts and problems of Mitchell's work, these being a real part of its value, precisely): fiction, political weapon, incipient science of the ideology of patriarchy (the 'incipient' is important)...Feminism is the necessary lever on psychoanalysis today, the dialectical pressure that forces it into truth (it always was, in Freud: the Dora case-history is an obvious text for this, strikingly read as such in many recent feminist accounts). Not that this resolves the argument as to 'whether there is a radical potential for feminism in Freudian psychoanalysis'[31] but it does indicate that the argument is important, that it is, indeed, a radical argument, that psychoanalysis is already political for feminism, and productively so ('it came into the arena of discussion in response to the internal needs of feminist debate').[32]

How one would say that and follow it through would be different according to context. Mine immediately was British feminism – all my references here were to that, Mulvey and Mitchell and then, in the paragraph above, the Editorial Board of *Feminist Review* and Jacqueline Rose. Things would be different if one's context was French, for example, with the reality of a very influential cultural establishment of psychoanalysis insistently reproducing versions of mastery and discipleship and anti-feminism which have sometimes been played out by women against other women (the 'Psychanalyse et Politique' group and its publishing outlet 'Des Femmes' registering the French phrase for 'Women's Liberation Movement' as its trademark and taking legal action to prevent other women using it). All of which, indeed, should be brought back into and made part of the British argument too so that, say, Lacanian theory *and practice* are examined (has anyone ever even commented on Jeanne Favret-Saada's moving account of her resignation from the Lacan School?).[33] It is difficult and contradictory to use psychoanalysis and doubtless that is reflected here, in the movement of these notes.

I started this note from Barthes, Mulvey, Mitchell: two feminists, one male...what? Individualist perhaps: 'I believe now that the only effective marginalism is individualism.'[34] But one of the things men learn from feminism is that women have had enough of being marginal, marginalized: patriarchal society is about marginalization, keeping women out or on the edges of its economy, its institutions, its decisions. To change things, moreover, involves not individualism but collective action, women together, what feminism is about. Of course, Barthes added that 'individualism' would have to be understood in new ways, 'more radical, more enigmatic' (but then 'enigmatic' is not a happy choice either). This was in the last interview he gave, four days before his death, entitled by the magazine in which it appeared 'The Crisis of Desire'.

Is the position of men to feminism marginal, an individualism? I think it is, and *at best*, despite the difficulties of the terms; not meaning by that to exclude shared actions and relations, simply saying that feminism has decentered men, something else they must learn, and that that means that there is no simple position, only a shifting marginalism, a new individualism in the sense that collective identity of men is no longer available (no longer available once you listen and respond to feminism). This, again, is not tragic (not to be lived as loss, along the 'if -only-I-were-a- woman-I-would-have-an-authentic-identity' lines), just a fact of life (of life politically, listening and responding to feminism). And perhaps we can come back to psychoanalysis here. I can think of any number of feminist women in Britain who are directly involved in psychoanalysis but no men. Obviously I don't mean that there are no men in psychoanalysis, only that the political–personal commitment to analysis, here where I live and work, seems common for women, rare for men. A reflection on male feminism should probably recognize that, this not to conclude that feminism should lead men into psychoanalysis but to move to consideration of whether and how the radical potential of psychoanalysis for feminism, the argument about that at least, actually involves men. Perhaps psychoanalysis with its exploration of subjectivity, its problematization of identity, can offer an individualism, away from the certainties of our representations of man and masculinity, that men too readily resist, refuse. The fiction to be gone through can tell a different story of ourselves, politically appropriate if we want to analyze and change the patriarchal positioning central to our lives.

In a graduate class at Yale concerned with Richardson's *Clarissa* a male student remarks affirmatively that of course he cannot conceive of anyone other than as 'a full human subject' – 'what else could one be?' The female teacher answers simply, 'well, you can be a victim.' It is like a little scenario of the center and the margin. What is difficult for men aware of feminism is not to imagine equality for women but to realize the inequality of their own position: the first is abstract and does not take me out of my position (naturally women should be equal with me); the second is concrete and comes down to the fact that my equality is the masking term for their oppression (women are not equal with me and the struggle is not for *that* equality).

Do I write male? What does that mean? We have learnt – from semiotics, psychoanalysis, deconstruction, the whole modern textual theory – not to confuse the sex of the author with the sexuality and sexual positioning inscribed in a text. There is no simple relation of direct expression between myself as male or myself as female and the discourse, writing, text I produce, this production involving me in the whole mesh of discursive orders of language, all the available forms and constructions with their particular positions, their particular terms of representation, all the defined senses of 'masculine', and 'feminine' (and in which I am anyway caught up from the start, given as a 'man' or 'woman').

But this cannot be allowed to end those initial questions, however much I might want to push responsibility away into a world of conventions and forms, inscriptions of position, into all that world of textuality of which we are invited to be the playfully deconstructing prisoners. I must recognize the facts of those forms and conventions and their implications in my position as a man in this society, a position which my writing risks reinscribing, confirming, prolonging. Just as women are not bound by the dominant discursive orders which nevertheless socially define them and against which, from which, beyond which their new reality has to be made, articulated, brought into being. Hence no doubt the strong emphasis from women on women's writing, female discourse, writing the body and so on, theoretically dubious (from the perspective of male theory?) with its potential essentialism (a kind of immediate expressive unity of woman, the female) and politically strong (elaborating a reality of . women speaking and writing out as women). For men, though, exactly because of the fundamental asymmetry that holds between them and women (their domination), there can be no equivalent: men's writing, male discourse, will simply be the same again; there is no politically progressive project that can work through that idea (unless perhaps in and from areas of gay men's experience, in a literature for that). 'Telling the truth about one's body: a necessary freeing subject for the woman writer', says Tillie Olsen.[35] What seems unlikely is that sentences could also be written for the male writer. The truth about men and their bodies *for the moment* is merely repetitive (this has to be put without any suggestion of some inverse romanticization of women and their bodies): the régime of the same, the eternal problem of the phallus, etc. (with its celebration from Lawrence on, through Miller and Mailer on into the present day). Taking men's bodies away from the existing representation and its oppressive effects will have to follow women's writing anew of themselves: for today, telling the truth about the male body as freeing subject is utopia, about the female body *actuality*.

So there I am between a male writing as oppression and a male writing as utopia, and still I am, here and now as you read in this page, a male writing. All I can do is pose each time the question of the sexual positioning of my discourse, of my relations to and in it, my definition as man, and then through it to the practice and reality of men and women, their relations in the world. To do this, not to elide the question, to give up the image of neutrality, is not to write male, not to run continually into terms of oppression, but it is at least, to grasp writing as an involvement in an ethics of sexual difference, which is a start today towards another male writing.

A woman reading is not the same as reading as a woman. In a long history women have been trained not to read as women, to repeat and conform to male readings, male tradition, a particular recognition of the canon of literature ('canon' with its strange appropriateness, ecclesiastical law and phallic weapon). Which is not to say that they have simply repeated, simply conformed, that there has not been misreading, other reading, in revolt, refusal; domination, after all, implies an edge of resistance, the elsewhere of what it seeks to hold down. And, of course, the dominant order has also in that long history decreed and tolerated set areas for reading as a woman, women's reading – the novel in late eighteenth-century England, the Hollywood 'woman's film' of the 1940s, there are many examples. Such areas are safe and unsafe: clearly defined and 'trivial' and at the same time a little uncertain just because women are there with their readings (hence the period attacks on novel-reading and its dangers, hence, differently, from the other side, the reoccupation of the 'woman's film' by feminist film theorists today).

. Reading as a woman is a place given, the available positions, 'women's' genres, styles, and so on, or an alternative project, a struggle to be won, all the pressures of women re-reading, of feminist criticism. 'A woman writing as a woman', Peggy Kamuf pointed out, involves a split: the repetition of the seemingly identical 'woman' in fact breaks the assumption of identity, 'making room for a slight shift, spacing out the differential meaning which has always been at work in the single term.'[36] The same goes for 'a woman reading as a woman'. To read *as* is to make the move of the construction of an identity in which the diverse, heterogeneous relations of experience are gathered up in a certain way, a certain form. A woman reading is different from reading as a woman, which, in turn, is not necessarily the same as reading as a feminist. Except that one can see the necessity in reverse: reading as a feminist involves reading as a woman (it involves a knowledge of what it is to be a woman both negatively, the assigned place of oppression, and positively, the force of the struggle against oppression) which includes a woman reading (reading as a woman takes up a woman's experience). Putting this necessary reversibility in these terms is then doubtless open to theoretical debate. Since sex is not immediate identity, since reading as a woman is construction, where is the necessary link between reading as a woman and being a woman? Since feminism is a social-political awareness of the oppression of women and a movement to end it, where is the necessary link between identity as a woman and being a feminist? Or, to put it another way, this circuit cuts out men.

A man reading is never now not the same as reading as a man. In a long history men have been trained simply to read, they have the acquired neutrality of domination, theirs is the security of indifference – it is women who are different, the special case. Reading as a man is not a project, it is the point of departure; which is why, say, for male modernist writers seeking an avant-garde dislocation of forms, a recasting of given identity into multiplicity, writing differently has seemed to be naturally definable as writing feminine, as moving across into a woman's place (Joyce provides an obvious instance, his two great novels ending in 'female' monologue or polylogue, Molly Bloom, Anna Livia). It is a point of departure which cannot be merely thrown off, forgotten. We can learn to read as women and we can learn to read as feminists; that is, we can learn women's reading, feminist readings, we can make connections that we never made before, come back critically on our point of departure. Yet we must recognize too that we are that point of departure, not in the sense that that is our identity, that we are just that (we are a history, a process that is unfinished), but in the sense that that is nevertheless where we are at, in this society that is our position. It would be nice to forget one is a man (and I am more prone to this fantasy than most) but we can't, we have to assume what being a man means. So the circuit of reading, the reversibility described above, cannot include us as it includes women, though we can go along with it, perhaps.

I think one has politically to accept the contradictions (not be put off by charges of theoretical impurity, incorrectness). The relation of sex to identity is not immediate, we are constructed as gendered individuals in a complex psycho-social history; 'male' and 'female,' 'masculinity' and 'femininity' are positions, places, terms of identification; we are unfinished, sexually heterogeneous, however much the orders of heterosexual law constrain and define; woman and man do not exist only men and women with all the shared experience that race and class can cut across much more decisively at many points, in many situations. *And* the relation of sex to identity is direct and powerful; men and women exist in radical separation, in difference that is produced as the ground of oppression; the shared experience is cut across by sexual difference, which sexual difference also cuts across race and classs; the women's movement, in other words, is a reality.

Thus when Elaine Showalter warns against overstating

the essentialist dilemma of defining the *woman* reader, when in most cases what is implied and intended is a *feminist* reader. Reading as a feminist, I hasten to add, is not unproblematic; but it has the important aspect of offering male readers a way to produce feminist criticism that avoids female impersonation. The way into feminist criticism for the male theorist, must involve a confrontation with what might be implied by reading as a man, and with a questioning or surrender of paternal privileges,[37]

I feel this is right; and I also feel that, hastening to add, she does run too quickly over the problematic nature of the idea of a man reading as a feminist. Male feminism is not just different from feminism (how ludicrous it would be to say 'female feminism'), it is a contradiction in terms. Or, at the very least, it is always also that. There is a female impersonation in a man reading as a feminist, whatever else there might be too. To think otherwise is to abstract the personal (and that much modern theory is keen on such abstraction says something politically about that theory): reading as a feminist and reading as a woman and a woman reading are bound up together, there is no bypassing one of the stages. I think Showalter also says this when she talks of the development by feminist critics of 'theories proved on our pulses' and repeats a warning that 'feminist techniques could be copied and lifted out of their personal and political contexts.'

I like the poems of Adrienne Rich, she says things exactly; and the titles of her collection to start with: *The Will to Change, Diving into the Wreck, The Dream of a Common Language, A Wild Patience Has Taken Me This Far...*[38]

What does it, can it mean for me to say that I like them? One poem is called 'Trying to Talk with a Man' (DW,3) but a common language is a dream: at times perhaps for anyone, man or woman, 'each/speaker of the so-called common language feels/the ice-floe split, the drift apart/as if powerless' (CL,16); certainly from woman to man, her rage no longer contained in 'the ordinary pact/of men & women' (DW,50), now focused in 'a world masculinity made/unfit for women or men' (DW,36). A world that is unfit for women or men but where women are absent and elsewhere: *'Could you imagine a world of women only,/*the interviewer asked. *Can you imagine/a world where women are absent.* (He believed/he was joking). Yet I have to imagine/at one and the same moment, both. Because/ I live in both' (CL,61). Unfit for women or men but where men own the streets, 'when did we ever choose/to see our bodies strung/in bondage and crucifixion across the exhausted air' (WP,3), where 'no-man's-land does not exist' (WP,4): 'A man's world. But finished' (DW,8). So where am I reading these poems? As a woman? (When all of them, this writing, tell me in their 'rage', their 'wild patience', their 'making for the open', that I am not). As a feminist? (When all of them, this writing, tell me stories, images, scenes, reactions, words that leave me no position, no place from which I could avoid by some identification or impersonation their reality, their politics; and 'What we're after/is not that clear to me, if politics/is an unworthy name' (WP,49). As a version of 'The phantom of the man-who-would-understand,/the lost brother, the twin' (CL,62)? (When the poet continues 'for him did we leave our mothers, /deny our sisters, over and over?'). Maybe the task of male critics is just to read (forget the 'as') and learn silence: 'Silence can be a plan/rigorously executed/the blueprint to a life/It is a presence/it has a history a form/Do not confuse it/with any kind of absence' (CL,17). But a silence broken by these poems, theirs not ours, 'these words, these whispers, conversations/from which time after time the truth breaks moist and green' (CL, 20).

Perhaps (the mode of these notes is 'perhaps'), perhaps male feminism should involve a fundamental *admiration*. The word, yes, is old-fashioned, is tangled up with ideas of love and courtship (the heroine's 'admirers' in this or that classic novel), is eminently deconstructible as the original senses are teased out and we find the notion of considering with astonishment and stupefaction moving into that of contemplating with reverence and esteem and gratified pleasure (one can feel psychoanalysis, the uncanny, just round the corner). But still, *admiration*, in the sense in which Irigaray has recently brought it back, thinking precisely of an ethics of sexual difference. She gets at it by rereading Descartes who in *Les Passions de l'Ame* makes admiration the first of all the passions, the 'sudden surprise' of the new and the different that precedes objectification of the other as this or that quality, this or that characteristic. Or as Irigaray explains it: 'What has never existed between the sexes. Admiration keeping the two sexes unsubstitutable in the fact of their difference. Maintaining a free and engaging space between them, a possibility of separation and alliance.'[39]

Admiration as utopia, what has never existed between the sexes; so how to open this space of a radical sexual difference that is not the old difference (psychoanalytic theory too readily turns admiration to the immobility of castration, a supposed male astonishment, the fright that Freud thinks no man is spared 'at the sight of a female genital', a male fixation, what Descartes describes as the body 'motionless as a statue', stopped rigid in single perception: 'astonishment is an excess of admiration that can never be other than bad')?[40] The question brings us back to the impossible relation of men to feminism, that relation only as a possible future, and to the recognition of male feminism as today a contradiction in terms, but then necessary as that, necessary for men to live as such. Perhaps in the end all one can say, indicating the core reality of male feminism, is what Irigaray says as so many others have said, part of the political consciousness of feminism: 'I will never be in a man's place, a man will never be in mine. Whatever the possible identifications, one will never exactly occupy the place of the other – they are irreducible the one to the other.'[41] Perhaps men could learn to realize that, no sadness, no anger, just an acceptance of the irreducible, something like Irigaray's admiration.

More pious words? Of course. I take Irigaray and use her writing to end mine, and with a word, 'admiration', as though that could do anything, could resolve any of the difficulties, any of the doubts I feel as I read over what I have written. But perhaps 'admiration' can say that too, that there is no ending, that *I* cannot resolve. And then I think that I wrote most of this in a hospital ward for women, the majority of them elderly, watching my mother for hours and days. There is every conventional reason not to mention that here and no real reason why I shouldn't. It had something to do with admiration and is at least a possibly real ending.

1984

I think now, at a distance, that such an ending has too many problems just to be left without comment, is not enough. I knew it then, it can be felt in the writing, even while I could anyway only end like that, falling off into silence and leaving the piece apparently held in an attitude of awed contemplation. The reference to my mother, to writing in hospital, is real but it is also an emotional location of the piece as legitimation, not that far from the kind of personal guarantee of which I am earlier critical. The final paragraph says something true at the same time that its truth cannot be turned into an end without some loss of truth, of the critical, political truth with which 'Male Feminism' and male feminism – is concerned.

The wider point here can be made by considering the use of Irigaray, the appearance of the notion of 'admiration'. I do not want to go back on this (on the contrary); simply, it has difficulties which were, wrongly, left aside. Again, what Irigaray says is true, yet when I quote it, use it, produce it in conclusion, I finish up with a false unity, a fetishizing elision – look, her! For difference and contradiction, I substitute silence, admiration as that; hence the last paragraph, nothing more to say.

'I will be never be in a man's place, a man will never be in mine. Whatever the possible identifications, one will never exactly occupy the place of the other – they are irreducible the one to the other.' Yes, but the irreducibility can quickly become not difference and contradiction but a gulf, as though between two species, and the implications of men in feminism – feminism which has to include men, their transformation, in its project – are cut short: just admiration, as of an object, the awed contemplation. The autonomy of feminism is converted into its separateness and the necessary acknowledgement by men of the former becomes my drift into fixation with the latter.

It is significant in this context that feminism itself is envisaged in the piece in a way which can tend to suggest it as a unified field, masking the various positions and movements and struggles that are its reality. My concern in the first instance was to write about feminism as the overall fact of the recognition and understanding by women of their oppression and their determination to act against it. From the perspective of the consideration of male feminism (only from that perspective) the alternatives within feminism, the different feminisms, seemed to me at the time secondary; the aim was to explore something of what is at stake in men's coming to terms with that fact of recognition, understanding, determination for change, with the whole process of women changing things for themselves and for us – a process which is plural and heterogeneous, not singular and homogeneous, but which is still nevertheless perceivable as this overall fact, feminism.

The other side of that perception, though, is the structure of being 'outside', the outsideness that admiration in part enacts, self-exclusion as value, an authentic male response (the reverse extreme to the 'more radical, most radical' gesture discussed in the piece). Running feminisms into feminism allows – goes with – a gender-defined object, feminism as women and women's. Which is right and wrong: right because feminism is gender-defined, and necessarily and crucially so; wrong because that gender definition is also problematic, is a debate within feminism about feminism that 'feminism' covers over (in its general social currency moreover 'feminism' has been taken over as the term for a new psychology of women, their reductive and controlling identification in the aftermath of a women's liberation movement now, hopefully, past). Which is right and wrong too for men specifically, for thinking about male feminism: right because feminism for us must involve awareness of *a* separateness, precisely that acknowledgement of women's autonomy, of *them*; wrong because that autonomy is not to be translated into exclusion, albeit in the deferential form this takes in the piece, but is rather to be seen as the very basis of our participation, where we start from, knowing one is a man, what that means.

It was with the consequences of this knowledge we gain from feminism that 'Male Feminism' was concerned. Its problems, brought up in the ending, are then those of the relations of such a knowledge to feminist practice – *what does feminism mean for men?* is abstracted too far from *what is feminism?* The insistence in the piece on the political–ethical reality of feminism for men, for me-as-a-man (an insistence which I believe to be important and needed, against the appropriative displacement of feminism into a set of ideas for a theoretical argument or a known politics, against men just assuming it is there for them to 'go into', to have 'positions' in, all the ways in which we avoid bringing it back questioningly onto ourselves) runs the risk of turning into a personal essentialism, outsider and object, ethics separating from politics as *I* stop in silence (admiration, contemplation, deference are the signs of this in the piece, the negative turn of the positive emphases from which they emerge). It is not that I would want now to change what I wrote, only that I need here to have drawn attention to the problems.[42]

Notes

1. CLAIRE PAJACZKOWSKA, 'The Heterosexual Presumption: A Contribution to the Debate on Pornography', *Screen*, 22, no. 1(1981), p. 92.

2. B. RUBY RICH, 'Anti-Porn: Soft Issue, Hard World', *Feminist Review* no. 13 (Spring 1983), p. 66.

3. ELIZABETH WILSON, *What Is To Be Done About Violence Against Women?* (Harmondsworth: Penguin, 1983), pp. 135-68.

4. STEPHEN HEATH, *The Sexual Fix* (London: Macmillan, 1982), p. 163.

5. SIGMUND FREUD, 'Analysis Terminable and Interminable', *The Standard Edition of the Complete Psychological Works of Sigmund Freud* (London: Hogarth, 1953-74), vol. XXIII, p. 252.

6. JACQUES DERRIDA, 'La Question du style', *Nietzsche aujourd'hui?* (Paris: Union Générale d'Editions, 1973), vol. I, pp. 299, 244.

7. ROSALIND COWARD, *Female Desire: Women's Sexuality Today* (London: Paladin, 1984), p. 227.

8. WILLIAM THACKERAY, *Vanity Fair* (first published 1848; Harmondsworth: Penguin, 1982), p. 659.

9. JACQUES LACAN, *Le Séminaire livre XX Encore* (Paris: Seuil, 1975), p. 75. Freud's question occurs in a letter to Marie Bonaparte, cit. Ernest Jones, *Sigmund Freud: Life and Work* vol. 2 (London: Hogarth, 1955), p. 468. Lacan's 1932 thesis containing the Aimée case and the 1933 essay on the Papin sisters published in the Surrealist review *Le Minotaure* can be found in Lacan, *De la psychose paranoïaque dans ses rapports avec la personnalité* (Paris: Seuil, 1975).

10. LACAN, seminar, 16 November 1976, *Ornicar?* no. 12/13 (1977), p. 12.

11. EUGÉNIE LEMOINE-LUCCIONI, *La Robe* (Paris: Seuil, 1983), p. 25.

12. JULIET MITCHELL, 'Feminine Sexuality: Interview with Juliet Mitchell and Jacqueline Rose', *m/f* no. 8 (1983), p. 15.

13. MICHÈLE MONTRELAY, intervention, Journées de l'Ecole Freudienne de Paris, Lille 1977, *Lettres de l'Ecole Freudienne*, no. 22 (March 1978), p. 144.

14. STEPHEN HEATH, 'Difference', *Screen*, 19, no. 3 (Autumn 1978), pp. 51-112.

15. MILLICENT GARRETT FAWCETT, *Women's Suffrage: A Short History of a Great Movement* (London: Jack, 1912), p. 16.

16. TERRY EAGLETON, *Walter Benjamin: or Towards a Revolutionary Criticism* (London: New Left Books, 1981), all quotations from pp. 99-100.

17. The translator of the Penguin Classics *Symposium* notes that 'It is almost universally and no doubt rightly held that Diotima is a fictitious personage, in spite of the apparently historical statements made about her by Socrates', Plato, *The Symposium* trans, William Hamilton (Harmondsworth: Penguin, 1975), p. 19. No doubt rightly since the voice-off is always anyway theory's fiction for itself.

18. See particularly LUCE IRIGARAY, *Speculum, de l'autre femme* (Paris: Minuit, 1974).

19. LACAN, *Le Séminaire livre XX Encore*, p. 69.

20. ANN SNITOW, CHRISTINE STANSELL AND SHARON THOMPSON eds, *Desire: The Politics of Sexuality* (London: Virago, 1984).

21. IRÈNE ROUBLEF, intervention, Journées des Cartels de l'Ecole Freudienne de Paris,

Paris 1975, *Lettres de l'Ecole Freudienne*, no. 18 (April 1976), p. 211.

22. PAUL BROWN AND CAROLYN FAULDER, *Treat Yourself to Sex* (Harmondsworth: Penguin, 1979), p. 81.

23. MONTRELAY, *L'Ombre et son nom* (Paris: Minuit, 1977), p. 151; subsequent quotation, p. 142.

24. GAYATRI SPIVAK, cit. Elaine Showalter, 'Critical Cross-Dressing: Male Feminists and The Woman of the Year', *Raritan*, III, no. 2 (1983/4) p. 133. (See this volume, p. 118).

25. BARTHES, 'Digressions', *Promesse*, no. 29 (1971), p. 27; TILLIE OLSEN, *Silences* (London: Virago, 1980), p. 255.

26. LACAN, *Le Séminaire Livre XI, Les quatre concepts fondamentaux de la psychanalyse* (Paris: Seuil, 1973) p. 240; trans. Alan Sheridan, *The Four Fundamental Concepts of Psycho-Analysis* (Harmondsworth: Penguin 1979), p. 266.

27. FREUD, 'Female Sexuality', *Standard Edition*, vol. XXI, p. 226; *New Introductory Lectures on Psycho-Analysis, Standard Edition*, vol. XX11, p. 134.

28. LACAN, 'L'Etourdit', *Scilicet*, no. 4 (1973), p. 47.

29. LACAN, seminar 15 March 1977, *Ornicar?*, no. 17/18 (1979), p. 9.

30. BARTHES, *Le Plaisir du texte* (Paris: Seuil, 1973), pp. 92-3; trans Richard Miller, *A Barthes Reader* ed. Susan Sontag (London: Jonathan Cape, 1982), p. 412; LAURA MULVEY, 'Visual Pleasure and Narrative Cinema', *Screen*, 16, no. 3 (Autumn 1975), p. 6; JULIET MITCHELL, *Women: The Longest Revolution* (London: Virago, 1984), p. 221.

31. Editorial, *Feminist Review*, no. 14 (Summer 1983), p. 1.

32. JACQUELINE ROSE, 'Femininity and its Discontents', *Feminist Review*, no. 14 (Summer 1983), p. 5.

33. JEANNE FAVRET-SAADA, 'Excusez-moi, je ne faisais que passer', *Les Temps modernes*, no. 371 (June 1977), pp. 2089-103.

34. BARTHES, 'La Crise du désir', *Le Nouvel Observateur*, 20 April 1980, p. 87.

35. OLSEN, *Silences*, p. 255.

36. PEGGY KAMUF, 'Writing like a Woman', *Women and Language in Literature and Society*, ed. Sally McConnell-Ginet, Ruth Borker and Nelly Furman (New York: Praeger, 1980), p. 298.

37. SHOWALTER, 'Critical Cross-Dressing: Male Feminists and The Woman of the Year', p. 143; subsequent quotations, pp. 133, 147 (See this volume, pp. 116-32). Showalter's article has been very much part of the writing of the present essay.

38. Quotations here are from: ADRIENNE RICH, *Diving into the Wreck* (New York: Norton, 1973) – DW: *The Dream of a Common Language* (New York: Norton, 1978) – CL: *A Wild Patience Has Taken Me This Far* (New York: Norton, 1981) – WP.

39. IRIGARAY, *Ethique de la différence sexuelle* (Paris: Minuit, 1984), p. 20.

40. DESCARTES, *Les Passions de l'Ame* (1649), *Oeuvres et lettres* (Paris: Gallimard 'Pléiade', 1953), p. 729.

41. IRIGARAY, *Ethique de la différence sexuelle*, pp. 19-20.

42. Letters from a number of people in response to the original publication of 'Male Feminism' have helped me think further about the issues it raises. I am specifically indebted to Paul Willemen for comments on its final paragraph and to Rosalind Delmar for sustained discussion.

Glossary of Terms

ANDROGYNY A conjoining of masculinity and femininity. For some critics (for example, Elaine Showalter) an interest in androgyny is viewed as a deviation from the crucial emphasis on the specificity of women, their needs and achievements. For others (for example, Toril Moi) the notion of androgyny is progressive, suggesting the deconstruction of fixed concepts of masculinity and femininity.

BINARY OPPOSITION (post-structuralist usage) The opposition of two terms in an hierarchical relationship. The first term is seen as positive, normative or prime: the second as negative, deviant or subordinate. For example, activity/passivity; rational/irrational. Hélène Cixous' claim is that the fundamental opposition is male/female.

BIOLOGISM The belief in an innate biological difference between men and women which to a greater or lesser extent determines their social behaviour. Biologism collapses the distinction between biology and gender. (See **gender**.)

BLACK FEMINISM Black feminism explores the specificity of black women's experience, critiques the racism it finds in the work of white feminists and deconstructs our understanding of racial terminology. Alice Walker in *In Search of Our Mothers' Gardens* (1983) substitutes for 'black feminism' the term 'womanism'.

ECRITURE FÉMININE (feminine writing) A term from French feminism, signifying a particular kind of writing – poetic, non-realist – which undermines the logic, truths, definitions of the dominant order. Feminine writing is available to both male and female writers, though there are social and psychoanalytical reasons why practitioners of feminine writing are more likely to be female. Hélène Cixous refuses to provide any neat definition of 'l'écriture féminine'. What concerns her is the openness and plenitude of such writing; to define is to control and limit.

FEMALE; FEMININE; FEMINIST In *A Literature of Their Own* (1977), Elaine Showalter employs these terms to describe three stages in the development of women's writing. In 'Toward a Feminist Poetics' (1979), she applies the term 'feminist' to the radical reading by women of texts by male authors. A current, widely accepted – but by no means unproblematic – definition is to view 'female' as a biological category, 'feminine' as a cultural construct and 'feminist' as a political position. (See **l'écriture féminine**.)

GENDER Feminists stress the distinction between 'sex', a matter of biology, and 'gender', the social construction of our concepts of masculinity and femininity. Hence Simone de Beauvoir's famous dictum: one is not born a woman; one becomes one.

GENDER STUDIES A study of the construction and meanings of masculinity and femininity in history and culture. Many feminists are worried that Gender Studies will eradicate Women's Studies and its specific emphasis on women and femininity.

GYNESIS A term coined by Alice Jardine in her study of the relationship between feminism and post-modernism, *Gynesis* (1985). 'Gynesis' describes the process by which 'woman', the feminine, that which has eluded discourse, is discovered and articulated.

GYNOCRITICISM Introduced by Elaine Showalter in her essay 'Toward a Feminist Poetics' (1979) to describe what she finds the most necessary form of feminist criticism: namely, the study of women's writing; the relating of that writing to female experience; and the development of critical theories and methodologies appropriate to women. She contrasts this mode of criticism with what she terms the 'feminist critique'. (See **female; feminine; feminist**.)

IMAGINARY Jacques Lacan describes as the 'Imaginary' the pre-Oedipal period, when the child feels at one with the mother and has no sense of its own difference. The Imaginary holds a pleasurable sense of unity, a narcissistic satisfaction, as the child identifies and fuses with other images. This period ends with the Oedipal crisis and the child's entry into the Symbolic Order. (See **Symbolic Order**.)

JOUISSANCE A term popular in French feminism to express a sense of pleasure, abandonment, orgasmic overflowing. But it also contains the meaning of the enjoyment of rights and property. Betsy Wing, the translator of Cixous and Clément (1986), understands the term as having '*simultaneously* sexual, political and economic overtones'. The same multiple meanings are present in the gloss to Julia Kristeva's use of the term (see p.83).

LIBERAL FEMINISM A reformist position, working within existing political structures to secure equal rights and equality of opportunity for women. (See **Marxist feminism, radical feminism**.)

MARGINAL The 'marginal' indicates the subordinate status of women under patriarchy – that is, consigned to the margins. But it can also suggest a location where the subordinated can contest the dominance of the centre. In deconstructive theory, therefore, the marginal offers a transformative potential.

MARXIST FEMINISM; SOCIALIST FEMINISM; MATERIALIST FEMINISM Feminists of these persuasions seek an alliance between class politics, gender politics and, increasingly, the politics of race. The place of the economic, problems of ideology, questions of aesthetic value are examples of issues debated within this approach. Newton and Rosenfelt (1985) suggest the term 'materialist feminism' as more encompassing than the other two, and more suited to an American context.

MASCULINISM A politics that seeks to maintain male control.

PATRIARCHY A social system which ensures the dominance of men and the subordination of women.

PHALLOCENTRISM A system which affirms the phallus as the principal signifier, the symbol of power. In terms of sexual difference phallocentrism seems to lead to defining masculinity as the norm and femininity as deviant.

RADICAL FEMINISM Radical feminism views the inequality between men and women as the primary form of exploitation, pre-dating class or racial antagonism. For radical feminism, change is impossible within the present social order. What is needed is a new social order based on woman-centred values and methods of organization. (See woman-centredness).

SEMIOTIC In Julia Kristeva's theory the 'semiotic' is a kind of language of tones, rhythms and sensations, expressive of the pre-Oedipal, the pre-Symbolic. The semiotic is not obliterated by entry into the Symbolic Order. On the contrary, the semiotic retains the potential to erupt and disrupt the meanings and norms of the dominant order. (See **Symbolic Order**.)

SEXUAL POLITICS Kate Millett asserts that relations between the sexes are not only personal and social, but also profoundly political. Sexual relations are relations of inequality: men establish and maintain their dominance over women through the institution of patriarchy. (See Patriarchy.)

SUBJECT; SUBJECT POSITION In contrast to the notion of a coherent identity or a human essence, psychoanalysis and post-structuralist theory offer the term 'subject', suggesting a sense of self which is unstable, constantly brought into question and reformed. The individual is not consistent but may occupy several different 'subject positions'.

SYMBOLIC ORDER In Lacanian theory, the child's Oedipus crisis and the acquisition of language marks its entry into the 'Symbolic Order', the order of signs and social and cultural life. The dyadic unity with the mother is broken and the child becomes subject to the Law of the Father. The repression of desire for the mother creates the unconscious. (See **Imaginary**.)

'WOMAN'; WOMEN In French feminism 'woman', like the feminine, constitutes a writing-effect, an excess which has escaped the control of the master narratives. In Anglo-American feminism 'women' refers to a group which can be identified biologically and which aims to be united politically.

WOMAN-CENTREDNESS A radical-feminist concept which claims that feminism should concentrate on female experience and interpretations and resist male definitions. The belief can lead to a position of separatism.

Notes On Authors

HÉLÈNE CIXOUS (1937–) is Professor of Literature at the University of Paris VIII and director of the research centre she founded in 1974: the Centre d'Etudes Féminines. Her work includes novels, plays, criticism, and autobiography. Among her publications in English are *The Exile of James Joyce* (London: John Calder, 1976); *Portrait of Dora* (London: John Calder 1979); and, with Catherine Clément, *The Newly Born Woman* (Manchester: Manchester University Press, 1986). Her most famous essay 'The Laugh of the Medusa' (1976) is reprinted in *New French Feminisms: An Anthology*, ed. Elaine Marks and Isabelle de Courtivron (Brighton, Sussex: Harvester Press Ltd., 1981). Some of Cixous's contributions to her research group are available in *Writing Differences: Readings from the Seminars(?) of Hélène Cixous*, ed. Susan Sellers (Milton Keynes: Open University Press, 1988).

CATHERINE CLÉMENT (1939–), formerly an editor for the Socialist newspaper *Le Matin*, is now in charge of cultural exchanges at the Bureau of Cultural Affairs in Paris. She writes both fiction and non-fiction, moving in her theoretical work between Marxism, feminism and psychoanalysis. Available in English are *The Lives and Legends of Jacques Lacan* (New York: Columbia University Press, 1983); with Hélène Cixous, *The Newly Born Woman* (Manchester: Manchester University Press, 1986); *The Weary Sons of Freud* (London: Verso, 1987): *Opera or the Undoing of Women* (Minneapolis: University of Minnesota Press, 1988).

STEPHEN HEATH is a Fellow of Jesus College, Cambridge and author of numerous works on cultural theory, particularly film theory. Translator of Roland Barthes *Image–Music–Text* (London: Fontana, 1977), he is also author of *Questions of Cinema* (London: Macmillan, 1981); and *The Sexual Fix* (London: Macmillan, 1982). Heath has edited, with Teresa de Laurentis, *The Cinematic Apparatus* (London: Macmillan, 1980); and, with Patricia Mellencamp, *Cinema and Language* (Los Angeles: University Publications of America, 1983).

MARY JACOBUS is Professor of English and Women's Studies at Cornell University. Her first book was *Tradition and Experiment in Wordsworth's 'Lyrical Ballads', 1798* (Oxford: Clarendon Press, 1976). Jacobus's interest in French theory since the mid-1970s has been illustrated in *Women Writing and Writing About Women* (London and Sydney: Croom Helm, 1979), a volume which she edited and to which she contributed; a collection of her own essays, *Reading Woman: Essays in Feminist Criticism* (London: Methuen, 1986); and *Romanticism, Writing, and Sexual Difference: Essays on THE PRELUDE* (Oxford: Clarendon Press, 1989).

PEGGY KAMUF (1947–) lectures in French at Miami University, Ohio. Author of many essays on feminism and French literature, she has also published *Fictions of Feminine Desire: Disclosures of Héloïse* (Lincoln: University of Nebraska Press, 1982) and *Signature Pieces: On the Institution of Authorship* (Ithaca: Cornell University Press, 1988).

CORA KAPLAN (1940–) is Professor of English at Rutgers University. She is editor of an anthology of women's poetry, *Salt and Bitter and Good: Three Centuries of English and American Women Poets* (New York: Paddington Press, 1975); editor of Elizabeth Barrett Browning's *Aurora Leigh and Other Poems* (London: Women's Press, 1978); and author of a collection of essays, *Sea Changes: Essays on Culture and Feminism* (London: Verso, 1986).

JULIA KRISTEVA (1941–) is both a psychoanalyst and Professor of Linguistics at the University of Paris VII. Among her many works are *About Chinese Women* (London: Marion Boyars, 1977); *Desire in Language: A Semiotic Approach to Literature and Art* (Oxford: Basil Blackwell, 1980); *The Powers of Horror: An Essay on Abjection* (New York: Columbia University Press, 1982); and *Revolution in Poetic Language* (New York: Columbia University Press, 1984). A representative sample of Kristeva's writing, including several complete essays, is available in *The Kristeva Reader*, ed. Toril Moi (Oxford: Basil Blackwell, 1986).

NANCY K. MILLER (1941–) is Professor of Women's Studies and Director of the Women's Studies Programme at Barnard College. She is the author of *The Heroine's Text: Readings in the French and English Novel, 1722–1782* (New York: Columbia University Press, 1980) and *Subject to Change: Reading Feminist Writing* (New York: Columbia University Press, 1988). She has edited *The Poetics of Gender* (New York: Columbia University Press, 1986) – a book in the Gender and Culture series which she co-edits with Carolyn Heilbrun.

KATE MILLETT (1934–) was a founding member in 1966 of the National Organisation of Women (NOW). She is a writer, sculptor and film-maker. Her most famous work is the classic text of feminist theory, *Sexual Politics* (New York: Avon, 1970). In addition, she has edited *The Prostitution Papers: A Candid Dialogue* (New York: Avon, 1973); written an autobiography, *Flying* (New York: Alfred A. Knopf,1974); *Sita* (New York: Farrar, Straus and Giroux, 1977); *The Basement: Meditations on a Human Sacrifice* (New York: Simon and Schuster, 1979); and *Going to Iran* (New York: Coward, McCann and Geoghegan, 1982).

TORIL MOI (1953–) is Adjunct Professor of Comparative Literature at the University of Bergen and Professor of Literature at Duke University. In addition to many essays in the fields of literature and psychoanalysis, she has written *Sexual/Textual Politics: Feminist Literary Theory* (London and New York: Methuen, 1985); and *Feminist Literary Theory and Simone de Beauvoir* (Oxford: Basil Blackwell, 1990). Her interest in French feminist theory is shown also in the works she has edited: *The Kristeva Reader* (Oxford: Basil Blackwell, 1986); and *French Feminist Thought: A Reader* (Oxford: Basil Blackwell, 1987). Moi is at present working on a study of Simone de Beauvoir.

ELAINE SHOWALTER (1941–) is Professor of English and Avalon Foundation Professor of the Humanities at Princeton University. Her major contribution to the development of feminist analysis includes *A Literature of Their Own: British Women Novelists from Brontë to Lessing* (New Jersey: Princeton University Press, 1977); and *The Female Malady: Women, Madness, and English Culture, 1830–1980* (New York: Pantheon Books, 1985). She is editor of and contributor to *The New Feminist Criticism: Essays on Women, Literature and Theory* (New York: Pantheon Books, 1985); and *Speaking of Gender* (New York and London: Routledge, 1989).

GAYATRI CHAKRAVORTY SPIVAK is Andrew W. Mellon Professor at the University of Pittsburgh. She has translated and introduced Jacques Derrida's *Of Grammatology* (Baltimore: Johns Hopkins University Press, 1976); and edited, with Ranajit Guha, *Selected Subaltern Studies* (Oxford: Oxford University Press, 1988). Some of her influential essays have been collected in *In Other Worlds: Essays in Cultural Politics* (New York and London: Methuen, 1987).

Further Reading

(1) Introductions

The easiest way to get a sense of the scope of feminist literary debate is to look at the surveys, readers and collections of essays that have been published in recent years. Each of the books listed below ranges across a variety of theoretical approaches to feminist literary studies.

CATHERINE BELSEY and JANE MOORE (eds.), *The Feminist Reader: Essays in Gender and the Politics of Literary Criticism* (Basingstoke and London: Macmillan Education, 1989).

MARY EAGLETON (ed.), *Feminist Literary Theory: A Reader* (Oxford: Basil Blackwell, 1986).

HESTER EISENSTEIN and ALICE JARDINE (eds.), *The Future of Difference* (Boston, Mass: G. K. Hall & Co., 1980).

GAYLE GREENE and COPPÉLIA KAHN (eds.), *Making a Difference: Feminist Literary Criticism* (London and New York: Methuen, 1985).

MARY JACOBUS (ed.), *Women Writing and Writing About Women* (London and Sydney: Croom Helm, 1979).

TORIL MOI, *Sexual/Textual Politics: Feminist Literary Theory* (London and New York: Methuen, 1985).

K. K. RUTHVEN, *Feminist Literary Studies: An Introduction* (Cambridge: Cambridge University Press, 1984).

ELAINE SHOWALTER (ed.), *The New Feminist Criticism: Essays on Women, Literature and Theory* (New York: Pantheon Books, 1985; London: Virago, 1986).

(2) Further Studies

MICHÈLE BARRETT (ed.), *Virginia Woolf: Women and Writing* (New York: Harcourt Brace Jovanovich, 1980; London: Women's Press, 1980).

_____ , *Women's Oppression Today: Problems in Marxist Feminist Analysis* (London: Verso, 1980).

Barrett's collection of Woolf essays on the context of women's writing and on individual women authors is a valuable supplement to *A Room of One's Own*. Her introduction to the collection and her work on ideology and cultural politics in *Women's Oppression Today* aim to create a dialogue between Marxism and feminism.

Simone de Beauvoir, *The Second Sex* (Paris: Gallimard, 1949; Harmondsworth, Middlesex: Penguin, 1972).
The historical and geographical span of this study is from early nomadic society to contemporary industrialisation. Along the way, de Beauvoir discusses biology, history, philosophy, psychoanalysis, myth and literature. Her theoretical base lies in Marxism and existentialism.

Hélène Cixous and Catherine Clément, *The Newly Born Woman* (Paris: Union Générale d'Editions, 1975; Manchester: University of Manchester Press, 1986).
Cixous and Clément are among the foremost voices in French feminist thinking. By turns poetic, utopian, analytical, autobiographical, argumentative, the authors discuss femininity, female sexuality, writing, the repressed, marginality. Cixous' essay, 'Sorties' has become one of the best known explications of 'l'écriture féminine'.

Mary Ellmann, *Thinking About Women* (New York: Harcourt Brace Jovanovich, 1968; London: Virago, 1979).
Ellmann uses humour to devastating effect in her sharp analysis of dominant concepts of femininity and of our proclivity to think always in terms of sexual analogy. Later critics, for instance Moi (1985), have found in Ellmann an early example of a deconstructive mode.

Jane Gallop, *The Daughter's Seduction: Feminism and Psychoanalysis* (New York: Cornell University Press, 1982). Published in Great Britain under the title *Feminism and Psychoanalysis: The Daughter's Seduction* (London: Macmillan, 1982).
Gallop's focus is the interrelation between feminist theory and the psychoanalysis of Jacques Lacan. In developing her thesis she discusses, among others, Kristeva, Cixous, Clément, Luce Irigaray, Michèle Montrelay – in short, the major names of French feminism.

Henry Louis Gates, Jr. (ed.), *Black Literature and Literary Theory* (New York and London: Methuen, 1984).
_____ (ed.), *'Race', Writing, and Difference* (Chicago and London: University of Chicago Press, 1986).
Gates's contributors utilize contemporary critical approaches – structuralist, post-structuralist, Marxist, feminist – to discuss the work of Black authors and the meanings of 'race' in writing. Black women writers and the perspective of feminism are well represented.

Sandra M. Gilbert and Susan Gubar, *The Madwoman in the Attic: The Woman Writer and the Nineteenth-Century Literary Imagination* (New Haven and London: Yale University Press, 1979).
Rebuking notions of literary paternity, this study of nineteenth-century women writers establishes a female literary continuity, based on common themes, images, anxieties and literary strategies. The madwoman becomes an emblem of repressed female anger and creative power.

Mary Jacobus, *Reading Woman: Essays in Feminist Criticism* (New York: Columbia University Press, 1986; London: Methuen, 1986).
In this collection, Jacobus deliberately eschews any of her pre-1978 writing so as to concentrate on the influence of French theory on feminist literary criticism. The ambiguity of her title suggests the volume's varied interests: women as readers, developing feminist critiques; reading women writers; reading 'woman' as a sign for sexual difference.

Alice A. Jardine, *Gynesis: Configurations of Woman and Modernity* (Ithaca and London: Cornell University Press, 1985). Jardine mediates between Anglo-American and French theories in an investigation of 'woman' and 'modernity'. Jardine's role in interpreting French theory for Anglo-American audiences has been significant.

Alice Jardine and Paul Smith (eds.), *Men In Feminism* (New York and London: Methuen, 1987).

This collection of essays reflects the diversity and vehemence of debate on the subject of men's relation to feminism. Within the context of contemporary feminist theory, questions are posed about writing, politics, the academy, power.

CORA KAPLAN, *Sea Changes: Culture and Feminism* (London: Verso, 1986).
From a basically socialist-feminist perspective, Kaplan engages with other critical discourses in an exploration of women's writing and cultural politics.

AUDRE LORDE, *Sister Outsider: Essays and Speeches* (New York: Crossing Press, 1984).
Lorde's perceptions as a Black, lesbian feminist are here applied to poetry and politics.

ELAINE MARKS and ISABELLE DE COURTIVRON (eds.), *New French Feminisms: An Anthology* (Brighton, Sussex: Harvester Press, 1981).
This was the first anthology to introduce French feminist writers to an Anglo-American audience. The volume includes a wide range of authors, a variety of critical positions and introductions which situate French feminism historically and culturally.

KATE MILLETT, *Sexual Politics* (New York: Doubleday, 1970; London: Virago, 1977).
Millett's sociological, historical and literary study examines the changing relationship of men and women from the mid-nineteenth century to the mid-twentieth. For Millett, misogyny in twentieth-century literature is indicative of an oppressive sexual politics throughout our culture and of the power of patriarchy to stifle change.

JULIET MITCHELL, *Women: The Longest Revolution: Essays on Feminism, Literature and Psychoanalysis* (London: Virago, 1984).
Mitchell's work moves between politics, literature and psychoanalysis. Her primary literary concern in this collection of essays is with the novel.

ELLEN MOERS, *Literary Women: The Great Writers* (New York: Doubleday, 1976; London: Women's Press, 1977).
Moers' study of women authors from the late eighteenth century onwards constructs a tradition of women's writing and emphasizes its distinctiveness. Her categories of 'heroinism' and the 'Female Gothic' have been employed by subsequent critics.

TORIL MOI (ed.), *The Kristeva Reader* (Oxford: Basil Blackwell, 1986).
_____ (ed.), *French Feminist Thought: A Reader* (Oxford: Basil Blackwell, 1987).
Moi's surveys bring together a diversity of material, much not anthologised elsewhere. Her introductions provide historical and theoretical contexts.

JUDITH NEWTON and DEBORAH ROSENFELT (eds.), *Feminist Criticism and Social Change: Sex, Class and Race in Literature and Culture* (New York and London: Methuen, 1985).
The materialist-feminist critique in this collection is related not only to gender but to other major determinants of class, race and sexual identity. The essays comprise both theoretical explorations and applied criticism on nineteenth- and twentieth-century texts.

TILLIE OLSEN, *Silences* (New York: Delacorte Press, 1978: London, Virago, 1980).
Influenced by both feminism and Marxism, Olsen explores the conditions of literary production and the circumstances of class, race and gender that can silence or restrict potential writers.

ADRIENNE RICH, *On Lies, Secrets, and Silence: Selected Prose 1966–1978* (New York: W. W. Norton & Co., 1979; London: Virago 1980).
_____ , *Blood, Bread, and Poetry: Selected Prose 1979–1985* (New York: W. W. Norton & Co., 1986: London: Virago 1987).
Rich's essays speak on women's writing, politics and women's education from a radical-feminist and lesbian position.

LILLIAN S. ROBINSON, *Sex, Class, and Culture* (Bloomington, Indiana: Indiana University Press, 1978; London: Methuen, 1986).
Robinson's essays, written between 1968–1977, link the approaches of Marxism and feminism in an understanding of theory, literature and the media.

SUSAN SELLERS (ed.), *Writing Differences: Readings from the Seminar of Hélène Cixous* (Milton Keynes: Open University Press, 1988).
Cixous, and members of the research group she founded, explore the play of the sexual difference in a range of literary texts from Shakespeare to *Alice in Wonderland*. Their 'loving' approach to the text depends on post-structuralist and psychoanalytical theories.

ELAINE SHOWALTER, *A Literature of Their Own: British Women Novelists from Brontë to Lessing* (New Jersey: Princeton University Press, 1977; London: Virago, 1978).
Showalter's aim is to uncover a female tradition of writing, to appreciate its distinctive qualities and to consider its relationship with the dominant tradition of male writing. In so doing, Showalter establishes an agenda for Anglo-American literary criticism.
_____ (ed.), *Speaking of Gender* (New York and London: Routledge, 1989).
This volume indicates the shift in the 1980s from readings that looked largely at femininity to a consideration of the significance of both femininity and masculinity in literary production and interpretation.

GAYATRI CHAKRAVORTY SPIVAK, *In Other Worlds: Essays in Cultural Politics* (New York and London: Methuen, 1987).
Spivak employs Marxism, feminism and deconstruction in an exploration of the relationship between cultures and a resolute critique of racism and imperialism. The literary text – from Dante to Margaret Drabble – forms part of that exploration.

JANET TODD, *Feminist Literary History: A Defence* (Cambridge: Polity Press, 1988).
In her analysis of feminist literary history over the last thirty years, Todd offers a defence of 'American socio-historical feminist criticism' against recent attacks from deconstructivist and psychoanalytical theories.

ALICE WALKER, *In Search of Our Mothers' Gardens: Womanist Prose* (New York: Harcourt Brace Jovanovich, 1983; London: Women's Press, 1984).
_____, *Living By the Word: Selected Writings 1973–1987* (New York: Harcourt Brace Jovanovich, 1988; London: Women's Press, 1988).
Walker's essays on Black politics, history and culture focus particularly on the significance of Black women's creativity. Her concept of 'womanism' unites feminism and Black activism.

CHRIS WEEDON, *Feminist Practice and Poststructuralist Theory* (Oxford: Basil Blackwell, 1987).
Weedon's introduction to poststructuralist thinking argues for post-structuralism's relevance to the practice of feminist politics and to feminist literary and cultural criticism.

VIRGINIA WOOLF, *A Room of One's Own* (London: Hogarth Press, 1929; London: Grafton Books, 1987).
Woolf's study of female literary production lends itself to a variety of theoretical interpretations – notably, gynocriticism, Marxism, deconstruction, psychoanalysis.

Index